NEW FORMATIONS

EDITOR:
David Glover

REVIEWS EDITOR
Alasdair Pettinger

EDITORIAL ASSISTANT
Alyson Pendlebury

EDITORIAL BOARD:
Timothy Bewes
Laura Chrisman
Jeremy Gilbert
Cora Kaplan
Scott McCracken
Bill Schwarz
Judith Squires
Jenny Bourne Taylor
Wendy Wheeler

ADVISORY BOARD:
Ien Ang
Angelika Bammer
Tony Bennett
Jody Berland
Homi Bhabha
Victor Burgin
Lesley Caldwell
Hazel Carby
Erica Carter
Iain Chambers
Joan Copjec
Lidia Curti
Tony Davies
James Donald
Simon Frith
Stuart Hall
Dick Hebdige
Colin Mercer
Edward Said
Renata Salecl
Gayatri Chakravorty Spivak
Valerie Walkerdine

New Formations is published
three times a year by
Lawrence & Wishart
99a Wallis Road, London E9 5LN
Tel: 0181-533 2506
Fax: 0181-533 7369
Website:www.l-w-bks.co.uk/
formation.html

ADVERTISEMENTS:
For enquiries/bookings contac
Lawrence & Wishart

SUBSCRIPTIONS:
For 1999, subscription rates to Lawrence &
are, for 3 issues
UK: Institutions £70, Individuals £35.
Rest of world: Institutions £75; Individuals £38.
Single copies: £14.99

CONTRIBUTIONS AND CORRESPONDENCE:
Send to:
The Editor, *New Formations*
Dept. of English, University of Southampton
Highfield, Southampton SO17 1BJ

BOOKS FOR REVIEW:
Send to:
Alasdair Pettinger
Scottish Music Information Centre
1 Bowmont Gardens
Glasgow, Scotland G12 9LR

Prospective writers are encouraged to contact the
editors to discuss their ideas and to obtain a copy of
our style sheet.
Manuscripts should be sent in triplicate; experts in
the relevant field will referee them anonymously.
The manuscripts will not be returned unless a
stamped, self-addressed envelope is enclosed.
Contributors should note that the editorial board
cannot take responsibility for any manuscript
submitted to *New Formations*.

ISSN   0 950 2376
ISBN   0 85315 9084

Text design and setting by Art Services, Norwich
Printed in Great Britain at the University Press,
Cambridge.

NOTES ON CONTRIBUTORS

Andrew Blake is Head of the School of Cultural Studies, King Alfred's College, Winchester. Recent publications include *The Land Without Music* (Manchester University Press 1997) and the edited collection *Living Through Pop* (Routledge 1999).

Fred Botting is Professor of English at the University of Keele. His books include *Making Monstrous: Frankenstein, Criticism, Theory* (1991), *Gothic* (1996), and *Sex, Machines and Navels: Fiction, Fantasy and History in the Future Present* (1999). He has co-edited two readers on George Bataille with Scott Wilson, and their *Holy Shit: the Tarantinian Ethics* will appear in 2000.

Steven Connor is Professor of Modern Literature and Theory at Birkbeck College, University of London. His works include *Postmodernist Culture* (1989), *Theory and Cultural Value* (1992), and *The English Novel in History 1950-1995*. He is currently completing two books, a cultural phenomenology of skin and a cultural history of ventriloquism and the dissociated voice.

Alan Durant is Professor of English Studies at Middlesex University, London. His published work ranges across linguistics, literary studies, media studies and music, and he is currently working on a book about questions of meaning in media regulation.

Rita Felski is Director of the Forum of Contemporary Thought and Professor of English at the University of Virginia. Her books include *Beyond Feminist Aesthetics: Feminist Literature and Social Change* (1989), *The Gender of Modernity* (1995) and *Doing Time:Critical Perspectives on Modernity and Postmodernity* (forthcoming).

Mariam Fraser is Lecturer in Sociology at Goldsmith's College, University of London. Her publications include *Identity without Selfhood: Bisexuality and Simone de Beauvoir* (Cambridge University Press, 1998). She is currently researching the brain, subjectivity and 'human-ness'.

Guy Hocquenghem (1946-1988) was a key figure in the history of gay theory and activism in France. Best known for his book *Homosexual Desire* (1972), he also published fiction, cultural criticism and autobiography. The paper published in this issue originally appeared in *Gai Pied Hebdo* in August 1987.

Syed Manzurul Islam is a Lecturer in the School of English at Cheltenham and Gloucester College of Higher Education. His previous publications include *The Ethics of Travel: From Marco Polo to Kafka* (1996) and *The Mapmakers of Spitafields*(1997). He is currently working on a novel.

Anny Brooksbank Jones teaches and researches in Spanish and Latin American culture at the University of Leeds. She has co-edited a volume on cultural politics (forthcoming) and *Latin American Women's Writing: Feminist Readings in Theory and Crisis* (1996). She is the author of *Women in Contemporary Spain* (1997) and is currently completing a book on Hispanic cultural studies.

Bill Marshall is Reader in French at the University of Southampton. He published the first monograph on Guy Hocquenghem in English in 1996.

Dick Pountain is currently a technical writer, Real World Editor of *PC Pro Magazine* and a director of Dennis Publishing Ltd. but he has also written on music, film, art and literature.

David Robins is a visiting professor at Middlesex University and the author of *Tarnished Vision* (OUP 1992), *We Hate Humans* (1984) and *Knuckle Sandwich* (1978 with P.Cohen).

Gregory Stephens is lecturer in Mass Communication and American Studies at the University of California Berkeley. His latest publication is *On Racial Frontiers: The 'New Culture' of Frederick Douglass, Ralph Ellison and Bob Marley* (Cambridge University Press, 1999).

Tim Youngs is the author of *Travellers in Africa* (1994) and editor of *Writing and Race* (1997). He edits the journal *Studies in Travel Writing* and is co-editor, with Peter Hulme, of *The Cambridge Companion to Travel Writing* (forthcoming).

CONTENTS
NUMBER 39   WINTER 1999-2000

Cool Moves

Lawrence and Wishart wish to acknowledge
the artist who supplied the cover photograph for
new formations 36, *Diana and Democracy*:
Cover photo © Layla Bates

EDITORIAL

David Glover

Nothing better illustrates the brittle cultural logic of the present than the trajectory of the term 'cool'. As Dick Pountain and David Robins show in their lead essay, in the 1990s 'cool' ceased to be a performative style of hedonistic disaffiliation assiduously cultivated by an oddly assorted collection of rebels and minorities and became instead one of the most important orientations to consumerism and marketing, the cynosure of style itself, particularly among the young and their imitators. For a brief moment 'cool' even came to signal a curious alliance between fashion-designers and spin-doctors around the fantasy-life of a nation under Blairism, the infamous re-branding of the United Kingdom as 'cool Britannia'. But 'cool' sits uncomfortably with the moralising civic rhetoric espoused by New Labour and championed by its leader. If Pountain and Robins are right in supposing that 'cool is the way to live with lowered expectations by going shopping', its intrinsically amoral appeal may yet prove to be the principal grave-digger of Blair's punitive democracy.

Questions of style and consumption also animate several of the other essays in this collection. In his essay on smoking 'in an age of techno-moral consumption', Fred Botting argues that the growing condemnation faced by cigarettes arises partly from the consummate hedonism that they offer, an excessive enjoyment of pure waste that reveals more about the uncanny compulsiveness of consumerist desire than almost any other act and must therefore be suppressed. Anathema to utilitarian and humanist forms of progressivism alike, smoking represents the last resort of an aesthetics of abjection, embodied in those 'beggarly figures, solitary or in groups, [who] huddle, cold and sodden, outside buildings, coughing and choking on foul clouds of smoke amid the detritus of soggy ash, crushed tobacco and butt-ends'. Scenes of bodily abjection also haunt Steven Connor's wide-ranging discussion of contemporary theorisations of skin. Thus the child's fascination with the scab, which quickly becomes a site of play, a controlling perpetuation of the wound as a mode of reconstituting the psyche in another register may have its parallels in the increasing prevalence of ritual piercing and marking of the skin - the ring or stud standing in for the scar - so closely linked to the contemporary staging of identity. Yet it is important to remember that these practices take place against the background of an insistent technological penetration of the body which calls into question the inviolability of the skin as the primary medium of individuation. Piercing or perforation can perhaps be read as a local symbolic counter to this threat.

From a different angle, the link between bodily control, identity and style forms the topic of Mariam Fraser's paper on the implications of mental impairment for the discourse of aesthetic originality. Looking at the last ten years of painter Willem de Kooning's life when he was suffering from Alzheimer's disease, Fraser suggests an alternative model to that of the authentic individual artist, preferring - like Deleuze - to think of creativity as a cluster of 'forces and affects', capacities that lend themselves to new critical engagements with the canvas.

The concept of everyday life has become almost ubiquitous in contemporary cultural theory; yet it is rarely subjected to sustained scrutiny. In her detailed examination of the history of the term, tracing its diverse origins in marxism and phenomenology, Rita Felski emphasises the need to recapture the ordinariness of the everyday, rather than elevating it into a primary setting for resistance or struggle. Under the routine conditions of modernity, everyday life enters into the very definition of humankind, especially through the medium of the home, shaping our knowledges and our habits: *la vie quotidienne* is the crucible of human agency, not the streetwise measure of its alienation. Felski's essay partially overlaps with Anny Brooksbank Jones's analysis of micro-cultural practices in Latin America, though they come to quite different conclusions. Focussing upon the flexibility of global marketing strategies, Brooksbank Jones shows how the multinational manufacturers of cosmetics provide low income women with a pleasurably hybridised sense of identity while drawing them into new networks of consumption. Her essay offers a valuable account of recent Latin American work on globalisation and cultural politics, which has hitherto been given scant attention in the Anglophone world.

The three remaining articles are each directly concerned with a politics and ethics that eschews false or disabling polarities. Gregory Stephens provides a case study of interracial 'sampling' in popular music through a detailed discussion of the independent film *Zebrahead*, a development that he suggests indicates 'new definitions of community allegiance and national citizenship'. In a lucid and rigorous essay, Syed Manzurul Islam attempts to theorise the possibility of a nomadic ethics for 'minoritarian' communities in the postcolonial era. Moving from Ibn Khaldun to Gilles Deleuze and from Nuruddin Farah to J. M. Coetzee, Islam insists upon the paradoxical necessity of a politics of minority rights and self-determination 'as part of a total liberatory movement' if such communities are to avoid being pulled on to the terrain of majority discourse, while still continuing to engage with the dominant centres of power. Finally, we publish the first English translation of the late Guy Hocquenghem's 1987 essay 'On Homo-sex, Or Is Homosexuality a Curable Vice?', together with an analysis by Bill Marshall of both its historical context and its implications for current gay politics. Like Islam and Stephens, Hocquenghem's argument also valorises a certain strategic predilection for the in-between or the tentative middle ground, in this instance for what he calls a distinctive 'homosexual sense', a situated mode of being that resists the absorption of gay identity into an indifferently straight world, while simultaneously refusing the pathologising fixedness of conventional understandings of homosexuality: 'an "innocent" or playful perversity', perhaps.

COOL RULES: ANATOMY OF AN ATTITUDE

Dick Pountain and David Robins

Believing that they had detected a scratch in new Labour's Teflon coating, our newspapers - both broad-sheet and tabloid - recently tussled with one another to support or rubbish the notion of cool Britannia (and to incorporate the greatest number of bad cool puns into their headlines). At the low-water mark of this debate, the *Independent on Sunday* babbled thus: 'Of course cool is important. Cool is the summation of all we aspire to. Cool is not an image, a way of looking, talking or doing. It is a way of being'.[1] *The Guardian* felt obliged to retaliate with a feature about 'The Myth of Cool', which opined that cool was just a conspiracy dreamed up by the UK record industry and an American ice-cream manufacturer.[2] While these antics were moderately amusing, and perhaps sold newspapers (though not nearly so many as murder and paedophilia do), they are not very helpful in understanding what cool actually means, and whether or not it is important. At the opposite pole of seriousness, the *New York Review of Books* carried a piece in which Mark Lilla of the Princeton Institute of Advanced Study discussed the twin revolutions that have transformed post-war America - the 'cultural' revolution of the 1960s and Reagan's laisser faire economic revolution of the 1980s - and severely criticised the inadequate understanding of these events by both right and left in American politics.[3] He characterises both their political responses as 'reactionary' in the purest sense: the right is stuck in a groove lambasting the moral laxity bequeathed by the 1960s, while the left rails helplessly against the cruel indifference of Reaganomics. The fact is, as Lilla puts it, that 'the Sixties happened, Reagan happened and for the foreseeable future they will together define our political horizon'. But according to Lilla young Americans have no difficulty in reconciling this contradiction in their daily lives, 'holding down day jobs in the unfettered global marketplace - the Reaganite dream, the left nightmare - and spending weekends immersed in a moral and cultural universe shaped by the Sixties'. This prompts Lilla to pose a dramatic question 'for which neither Tocqueville, nor Marx, nor Weber have prepared us: what principle in the American creed has simultaneously made possible these seemingly contradictory revolutions? How have our notions of equality and individualism been transformed to support a morally lax yet economically successful capitalist society?'

At the risk of some immodesty toward the shades of Tocqueville, Marx and Weber we are tempted to offer Lilla a single word answer: cool. Far from being a mere matter of sartorial style, or a passing behavioural fad, we believe that cool represents a sea-change in the group psychology of Western societies, as it appears to be usurping the work ethic to install itself as the

1. Eleanor Bailey, 'What's Really Cool', the *Independent on Sunday* , Real Life Section, 19.4.1998, p1.

2. 'The Myth of Cool' , the *Guardian* , G2 Section, 8.6.1987, p2.

3. Mark Lilla, 'A Tale of Two Reactions', the *New York Review of Books* , 14.5.1998, p4.

dominant mindset of advanced consumer capitalism. Cool (also known as hip) may have started out as a rebellious attitude, adopted by small minorities who rejected the values of mainstream society, but it is mutating to become the mainstream. This has consequences, not least for a new Labour which so ill-advisedly flirted with the idea. The brutal fact is that the cool attitude is an obstacle to several of the more important goals of new Labour's programme: namely the promotion of work and family, and the reduction of violent crime and drug abuse.

NARCISSUS UNCHAINED

For most white people the history of cool starts after World War Two. That very hot war destroyed or disrupted the lives of millions of men and women throughout Europe, America and Asia, and after the armistice demobilisation for the survivors meant a welcome return to the tranquillity of domestic life. In the UK such people built the welfare state which promised security against a repeat of such calamities. For a few however the experience of war had poisoned the very idea of domesticity and respectability, and they concluded that 'society' itself was to blame, and to be shunned.

The deferred gratification offered by work and family no longer seemed like such a good deal - especially after the start of the Cold War and the nuclear arms race - better to live fast and live now. Lowered future expectations lead to an opting out of civic duties and the pursuit of immediate pleasures. In the USA disgruntled ex-GIs formed the first outlaw motorcycle gangs, and the beat poets began to shout their passionate and dissident verse in coffee bars.

Cool took its name from its nonchalance, quite the opposite of the righteous indignation traditionally associated with rebellion. This post-war cool may have been new to white people, but it borrowed heavily from an aesthetic that had already been honed between the wars by black jazz and blues musicians, who used it as a defence against the racial discrimination and patronisation of the white-owned entertainment business. You could parody the original meaning of cool as: 'I'm excluded, but I make a virtue of my exclusion; I'm prettier, sexier, and have more style than you; I don't care what you think or say about me, and I've nothing to say to you'. Such an attitude could be equally adaptive for New Orleans prostitutes, itinerant blues musicians, criminals, beboppers, disillusioned GIs, or teenagers revolting against their parents' culture - in fact for anyone who had lost respect for their society's dominant value system under pressure of war, persecution or corruption. Right from the start the term 'cool' carried connotations of anti-establishment and anti-authority, and was associated with the louche, the bizarre and the criminal.

We describe this cool attitude as being constructed from four principal personality traits: *detachment, narcissism, irony* and *hedonism*.

Detachment - the retreat from social entanglements, is expressed verbally by the language of cool (nowadays by those ubiquitous phrases such as 'Yeah, right ... ' or 'Whatever ... ') and by that sartorial emblem of cool, the wearing of dark glasses.

Narcissism - in the strong psychoanalytic sense, rather than just vanity - was explored by the late Christopher Lasch in *The Culture of Narcissism*.[4] Lasch identified a new 'liberated' (or in our terms cool) personality type characterised by charm, protective emotional shallowness, promiscuous pansexuality, avoidance of dependence, inability to mourn, and dread of old age and death. He attributed the phenomenon to changes in child rearing practices: crudely put, children constructed 'fantasies of beauty and omnipotence to counteract their threatening feelings of impotent rage'. Affluent parents were offering excessive attention (i.e. 'spoiling' their children) while withholding deep emotional support because they 'gave priority to their own right to self-fulfilment'. Thanks to the bomb and decreasing job security they lacked the faith in the future required for successful child rearing.

4. Christopher Lasch, *The Culture of Narcissism*, Warner Books, New York 1979.

Irony - the stratagem of stating one's thoughts indirectly, usually by uttering their exact opposite - is a verbal weapon, equally effective for aggression or defence, which is central to the protective cool persona. So-called 'sick' comedians like Lenny Bruce and Richard Pryor probed the extremities of a dark, ironic humour which nowadays has captured the culture of TV and film so thoroughly that any display of directness or sincerity has become almost impossibly un-cool. You can express almost any opinion (and its opposite) in the name of irony, as viewers of *Have I Got News for You* well know. Or consider Quentin Tarantino's *Pulp Fiction* - it takes genius, of a sort, to make removing splattered brains from a car-seat seem genuinely funny.

Hedonism - needs little explanation, except to point out that a cool good time almost always involves consuming drugs; from tobacco and alcohol to heroin and cocaine. The original 1950s cool adopted heroin as the drug of choice, because opiates effortlessly produce the emotionally detached state that cool seeks - one could almost describe cool as the abstraction of opiate intoxication.

A structural problem for cool is that detachment, if pursued to its limits, would lead to total social atomisation. There is however a countervailing tendency in cool that encourages the formation of tight peer groups and subcultures, unified by a shared definition of what is cool. It's easier to understand this mechanism by looking at cool's alternative label hip, which originally meant knowingness, as in 'I'm hip to that'. Hip expresses shared knowledge of a secret that is denied to 'the squares' – i.e. members of the respectable society - that bonds the hip together. The overt content of that secret might concern drugs, crime, forbidden sexual practices, or the appreciation of a certain musical style. In the background though there's always the suggestion of a bigger, seldom verbalised, more abstract secret: namely the perceived 'hypocrisy' of straight society, a shared belief that society's taboos have no rational basis, and are in any case regularly broken by even its most supposedly respectable members.

This 'big secret' has many facets - reflecting many smaller 'hypocrisies' - and it can encompass all aspects of life. Sex: even the president of the USA, even your preacher, even your parents do it. Family: they fuck you up, your mum and dad. Money: everyone's out to rip you off (a blurred perception of the hidden extraction of surplus value). Politics: the good guys never win. Crime: the only real crime is getting caught. Drugs: they tell us drugs are nasty, but we know drugs feel good, so they are either liars or hypocrites. Death: we're all going to die. Cool may fear death, but for that very reason it wants to laugh in its face, hence the historic association with fast motorbikes, guns, needles, alcoholism and suicide.

It's no coincidence that this picture of cool constitutes almost the antithesis of the Christian virtues of faith, hope and charity, or the more specifically Protestant virtues of hard work, thrift and self-discipline. Nor does it have much in common with the secular virtues of old time labourism Labour which one might characterise as compassion, modesty and temperance (the latter to be taken in moderation of course). Advanced capitalism perhaps no longer needs such puritanical notions of virtue to maintain its labour discipline, and cool may just be the new mode of individualism, better adapted to a life of service and consumption rather than production.

Of course we don't claim to have discovered cool. Indeed a whole industry of style commentators continually fondles its contours and invents new names for its various extremities (like the proverbial blind men exploring an elephant): girl power, middle youth, new lads, new men and the rest. Our claim is only to have taken a step back in order to observe the whole beast.

THAT'S COOL TOO

In the 1960s genuinely radical oppositional political movements erupted, in the USA around civil rights, and throughout the Western world in opposition to the nuclear arms race and the Vietnam war. Alongside these political movements grew up a hedonistic counterculture based on a burgeoning Rock and Roll that conquered the whole of the popular music industry. The flamboyant hippy style looked very different from the button-down shirts and shades of 1950s jazz musicians like Chet Baker or Miles Davis, but those transgressive and hedonistic attitudes of 1950s cool appealed to this new generation, which readily adopted and adapted them. Where 1950s cool had cultivated a rather unworldly detachment from commercial concerns though, hippiedom (anti-materialistic oriental gurus notwithstanding) steered cool in an altogether more materialistic direction toward the market place. The 'Hidden Persuaders' of Madison Avenue became hip themselves; hip to the fact that hip was a way into the hearts and wallets of the newly affluent younger generation that formed the key market for clothing, music and soft drinks. Thomas Frank in *The Conquest of Cool* has written the first detailed study of this transformation of the US business culture, and the rise of hip consumerism: 'What happened in the sixties is that hip (or cool) became central to the way capitalism understood itself and explained itself to the public'.[5] Marketeers discovered that the cliquey solidarity implicit in cool made possible new strategies, based on branding and differentiation, which still rule the industry today; Nike vs Reebok vs Adidas.

5. Thomas Frank, *The Conquest of Cool*, University of Chicago Press, Chicago 1997, p26.

The democratic and collectivist spirit of the 1960s transformed cool in another very significant way, mostly thanks to the ambiguous influence of Andy Warhol. A successful commercial artist with avant-garde pretensions, it was Warhol who first understood that bourgeois high culture could be subverted by making it easier, rather than more difficult as the modernist movement had presumed. He elevated the ephemera of consumer society, like his famous soup cans, to the status of already-art, but without any of the 'difficult' satirical content of Dada and Surrealism or Duchamp's ready-mades. A Warhol work came with just a bland 'here it is, isn't it cool' and the implied message that anyone could do this - high art reduced to decoration. Everyone can 'understand' a Warhol's Marilyn. Since Warhol, irony has become the safest road into an artistic career, as witnessed in Jeff Koons, Damien Hirst and BritArt.

The post-war cool aesthetic had largely been forged in the cinema, its iconic figures actors like Bogart and Bacall, James Dean, Marlon Brando, Marilyn Monroe and Robert Mitchum. Warhol grasped the fact that this star system was quite as 'élitist' as any branch of bourgeois high art, depending as it did on good looks and some notion of acting talent. He ruthlessly stripped away at least the latter from his own movies, and issued the famous sound-bite that became his only manifesto: 'in future, everyone will be famous for 15 minutes'. Far from making Hollywood stars into sacred icons, Warhol reduced them to commodities, and his democratisation of art was complete. Any residual awe or deference toward seriousness of artistic purpose that might have survived in the populace was punctured forever. What Warhol started was completed by a couple of inspired hippies who invented the board game *Trivial Pursuit*: art and scholarship could both now be effortlessly absorbed into show business. We are still living through the consequences of Warhol's revolution, a popular outpouring of kitsch, voyeurism and exhibitionism: Yoof TV, porn and *Hello* magazine. Warhol drew on the narcissism at the heart of cool and seduced pop culture into falling in love with itself, free from any taint of critical thought. We're all stars now, but stars that have been brought down to earth.

During the 1960s and 1970s Hollywood adopted cool as its personal philosophy - a dandy worldview for anyone who lives by constantly reinventing themselves, never forming any permanent bonds. The audience became aware that the non-committal cool sex portrayed on screen by the likes of Warren Beatty and Jack Nicholson was happening off-screen in their real lives too.

Cool soon became the attitude to cultivate if you wanted to score, and so began that 'flight from feeling', from the messiness of real intimacy, into the world of the easy lay, the casual divorce, and non-possessive relationships (remember those doomed open marriages of the late 1960s and 1970s?)

COOL CONSUMERS

Far from being the pose of a tiny minority in revolt against 'square' life, by the 1990s cool has become the majority attitude among young people (and more to the point, among those who want to sell things to them). Given a complete loss of faith in radical political alternatives, cool is now primarily about consumption. This is the missing 'cement' that fills the gaping contradiction of Mark Lilla's question - cool is the way to live with lowered expectations by going shopping.

Those who have mastered cool best are the vendors of music, soft drinks, snack foods and sports wear, the life staples of the young. Most of the senior executive positions in the mass media, marketing and advertising industries are now occupied by a generation that came of age in the late 1960s, and this mediocracy knows how to deploy cool as a selling tool, how to manipulate its icons, because it makes sense to them: it reflects their own values. Cool is now the dominant attitude of media professionals - movie directors and script writers, television executives, record company chiefs, magazine editors, computer game designers and advertising creatives - who share with their potential customers a taste for cynicism, sensuality, self-obsession, social indifference and mindless (but ironic) cruelty.

Among pre-pubescent and early-teenagers, cool has immense appeal as the antidote to their ultimate fear, of being embarrassed - in the solipsistic world of Beavis and Butthead everything is cool or it sucks, period. Among young adults cool is the liberated way to consume: 'Most of what they are trying to sell me is crap, but I'm cool, I know the difference'. The level of irony and self-reference in youth-oriented commercials renders them both irresistible and irrefutable, since if you don't like them it can only be because you don't 'get' them (because you're not cool). Personal taste is elevated into a complete ethos: you are what you like, and what you therefore buy.

Cool is accessible to any kid whose parents can afford the price of (or who can steal) a pair of fashion trainers, and all without requiring any tiresome study. However cool is at root anti-family - your parents are almost by definition un-cool and you can only construct a cool persona for yourself outside of the too-warm and inevitably intrusive relationships and responsibilities of family life. Lasch's narcissistic parents now have to compete with TV cartoons, adverts, liberal teachers and the peer group - itself defined in terms of consumption (do you wear Stussy?) - for influence on their children's imaginations. Hence cool reproduces itself, as indeed it must if it is to become the new norm. Cool parents produce cool children, by spoiling them while offering only the shallowest of emotional education.

Mere government fiat is not going to break this cycle.

THE DRUGS DO WORK

Cool may have conquered popular culture, but politics is another world - a world in which one has to confront strongly held principles (or at least strongly defended interests) and as such is deeply un-cool. The media got it laughably wrong when they attached the cool label (the cool Treasury even) to Tony Blair's plans to harness the enthusiasm of disaffected youth. Transforming Britain into cool Britannia and Labour into the cool party was always a non-starter. We understand that Blair himself dislikes the cool sobriquet, which we hope is because he has understood this massive contradiction: while the thrust of his project is to shore up the traditional family, as a step toward halting the disintegration of community and the rise of crime, cool stands for precisely the opposite values. It's intrinsically anti-social, anti-family, pro-drug, anti-caring and most of all anti-authority. Ironic detachment is a poor adhesive for a society, and it's more than coincidence that criminals choose 'he's cool' to indicate when someone is one of them.

Today's cool maintains the traditional association with drug taking, spanning the full range from weed and speed, through 'E's, to fashionable junkie chic. Heroin abuse is on a steep increase today, and among ever younger age groups. The consequences of drug use are strongly conditioned by economic and social class, so that while a heroin habit might be a major inconvenience to a Fulham socialite, it is usually terminal for kids on a housing estate in Leeds or Glasgow, for whom jail or the mortuary are the most probable destinations. A triumph for cool means living permanently with the negative effects of both drug abuse and the penal policies that governments apply in pursuing their futile 'war on drugs': among black US youth one-in-six passes through the jail system, and gunshot has become the prime cause of death.

Can New Labour recapture young people's hearts and minds? It's unlikely that Labour would want (or could afford) to buy their affections by restoring unemployment benefits, and the party is equally unlikely to compromise with cool by, say, legalising cannabis. That only leaves some 'big idea' that could make Caring cool, but that's almost an oxymoron. Blair's project needs some traction to haul young minds back from the more nihilistic and destructive aspects of cool, but it's hard to see where it will come from: trying to encompass cool within a moralising, Christian socialist framework may prove too much even for a spin-master of Blair's undoubted abilities (and it will do nothing for Jack Straw's career prospects).

STAY COOL

Far from being a friend to social democracy, or indeed any kind of socialism, cool may prove to be its grave-digger - one could even argue that the effect of all those black-market Beatles albums and Levi jeans contributed significantly to the collapse of morale of Eastern bloc Communism. Cool represents a free market in personal relations and sexuality, and like it or not, many people all over the world now aspire to that freedom. What's more, they are unlikely to be gainsaid by mere moralising, for it would require dictatorship (perhaps following a colossal economic crash) or the military triumph of some religious fundamentalism to divert them from it. The USA, as Mark Lilla pointed out, must be our model for what happens when a society embraces the free market both in labour and leisure, while losing interest in party politics: unprecedented prosperity for the many, misery for the few, Wall Street at an all-time high, and a total lack of any truly oppositional - as opposed to knee-jerk reactionary - politics. Thomas Frank described this latest phase of capitalism in rather more radical terms as the 'construction of cultural machines that transform alienation and despair into consent'. The maintenance of a healthy democracy requires a perceptible difference between the parties of left and right and real confrontations over real issues: in this light the prospect of an apolitical cool generation is alarming. Cool tends to prefer images of rebellion offered by glamorous terrorists and wasted rock musicians to the hard slog of real politics, but we'd all do well to remember that Adolf Hitler was also a rebel with artistic pretensions, a distinctive haircut, big trousers and kinky boots.

CODA

February 1999: James Brown, the founder of *Loaded* magazine, resigned as editor of *GQ* following an article in the new lad stylesheet which called the Nazis and Field Marshal Rommel 'the sharpest men of the century'.

This article is extracted from Cool Rules: Anatomy of an Attitude *by Dick Pountain and David Robins, to be published by Reaktion Books in spring 2000.*

THE INVENTION OF EVERYDAY LIFE

Rita Felski

Everyday life is the most self-evident, yet the most puzzling of ideas. It is a key concept in cultural studies and feminism and an important reference point in other scholarly fields, part of a growing interest in micro-analysis and history from below. Yet those who use the term are often reluctant to explain exactly what it means. While doing the research for this paper, I was struck by how many recent books mention everyday life in the title and how few list everyday life in the index. This reticence may well be intentional; recourse to the everyday often springs from a sense of frustration with academic theories and hair-splitting distinctions. After all, everyday life simply *is*, indisputably: the essential, taken-for-granted continuum of mundane activities that frames our forays into more esoteric or exotic worlds. It is the ultimate, non-negotiable reality, the unavoidable basis for all other forms of human endeavour. The everyday, writes Guy Debord, 'is the measure of all things'.[1]

The powerful resonances of such appeals to everyday life are closely connected to its fuzzy, ambiguous meanings. What exactly does it refer to? The entire social world? Particular behaviours and practices? A specific attitude or relationship to one's environment? At first glance, everyday life seems to be everywhere, yet nowhere. Because it has no clear boundaries, it is difficult to identify. Everyday life is synonymous with the habitual, the ordinary, the mundane, yet it is also strangely elusive, that which resists our understanding and escapes our grasp. Like the blurred speck at the edge of one's vision that disappears when looked at directly, the everyday ceases to be everyday when it is subject to critical scrutiny. 'The everyday escapes', writes Blanchot, 'it belongs to insignificance'.[2]

Yet everyday life is also a concept with a long history. Beyond the often cited work of Michel de Certeau, there is an extensive tradition of writing on the everyday. This includes not just the work of Henri Lefebvre, but also of philosophers and sociologists such as Lukacs, Heidegger, Heller, Schutz, Goffman, and Habermas amongst others. The fact that much of this writing has not been taken up in feminism and cultural studies may be partly due to its often abstract philosophical character. Given the current interest in the concrete and the particular, and the enormous variations in human lives across cultural contexts, in what sense is it meaningful to talk about everyday life in general?[3]

As a result of this focus on the particular, however, everyday life is rarely taken under the microscope and scrutinised as a concept. Like any analytical term, it organises the world according to certain assumptions and criteria. For example, everyday life bears a complicated relationship to the distinction

1. Quoted in Peter Osborne, *The Politics of Time: Modernity and Avant-Garde*, Verso, London 1995, p192.

2. Maurice Blanchot, 'Everyday Speech', *Yale French Studies*, no. 73, 1987, p14.

3. See, however, Roger Silverstone's *Television and Everyday Life*, Routledge, London 1994, which draws extensively on sociology, phenomenology and anthropology, and Meaghan Morris, 'On the Beach' in *Cultural Studies*, Lawrence Grossberg, Cary Nelson, and Paula Treichler (eds), Routledge, New York 1992. See also Dorothy Smith, *The Everyday World as Problematic: A Feminist Sociology*, Open University Press, Milton Keynes 1987 for a brief discussion of Schutz, Kristin Ross, *Fast Cars, Clean Bodies: Decolonization and the Reordering of French Culture*, MIT Press, Cambridge 1995 for a feminist application of Lefebvre, and Nancy Fraser 'What's Critical about Critical Theory? The Case of Habermas and Gender', *New German Critique*, no. 35, 1985 for a feminist critique of Habermas's conception of the life-world. As this article was going to press, I discovered Laurie Langbauer's stimulating *Novels of Everyday Life: The Series in English Fiction 1850-1930*, Cornell University Press, Ithaca 1999. Though she comes

to slightly different
conclusions,
Langbauer's survey
of different
theoretical
conceptions of
everyday life and
their relationship to
questions of gender
reveals intriguing
parallels to my own
discussion.

4. Henri Lefebvre,
*Everyday Life in the
Modern World*,
Transaction, New
York 1984, p38. For
the history of writing
on daily life, see
Alvin W. Gouldner,
'Sociology and the
Everyday Life', in
The Idea of Social
Science, Lewis A.
Coser (ed),
Harcourt, Brace,
Jovanovich, New
York 1975.

5. Thomas Moore,
*The Re-enchantment of
Everyday Life*, Harper
Collins, New York
1996.

between private and public; it includes domestic activities but also routine forms of work, travel and leisure. Furthermore, everyday life is not simply interchangeable with the popular: it is not the exclusive property of a particular social class or grouping. Bismarck had an everyday life and so does Madonna. What then, does the term signify? What are its parameters? To what is it opposed?

Lefebvre argues that everyday life is a distinctively modern phenomenon that only emerged in the nineteenth century. The claim seems counter-intuitive, going against the presumed universality of the everyday. There is in fact a long history of writing on daily life extending from ancient Greece to medieval Christianity to the Enlightenment.[4] But it is true that everyday life becomes increasingly important in the nineteenth century as an object of critical reflection and representation in literature and art. What is the cause of this new visibility? Lefebvre points to the impact of capitalism and industrialisation on human existence and perception. As bodies are massed together in big cities under modern conditions, so the uniform and repetitive aspects of human lives become more prominent. Similarly, Alvin Gouldner suggests that the rapidly changing fabric of ordinary lives creates a new awareness of the mundane. That which was previously taken for granted becomes newly visible, in both its new and its traditional, disappearing forms.

Everyday life is also a secular and democratic concept. Secular because it conveys the sense of a world leached of transcendence; the everyday is everyday because it is no longer connected to the miraculous, the magical or the sacred. (Hence, a recent New Age bestseller is entitled *The Re-Enchantment of Everyday Life*).[5] Democratic because it recognises the paramount shared reality of a mundane, material embeddedness in the world. Everyone, from the most famous to the most humble, eats, sleeps, yawns, defecates; no one escapes the reach of the quotidian. Everyday life, in other words, does not only describe the lives of ordinary people, but recognises that every life contains an element of the ordinary. We are all ultimately anchored in the mundane.

At the same time, some groups, such as women and the working class, are more closely identified with the everyday than others. Everyday life is not just a material by-product of capitalism, as Lefebvre argues, but also a term that is deployed by intellectuals to describe a non-intellectual relationship to the world. For Lukacs and Heidegger, for example, the everyday is synonymous with an inauthentic, grey, aesthetically impoverished existence. Lefebvre views it with more ambivalence; everyday life is a sign of current social degradation under capitalism, but it is also connected to bodily and affective rhythms and hence retains a utopian impulse. More recently, for some scholars in cultural studies, history, and related fields, everyday life has emerged as an alternative to theory and an arena of authentic experience. Faced with a legitimation crisis about the value and purpose of humanities scholarship, intellectuals have often found an alibi in the turn to the ordinary. Everyday life, in other words, is rarely viewed with neutrality.

The concept is marked by a rich history of hostility, envy and desire, expressing both nostalgia for the concrete and disdain for a life lacking in critical self-reflection.

Yet as a term, everyday life remains strangely amorphous. As Lefebvre notes, it is often defined negatively, as the residue left over after various specialised activities are abstracted. One of these activities is philosophy. Conventionally, scholars have opposed everyday life to critical reflection and speculation. It is synonymous with the ' natural attitude' rather than the 'theoretical attitude', with the realm of common-sense and taken-for-grantedness rather than hard-headed scepticism.[6] A second influential distinction is between the everyday and the aesthetic. This distinction is addressed in Alice Walker's well-known story 'Everyday Use', which turns on the differing attitudes of two daughters to some old family quilts. For one daughter they are simply useful objects in her daily life, while for her college-educated sister they have become examples of authentic folk art, to be hung on the wall and admired.[7] To contemplate something as art is to remove it, at least temporarily, from the pragmatic needs and demands of the quotidian. Finally, everyday life is typically distinguished from the exceptional moment: the battle, the catastrophe, the extraordinary deed. The distinctiveness of the everyday lies in its lack of distinction and differentiation; it is the air one breathes, the taken-for-granted backdrop, the commonsensical basis of all human activities. 'The heroic life', writes Mike Featherstone, 'is the sphere of danger, violence and the courting of risk whereas everyday life is the sphere of women, reproduction and care'.[8]

As Featherstone's statement makes clear, gender has been an important factor in conceptions of everyday life. Lefebvre, like some other theorists, regards women as the quintessential representatives and victims of the quotidian. 'Everyday life weighs heaviest on women', he writes. 'Some are bogged down by its peculiar cloying substance, while others escape into make-believe … They are the subject of everyday life and its victims'.[9] Women, like everyday life, have often been defined by negation. Their realm has not been that of war, art, philosophy, scientific endeavour, high office. What else is left to woman but everyday life, the realm of the insignificant, invisible yet indispensable?

Such a negative view of the quotidian is, however, open to criticism. Both feminism and cultural studies have questioned the view that the everyday exists only as something to be transcended, as the realm of monotony, emptiness and dull compulsion. Furthermore, such a division between the everyday and the non-everyday slides imperceptibly into a ranking of persons: those exemplary individuals able to escape the quotidian through philosophy, high art or heroism versus the rest of humanity. Recent scholarship has argued, by contrast, that critical thinking is not simply the province of philosophers, that aesthetic experience need not be severed from everyday life, and that there are other forms of heroism besides war or Oedipal conflict.

6. Alfred Schutz and Thomas Luckmann, *The Structures of the Life-World*, vol. 1, Northwestern University Press, Evanston 1983.

7. Alice Walker, 'Everyday Use', in *Love and Trouble: Stories of Black Women*, Harcourt, Brace, Jovanovich, New York 1973.

8. Mike Featherstone, 'The Heroic Life and Everyday Life', *Theory, Culture and Society*, 9:1, 1992, p165.

9. Lefebvre, *Everyday Life in the Modern World*, 1984, *op. cit.*, p73.

Is it possible to think about the everyday in ways that do not simply treat it as negative or residual? A driving impulse behind some cultural studies scholarship has been the desire to invert this perception and to invest the everyday with supreme value and significance. In particular, De Certeau's *The Practice of Everyday Life* has inspired numerous readings of daily life as synonymous with acts of resistance and subversion. Yet this new account of the everyday often loses sight of the mundane, taken-for-granted, routine qualities that seem so central to its definition - the very everydayness of the everyday. By contrast, the phenomenological and sociological writing on everyday life focuses explicitly on this very question. From a reading of the work of Lefebvre, Heller and Schutz, I want to piece together an alternative definition of everyday life grounded in three key facets: time, space and modality. The temporality of the everyday, I suggest, is that of repetition, the spatial ordering of the everyday is anchored in a sense of home and the characteristic mode of experiencing the everyday is that of habit.

This vision of the everyday is interesting for several reasons. First of all, as I have suggested, it differs markedly from the way in which everyday life is conceptualised in contemporary cultural studies, where writers often rhapsodise about subversion, indeterminacy, nomadism and the like. I would like to explore these differences and to bring the various traditions of scholarship on everyday life into a more explicit dialogue. Second, the association of the everyday with repetition, home and habit often involves assumptions about gender and women's relationship to the modern world. These assumptions become most explicit in Lefebvre's sociological and Marxist-oriented account of everyday life. While I have found many of his insights useful, I want to question his view that the habitual, home-centred aspects of daily life are outside, and in some sense antithetical to, the experience of an authentic modernity.

REPETITION

Everyday life is above all a temporal term. As such, it conveys the fact of repetition; it refers not to the singular or unique but to that which happens 'day after day'. The activities of sleeping, eating, and working conform to regular diurnal rhythms that are in turn embedded within larger cycles of repetition: the weekend, the annual holiday, the start of a new semester. For Lefebvre, this cyclical structure of everyday life is its quintessential feature, a source of both fascination and puzzlement. 'In the study of the everyday', he writes, 'we discover the great problem of repetition, one of the most difficult problems facing us'.[10] Repetition is a problem or, as he says elsewhere, a riddle, because it is fundamentally at odds with the modern drive towards progress and accumulation.

Lefebvre returns repeatedly to this apparent contradiction between linear and cyclical time. Linear time is the forward-moving, abstract time of modern industrial society; everyday life is, on the other hand, characterised by

10. Henri Lefebvre, 'The Everyday and Everydayness', in *Yale French Studies*, no. 73, 1987, p10.

natural, circadian rhythms which, according to Lefebvre, have changed little over the centuries.[11] These daily rhythms complicate the self-understanding of modernity as permanent progress. If everyday life is not completely outside history, it nevertheless serves as a retardation device, slowing down the dynamic of historical change. Lefebvre resorts at several points to the concept of uneven development as a way of explaining this lack of synchronicity. Because of its reliance upon cyclical time, everyday life is *belated*; it lags behind the historical possibilities of modernity.

Time, writes Johannes Fabian, 'is a carrier of significance, a form through which we define the content of relations between the Self and the Other'.[12] In other words, time is not just a measurement but a metaphor, dense in cultural meanings. Conventionally, the distinction between 'time's arrow' and 'time's cycle' is also a distinction between masculine and feminine. Indeed, all models of historical transformation - whether linear or cataclysmic, evolutionary or revolutionary - have been conventionally coded as masculine. Conversely, woman's affinity with repetition and cyclical time is noted by numerous writers. Simone de Beauvoir, for example, claims that 'woman clings to routine; time has for her no element of novelty, it is not a creative flow; because she is doomed to repetition, she sees in the future only a duplication of the past'.[13] Here, repetition is a sign of women's enslavement in the ordinary, her association with immanence rather than transcendence. Unable to create or invent, she remains imprisoned within the remorseless routine of cyclical time. Lefebvre's perspective is less censorious: women's association with recurrence is also a sign of their connection to nature, emotion and sensuality, their lesser degree of estrangement from biological and cosmic rhythms. Julia Kristeva concurs with this view in seeing repetition as the key to women's experience of extra-subjective time, cosmic time, *jouissance*.[14]

Why are women so persistently linked to repetition? Several possibilities come to mind. First of all, women are almost always seen as embodied subjects, their biological nature never far from view. Biorhythmic cycles affect various aspects of male and female behaviour, yet menstruation and pregnancy become the pre-eminent, indeed the only, examples of human subordination to natural time and a certain feminine resistance to the project of civilisation. Second, women are primarily responsible for the repetitive tasks of social reproduction: cleaning, preparing meals, caring for children. While much paid work is equally repetitive, only the domestic sphere is deemed to exist outside the dynamic of history and change. For example, in his well-known discussion of industrial time, E. P. Thompson suggests that women's everyday lives conform to a pre-modern temporal pattern. 'The rhythms of women's work in the home are not wholly attuned to the measurement of the clock. The mother of young children has an imperfect sense of time and attends to other human tides. She has not yet altogether moved out of the conventions of "pre-industrial" society'.[15]

Finally, women are identified with repetition via consumption. For Marxist

11. Henri Lefebvre, *Critique de la vie quotidienne vol. 2*, L'Arche, Paris 1961, p54.

12. Johannes Fabian, *Time and the Other: How Anthropology Makes its Object*, Columbia University Press, New York 1983, pix.

13. Simone de Beauvoir, *The Second Sex*, Picador, London 1988, p610.

14. Lefebvre, *Everyday Life in the Modern World*, 1984, *op. cit.*, p17; Julia Kristeva, 'Women's Time', in *Feminist Theory: A Critique of Ideology*, Nannerl O. Keohane, Michelle Z. Rosaldo and Barbara C. Gelpi (eds), University of Chicago Press, Chicago 1982. See also *Taking our Time: Feminist Perspectives on Temporality*, Frieda Johles Forman (ed), Pergamon Press, Oxford 1989 for similar arguments.

15. E. P. Thompson, 'Time, Work-Discipline and Industrial Capitalism', *Past and Present*, 38, 1957, p79.

scholars of the everyday, commodification is its paramount feature, evident in ever greater standardisation and sameness. As the primary symbols and victims of consumer culture, women take on the repetitive features of the objects that they buy. Femininity is formed through mass production and mass reproduction, disseminated through endless images of female glamour and female domesticity. Women become the primary emblem of an inauthentic everyday life marked by the empty homogeneous time of mass consumption.

The different aspects of women's association with repetitive time are captured in a suggestive passage that is quoted by Lefebvre, from a novel by the popular American writer, Irwin Shaw. As the hero of Shaw's novel walks down Fifth Avenue looking at women shopping, he idly imagines a museum exhibit devoted to the theme of modern femininity. Like the tableaux at the Museum of Natural History, with their stuffed bears opening honeycombs against a background of caves, this diorama would display modern American women in their natural habitat and engaged in their most typical activities. What would such an exhibition consist of? It would display to the curious viewer 'a set of stuffed women, slender, high-heeled, rouged, waved, hot-eyed, buying a cocktail dress in a department store'. While these women engaged in democratic acts of mass consumption, 'in the background, behind the salesgirls and the racks and shelves, there would be bombs bursting, cities crumbling, scientists measuring the half-life of tritium and cobalt'.[16]

16. Henri Lefebvre, *Critique of Everyday Life*, vol. 1, Verso, London 1991, p28.

This image eloquently crystallises the gendering of time. In the background, dwarfing the indifferent shoppers, is the technological sublime of science and war. This is cataclysmic time: the catastrophe of nuclear explosion, mass destruction, monumental history. But the female customers remain caught within the repetitive time of everyday life; passionate yet compliant consumers, they continue to buy dresses, oblivious to the possibility of catastrophe. They are governed by a law of repetition that is both social and natural. Creatures of artifice, they embrace the capitalist imperative to 'shop until you drop'. Yet they also embody the inexorable rhythms of nature. Like the stuffed animals at the museum, their behaviour is framed as the inevitable result of natural instinct combined with appropriate environment. Indistinguishable members of the species woman, they are caught within a repetitive cycle of natural desire.

Such visions of the horror of repetition, we need to recognise, are distinctively modern. For most of human history, activities have gained value precisely because they repeat what has gone before. Repetition, understood as ritual, provides a connection to ancestry and tradition; it situates the individual in an imagined community that spans historical time. It is thus not opposed to transcendence, but is the means of transcending one's historically limited existence. In the modern era, by contrast, to repeat without questioning or transforming is often regarded as laziness, conservatism, or bad faith. This disdain for repetition fuels existentialism's critique of the unthinking routines of everyday life, its insistence on the importance of creating oneself anew at each moment. It is behind the shock of the new in modern art that is intended to liberate us from our habitual, entrenched, perceptions. And it is evident in Freud's view of repetition as a form of pathology, linked to the dark, anti-social urge of the death drive. Repetition is seen as a threat to the modern project of self-determination, subordinating individual will to the demands of an imposed pattern.

Yet the attempt to escape repetition is a Sisyphean project, for, as Lefebvre rightly insists, it pervades the everyday. He further argues that daily life is 'situated at the intersection of two modes of repetition: the cyclical, which dominates in nature, and the linear, which dominates in processes known as "rational"'.[17] Here, as elsewhere, Lefebvre conceives of repetition as taking one of two forms: natural bodily rhythms or the regimented cycles of industrial capitalism. Yet many everyday routines cannot easily be fitted into either of these categories. They are neither unmediated expressions of biological drives nor mere reflexes of capitalist domination but a much more complex blend of the social and the psychic. Continuity and routine are crucial to early child development and remain important in adult life. Repetition is one of the ways in which we organise the world, make sense of our environment and stave off the threat of chaos. It is a key factor in the gradual formation of identity as a social and intersubjective process. Quite simply, we become who we are through acts of repetition. While recent cultural criticism has stressed the innovative dimensions of the everyday, it has paid much less attention to the need for routine in the organisation of daily life.[18]

17. Lefebvre, 'Everyday and Everydayness', 1987, *op. cit.*, p10.

Furthermore, there is a tendency, clearly visible in the work of Lefebvre, to equate repetition with domination and innovation with agency and resistance. Yet this is to remain trapped within a mindset which assumes the superior value of the new. In our own era, however, the reverse is just as likely to be true. Within the maelstrom of contemporary life, change is often imposed on individuals against their will; conversely everyday rituals may help to safeguard a sense of personal autonomy and dignity, or to preserve the distinctive qualities of a threatened way of life. In other words, repetition is not simply a sign of human subordination to external forces but also one of the ways in which individuals engage with and respond to their environment. Repetition can signal resistance as well as enslavement.

18. See, Silverstone's *Television and Everyday Life* for a systematic engagement with these issues.

Finally, Lefebvre's often illuminating discussion of the quotidian is weakened by his persistent opposition of cyclical and linear time, the everyday and the modern, the feminine and the masculine. Yet the passing of time surely cannot be grasped in such rigidly dualistic terms. Thus acts of innovation and creativity are not opposed to, but rather made possible by, the mundane cycles of the quotidian. Conversely, even the most repetitive of lives bears witness to the irreversible direction of time: the experience of ageing, the regret of past actions or inactions, the premonition of death. The temporality of everyday life is internally complex: it combines repetition and linearity, recurrence with forward movement. The everyday cannot be

19. Osborne, *The Politics of Time*, 1995, *op. cit.*, p198.

opposed to the realm of history, but is rather the very means by which history is actualised and made real.[19] Thus repetition is not an anachronism in a world of constant flux, but an essential element of the experience of modernity. Rather than being the sign of a uniquely feminine relationship to time, it permeates the lives of men as well as women.

HOME

While everyday life expresses a specific sense of time, it does not convey a particular sense of space. In fact, everyday life is usually distinguished by an absence of boundaries, and thus a lack of clear spatial differentiation. It includes a variety of different spaces (the workplace, the home, the mall) as well as diverse forms of movement through space (walking, driving, flying). Moreover, our everyday experience of space is now powerfully affected by technology; thanks to television, telephones and computers we can have virtual knowledge of places and cultures quite remote from our own.

In spite of these varied locations, several philosophers of everyday life focus on the home as its privileged symbol. Agnes Heller writes: 'Integral to the average everyday life is awareness of a fixed point in space, a firm position from which we "proceed" (whether every day or over larger periods of time) and to which we return in due course. This firm position is what we call "home"'.[20] Like everyday life itself, home constitutes a base, a taken-for-granted grounding, which allows us to make forays into other worlds. It is central to the anthropomorphic organisation of space in everyday life; we experience space not according to the distanced gaze of the cartographer, but in circles of increasing proximity or distance from the experiencing self. Home lies at the centre of these circles. According to Heller, familiarity is an everyday need, and familiarity combines with the promise of protection and warmth to create the positive everyday associations of home.

20. Agnes Heller, *Everyday Life*, Routledge and Kegan Paul, London 1984, p239.

Home is also important to Lefebvre's discussion of everyday life, but his attitude is more ambivalent. Home becomes an occasion for meditating on his own discomfort with the everyday lives of others. Describing a suburban development at the outskirts of Paris, he is unable to suppress his own sense of irritation. 'The owners' superficiality oozes forth in an abundance of ridiculous details: china animals on the roofs, glass globes and well-pruned shrubs along the miniature paths, plaques adorned with mottos, self-important pediments'.[21] Home is a symbol of complacency, pretentiousness and petit-bourgeois bad taste. Yet Lefebvre is also critical of his own reaction. He admits that going into one of these suburban houses would probably seem like entering heaven to the migrant workers at Renault. 'Why should I say anything against these people who - like me - come home from work everyday? They seem to be decent folk who live with their families, who love their children. Can we blame them for not wanting the world in which they live reasonably at home to be transformed?'[22]

21. Lefebvre, *Critique of Everyday Life*, 1991, *op. cit.*, p43.

22. *Ibid.*, p43.

This is surely a key citation in understanding the spatial dimensions of theories of everyday life. Home is not just a geographical designation, but a resonant metaphysical symbol. Lefebvre perceives the petit-bourgeois individual to be reasonably at home in the world. Being at home in the world is an implicit affront to the existential homelessness and anguish of the modern intellectual. Adorno writes: 'Dwelling, in the proper sense, is now impossible ... It is part of morality not to be at home in one's home'.[23] The vocabulary of modernity is a vocabulary of anti-home. It celebrates mobility, movement, exile, boundary crossing. It speaks enthusiastically about movement out into the world, but is silent about the return home. Its preferred location is the city street, the site of random encounters, unexpected events, multiplicity and difference. David Harvey, for example, sketches an image of the city as the 'place of mystery, the site of the unexpected, full of agitations and ferments'.[24] This chaotic ferment is in tune with the spirit of the critic, described as a restless analyst, constantly on the move. Home, by contrast, is the space of familiarity, dullness, stasis. The longing for home, the desire to attach oneself to a familiar space, is seen by most theorists of modernity as a regressive desire.

Home is, of course, a highly gendered space. Women have often been seen as the personification of home and even as its literal embodiment. Houses are often imagined as quasi-uterine spaces; conversely, the female body, notes Freud, is the 'former home of all human beings'.[25] As a result, feminists have often been eager to demystify the ideal of home as haven. One nineteenth-century female novelist, for example, imagined a utopian future in which the word 'home' would no longer exist.[26] Modern feminism, from Betty Friedan onwards, has repeatedly had recourse to a rhetoric of leaving home. Home is a prison, a trap, a straitjacket. In recent years, this critique of home has intensified: the discourse of contemporary feminism speaks enthusiastically of migrations, boundary crossings, nomadic subjects. Much of the same language pervades cultural studies. De Certeau dedicates *The Practice of Everyday Life* to 'a common hero, an ubiquitous character, walking in countless thousands on the streets'. His image of the agile pedestrian, adeptly weaving a distinctive textual path across the grid of city streets, has become a resonant symbol of the contemporary subject. Freedom and agency are traditionally symbolised by movement through public space. Cultural studies, in stressing the resistive dimensions of daily life, has drawn heavily on such images of mobility, as in Larry Grossberg's references to nomadic subjects 'wandering through the ever-changing places and spaces, vectors and apparatuses of everyday life'.[27]

In response, Janet Wolff has suggested that such metaphors are masculine and hence problematic for feminism. She notes the persistent association of maleness with travel and femininity with stasis. But, as she also acknowledges, women have always travelled, and they now do so in vast numbers, as tourists, researchers, aid workers, guest workers, refugees. To describe metaphors of travel as inherently alienating to women seems too simple. Wolff also ignores the geopolitical dimensions of such metaphors.

23. Theodor Adorno, *Minima Moralia: Reflections from Damaged Life*, Verso, London 1974, pp38-39.

24. David Harvey, *Consciousness and the Urban Experience*, Basil Blackwell, Oxford 1985, p250.

25. Sigmund Freud, *The Uncanny*, in *Sigmund Freud vol. 14: Art and Literature*, Penguin, Harmondsworth 1985, p368.

26. Dolores Hayden, *The Grand Domestic Revolution: A History of Feminist Designs for American Homes, Neighborhoods and Cities*, MIT Press, Cambridge 1981, p137.

27. Lawrence Grossberg, 'Wandering Audiences, Nomadic Critics', *Cultural Studies*, 2, 3, 1988, p384.

28. Janet Wolff, 'On the Road Again: Metaphors of Travel in Cultural Criticism', *Resident Alien: Feminist Cultural Criticism*, Yale University Press, New Haven 1995.

29. Doreen Massey, 'A Place Called Home?' *New Formations* 17, Lawrence and Wishart, London 1992, p8.

30. Doreen Massey, 'Politics and Space/Time', *New Left Review*, 196, 1992, pp65-84.

31. Beverley Skeggs, *Formations of Class and Gender*, Sage, London 1997.

The new feminist interest in nomadism, travelling and boundary crossing derives at least partly from greater interest in exploring the geographical, ethnic and cultural differences amongst women.[28]

Still, it is true that such metaphors are partial, casting light upon particular aspects of experience only to relegate other parts of daily life to the shadows. In spite of the hyperbole in postmodern theory about nomadism, hyperspace and time-space compression, writes Doreen Massey, 'much of life for many people, even in the heart of the first world, still consists of waiting in a bus-shelter with your shopping for a bus that never comes'.[29] Similarly, Massey questions the assumption that postmodern global space has done away with the need for home and has left us placeless and disoriented. She notes the continuing importance of place and locality in everyday life, while questioning the belief that a desire for home is inauthentic or reactionary. This assumption, she argues, arises out a recurring tendency to see space and time as ontological opposites rather than as interconnected dimensions of human experience. Time, typically, is equated with history, movement and change, whereas space is seen as static, ahistorical and conservative.[30]

The everyday significance of home clearly needs to be imagined differently. First of all, home is, in de Certeau's terms, an active practising of place. Even if home is synonymous with familiarity and routine, that familiarity is actively produced over time, above all through the effort and labour of women. Furthermore, while home may sometimes seem static, both the reality and the ideology of home change dramatically over time. Second, the boundaries between home and non-home are leaky. The home is not a private enclave cut off from the outside world, but is powerfully shaped by broader social currents, attitudes, and desires. Think, for example, of the Martha Stewart phenomenon. Here we see a distinctively new vision of the home as *Gesamtkunstwerk*, a highly stylised and labour-intensive blend of folkloric authenticity and postmodern chic.

Finally, home, like any other space, is shaped by conflicts and power struggles. It is often the site of intergenerational conflicts, such that an adolescent sense of identity can be predicated upon a burning desire to leave home. It can be a place of female subordination as well as an arena where women can show competence in the exercise of domestic skills. Home is often a place for displaying commodities and hence saturated by class distinctions; a recent ethnography of working-class women notes their embarrassment at the perceived insufficiency of their home.[31] Home also acquires particularly poignant meanings for migrants and their descendants. In *Zami*, for example, Audre Lorde shapes the meaning of a life story around changing definitions of home. As a child, Lorde absorbs her mother's nostalgic yearning for her Caribbean homeland, as a young adult she must leave her mother's house in order to help create a 'house of difference' in the New York lesbian community, and finally she arrives at a vision of home informed by both her American lesbian identity and her Caribbean heritage.[32]

As this example suggests, the idea of home is complex and temporally fluid. Home should not be confused with a fantasy of origin; any individual life story will contain different and changing visions of home. My definition is intentionally minimal; it includes any often visited place that is the object of cathexis, that in its very familiarity becomes a symbolic extension and confirmation of the self. As Roger Silverstone argues, home is 'an investment of meaning in space'.[33] Such a familiar location fulfils both affective and pragmatic needs. It is a storage place, both literally and symbolically; home often contains many of the objects that have helped to shape a life-history, and the meanings and memories with which these objects are encrypted. Home is, in Mary Douglas's phrase, a 'memory machine'.[34] In this regard, Heller's focus on home as central to the spatial organisation of everyday life provides a useful corrective to the current infatuation with mobility and travel.

A number of feminist scholars, while not explicitly concerned with everyday life, are developing alternative visions of the symbolism and politics of home. bell hooks, for example, suggests that the history of home has very different meanings for African-American women as well as for men. 'Historically, African American people believed that the construction of a homeplace, however fragile and tenuous (the slave hut, the wooden shack) had a radical political dimension. Despite the brutal reality of racial apartheid, of domination, one's homeplace was the one site where one could freely confront the issue of humanisation, where one could resist'.[35] The title of an early black feminist anthology, *Home Girls*, underscores this more positive, though by no means uncritical, vision of home as a potential source of warmth and strength.[36]

In a recent essay, Iris Marion Young also makes a thoughtful case for rethinking feminist attitudes to house and home. Questioning the nostalgic longing for home as a place of stable identities predicated on female self-sacrifice, she nevertheless wants to recognise the symbolic richness and cultural complexity of 'home-making' (which is not just housework). Home, she argues, is a specific materialisation of the body and the self; things and spaces become layered with meaning, value and memory. This materialisation does not fix identity but anchors it in a physical space that creates certain continuities between past and present. 'Dwelling in the world means we are located among objects, artifacts, rituals, and practices that configure who we are in our particularity'.[37] Young explicitly tackles the oppressive aspects of home in a moving account of her own mother's failure to conform to the ideal of the 1950s housewife and its tragic consequences. Yet she also wants to insist that home can be a place of important human values, including safety, individuation, privacy and preservation, that need to be reclaimed, rather than disdained by feminism.

A masculinist cultural tradition, Meaghan Morris suggests, has perceived home as the site of both 'frustrating containment (home as dull) and of

32. Audre Lorde, *Zami: A New Spelling of my Name*, Sheba Feminist Publishers, London 1982.

33. Silverstone, *Television and Everyday Life*, 1994, op. cit., p28.

34. Mary Douglas, 'The Idea of a Home: A Kind of Space', in *Home: A Place in the World*, Arien Mack (ed), New York University Press, New York 1993, p268.

35. bell hooks, 'Homeplace: A Site of Resistance', in *Yearning: Race, Gender and Cultural Politics*, South End Press, Boston 1990, p42.

36. Barbara Smith (ed), *Home Girls: A Black Feminist Anthology*, Kitchen Table: Women of Color Press, New York 1983.

37. Iris Marion Young, 'House and Home: Feminist Variations on a Theme', *Intersecting Voices: Dilemmas of Gender, Political Philosophy and Policy*, Princeton University Press, Princeton, New Jersey 1997, p153.

38. Meaghan Morris, 'At Henry Parkes Motel', *Cultural Studies*, 2, 1, 1988, p12.

39. 'The domestic has become a complex and contradictory reality ... Do-it-yourself decoration and house improvement, the increasing personalisation of media and information technologies, consumption itself in all its various manifestations, the intensification of the home as a leisure centre, as well as a place of paid work, all signify its changing status'. Silverstone, *Television and Everyday Life*, 1994, *op. cit.*, p51. For one case study of the gender politics of home, see Lesley Johnson, 'As Housewives we are Worms': Women, Modernity and the Home Question', *Cultural Studies*, 10, 3, 1996: 449-463. Jane Juffer's recent book *At Home with Pornography: Women, Sex and Everyday Life*, New York University Press, New York 1998 is an important contribution to rethinking the meanings of home, modernity and space as well as redefining feminist approaches to pornography.

40. Lefebvre, *Everyday Life in the Modern World*, 1984, *op. cit.*, p24.

41. Samuel Beckett, *Proust and Three Dialogues*, John Calder, London 1965, p19.

truth to be rediscovered (home as real).'[38] In both cases, it has been seen as existing outside the flux and change of an authentically modern life. Yet home is not always linked to tradition and opposed to autonomy and self-definition: on the contrary, it has been central to many women's experience of modernity. A feminist theory of everyday life might question the assumption that being modern requires an irrevocable sundering from home, and might simultaneously explicate the modern dimensions of everyday experiences of home.[39]

HABIT

The temporality of everyday life and its spatial anchoring are closely connected. Both repetition and home address an essential feature of everyday life: its familiarity. The everyday is synonymous with habit, sameness, routine; it epitomises both the comfort and boredom of the ordinary. Lefebvre writes: 'The modern ... stands for what is novel, brilliant, paradoxical ... it is (apparently) daring, and transitory', whereas 'the quotidian is what is humble and solid, what is taken for granted ... undated and (apparently) insignificant'.[40]

The idea of habit crystallises this experience of dailiness. Habit describes not simply an action but an attitude: habits are often carried out in a semi-automatic, distracted, or involuntary manner. Certain forms of behaviour are inscribed upon the body, part of a deeply ingrained somatic memory. We drive to work, buy groceries, or type a routine letter in a semi-conscious, often dream-like state. Our bodies go through the motions while our minds are elsewhere. Particular habits may be intentionally cultivated or may build up imperceptibly over time. In either case, they often acquire a life of their own, shaping us as much as we shape them.

'Habit', writes Samuel Beckett dourly, 'is the ballast that chains the dog to its vomit'.[41] Modern literature has exposed these congealed patterns of daily life and questioned the sleep-walking demeanour inspired by the tyranny of habit. Its relationship to the everyday is often paradoxical, seeking to both preserve and negate it. On the one hand, literature is often passionately interested in the ordinary; think of the great realist novels of the nineteenth century, the encyclopaedic scope of *Ulysses* as an 'inventory of everyday life',[42] the domestic details of a postmodern novel such as *White Noise*. On the other hand, it also tries to redeem the everyday by rescuing it from its opacity, de-familiarising it and making us newly attentive to its mysteries. Yet this very act of magnifying and refracting taken-for-granted minutiae transcends the very dailiness it seeks to depict. Literature's heightened sensitivity to the microscopic detail marks its difference from the casual inattentiveness marking the everyday experience of everyday life.

A similar critique of habitual perception lies at the heart of contemporary critical theory. From Barthes, Althusser and others we have learned to see the taken-for-granted as the ruse of bourgeois ideology. Judith Butler has shown that sedimented practices are the means by which repressive regimes of gender do their work. Postmodern accounts of the 'aestheticisation of everyday life', the invasion of our inner selves by the images and slogans of the mass media, only intensify this suspicion of everyday beliefs and attitudes. There is nowhere to run and nowhere to hide: no sanctum of the ordinary that escapes the tentacular grip of late capitalist consumer culture. The commonsense assumptions and routines by which we organise our lives are insidious precisely because they seem natural; their power can only be countered by ongoing critical vigilance. The work of theory is to break the spell of the habitual and the everyday.

Phenomenological studies of everyday life are, by contrast, much less censorious of habit. Indeed, they suggest that everyday life is self-evident and that this is necessary rather than unfortunate. Everyday life simply *is* the routine act of conducting one's day-to-day existence without making it an object of conscious attention. 'The reality of everyday life is taken-for-granted *as* reality. It does not require additional verification over and beyond its simple presence. It is simply *there*, as self-evident and compelling facticity. I *know* that it is real. While I am capable of engaging in doubts about its reality, I am obliged to suspend such doubt as I routinely exist in everyday life'.[43]

In other words, everyday life is the sphere of what Schutz calls the natural attitude. This does not mean that the forms of everyday life are inevitable or unchanging. Long before the current interest in gender as performance, ethnographers such as Goffman were describing the performance of self in daily life and noting the socially constructed and conventional nature of our identities. The point is, however, that such performances are for the most part automatic, conducted with a constant, but semi-conscious vigilance. Unless a specific problem emerges to demand our attention, we rarely pause to reflect upon the mundane ritualised practices around which much of our everyday life is organised. As Berger and Luckmann point out, 'our natural attitude of daily life is pervasively determined by a *pragmatic motive*'.[44]

Agnes Heller also insists on this point, claiming that it is impossible in principle to adopt a critical, self-reflexive attitude towards all aspects of everyday life. She writes: 'we would simply not be able to survive in the multiplicity of everyday demands and everyday activities if all of them required inventive thinking … Disengagement is an indispensable precondition for … continued activity'.[45] Heller's defense of habit is a pragmatic one; in order to survive in the world and get things done, we depend on routine. Certain facets of everyday life can be called into question, but it is simply impossible to doubt everything at once. Heller insists: 'It is absolutely imperative that in certain types of activity our praxis and our thinking should become repetitive'.[46] Habit is the necessary precondition for impulse and innovation.

Of course, phenomenological studies of everyday life are concerned with description rather than explanation and thus do not address

42. Lefebvre, *Everyday Life in the Modern World*, 1984, *op. cit.*, p3.

43. Peter Berger and Thomas Luckmann, *The Social Construction of Reality: A Treatise in the Sociology of Knowledge*, Penguin, Harmondsworth 1967, p37.

44. Schutz and Luckmann, *The Structures of the Life-World*, 1983 vol. 1, p6.

45. Heller, *Everyday Life*, 1984, *op. cit.*, p129.

46. *Ibid.*, p259.

questions of politics and power. An over-reliance on habit can be personally constraining and socially detrimental, promoting a complacent acceptance of the way things are. In this sense, habit can serve conservative ends. Yet contemporary theory tends to overpoliticise the routines of everyday life in presenting the 'natural attitude' as nothing more than a vehicle of ideology. At its most extreme, this results in a denunciation of any form of fixity in favour of permanent flux. Habit becomes the enemy of an authentic life.

This is, however, to see habit only as a straitjacket and constraint, and to ignore the ways in which routines may strengthen, comfort and provide meaning. Furthermore, the distracted performance of routine tasks is surely a quintessential feature of the everyday, occurring across a wide range of histories and cultures. This is not to deny the vast differences between particular experiences of everyday life nor the fact, stressed by Foucault and Elias, that the modern era has led to distinctively new forms of internalised discipline. It is, however, to argue that the ritualised activity known as habit constitutes a fundamental element of being-in-the-world whose social meanings may be complex and varied.

From such a perspective, habit is not something we can ever hope to transcend. Rather it constitutes an essential part of our embeddedness in everyday life and our existence as social beings. For example, the contemporary city may constitute a chaotic labyrinth of infinite possibilities, yet in our daily travels we often choose to carve out a familiar path, managing space and time by tracing out the same route again and again. Furthermore, habit is not opposed to individuality but intermeshed with it; our identity is formed out of a distinctive blend of behavioural and emotional patterns, repeated over time. To be suddenly deprived of the rhythm of one's personal routines, as often happens to those admitted to hospitals, prisons, retirement homes or other large institutions, can be a source of profound disorientation and distress. Furthermore, even the most esoteric and elevated of activities contain routinised elements. Lefebvre notes that no cultural practice escapes the everyday: science, war, affairs of state, philosophy all contain a mundane dimension.[47]

Paula Treichler has observed that cultural studies pays little attention to the daily life of academics, as if everyday life were something that only others experience.[48] As a result, everyday life often has the lure of the exotic. Cultural critics now treat it with reverential respect and endow it with the complexity and ambiguity previously attributed to the modern work of art. Within some versions of cultural studies, daily life constantly seethes with subversive energies. Yet everyday life is not just the realm of the other but of the self, not just the realm of transgression but also of familiarity, boredom and habit. To recognise that we all inhabit everyday life is not to deny social differences but simply to acknowledge a common grounding in the mundane.

Conversely, no life is defined completely by the everyday. Here I

47. Lefebvre, *Critique de la vie quotidienne*, 1961, *op. cit.*, p61.

48. John Fiske, 'Cultural Studies and the Culture of Everyday Life: Discussion,' in *Cultural Studies*, Lawrence Grossberg, Cary Nelson and Paula Treichler (eds), Routledge, New York 1992, p167.

disagree with the common claim that only the élite are free to transcend the quotidian, that 'most persons have *nothing but* that ordinary everyday life'.[49] This is to impose a fantasy of sameness and profound limitation onto the lives of ordinary individuals. Surely every life contains epiphanic moments, experiences of trauma and points of departure from mundane routines: religious ecstasy, sexual passion, drug-taking, childbirth, encounters with death or simply moments of distanced and thoughtful reflection on the meaning and purpose of one's life. Such heightened, intense, and often self-conscious episodes break just as dramatically with everyday routines as do the afore-mentioned realms of philosophy, high art or male heroism. It is hard to see how any specific transcendence of everyday life can be deemed more or less genuine than any other. Every life, in other words, contains elements of both the everyday and the non-everyday, though some lives are clearly more anchored in the mundane than others.

Everyday life, furthermore, does not afford any automatic access to the 'realness' of the world. Of course, it is true that daily life does involve certain forms of practical knowledge and skills without which we could not survive. Yet the assertion that everyday life is the realm of the concrete rather than the abstract needs to be qualified.[50] As both Heller and Schutz point out, everyday life is also the sphere of typification, that is, of a reliance on type, analogy and generality. Precisely because we cannot pause to question everything in the daily rush, we often depend upon common-sense assumptions and pre-existing schema that may not be supported by empirical evidence. According to Schutz, to live in the life-world is to take pre-existing knowledge as simply given 'until further notice', until a particular encounter or event serves to render it problematic. Heller suggests that everyday thinking is often fetishistic, accepting things and institutions as they are and bracketing them off from their origins.[51]

Of course we may also question our own beliefs; the everyday includes the ever-present possibility of innovation and change. Furthermore, everyday life should not be conceptualised as a homogeneous and predictable terrain. It embraces a diverse range of activities, attitudes and forms of behaviour; it contains 'broken patterns, non-rational and duplicitous actions, irresolvable conflicts and unpredictable events'.[52] Nevertheless, we typically conduct our daily lives on the basis of numerous unstated and unexamined assumptions about the way things are, about the continuity, identity and reliability of objects and individuals. For Schutz and Heller this is a necessary condition of everyday life rather than a moral or political failing. They would agree with Wittgenstein that theoretical critique is a specific language game that cannot provide a guide for the conduct of an entire life. The everyday is not necessarily more real, more authentic or more immediate than the non-everyday, but it has a certain pragmatic priority simply because it is 'what we are, first of all, and most often'.[53]

49. Dorothee Wierling, 'The History of Everyday Life and Gender Relations: On Historical and Historiographical Relationships', in *The History of Everyday Life*, Alf Lüdtke (ed), Princeton University Press, Princeton, N.J. 1995, p151.

50. Fiske, 'The Culture of Everyday Life', in *Cultural Studies*, 1992, *op. cit.*

51. Schutz and Luckmann, *Structures of the Life-World*, 1983 vol. 1, p8; Heller, *Everyday Life*, 1984, *op. cit.*, p52.

52. Silverstone, *Television and Everyday Life*, 1994, *op. cit.*, p7.

53. Blanchot, 'Everyday Speech', 1987, *op. cit.*, p12.

In conclusion I want to draw together the various threads of my argument and to elaborate on its implications. How useful is the idea of everyday life? What exactly does it mean? How should it be applied? While much of my paper has focused on the contrasting definitions of everyday life in sociology and cultural studies, I now want to make more explicit connections to feminist scholarship.

Feminism has, of course, traditionally conceived itself as a politics of everyday life. In practice, this has meant very different things. On the one hand feminists have deployed a hermeneutics of suspicion vis-à-vis the everyday, showing how the most mundane, taken-for-granted activities - conversation, housework, body language, styles of dress - serve to reinforce patriarchal norms. The feminist gaze reveals the everyday world as problematic, in Dorothy Smith's phrase;[54] it is here, above all, that gender hierarchy is reproduced, invisibly, pervasively and over time. This sensitivity to the power dynamics of everyday life has been heightened by the impact of poststructuralist thought, with its suspicion of any form of fixity. As a result, much current feminist scholarship is involved in a persistent questioning of the commonsensical, taken-for-granted and mundane.

54. Smith, *The Everyday World as Problematic, op. cit.*

On the other hand, everyday life has also been hailed as a distinctively female sphere and hence as a source of value. The fact that women traditionally cook, clean, change diapers, raise children and do much of the routine work of family reproduction is perceived by some feminists as a source of strength. Because of this grounding in the mundane, it is argued, women have a more realistic sense of how the world actually operates and are less estranged from their bodies and from the messy, chaotic, embodied realities of life. Thus, from the perspective of feminist standpoint theory, women's connection to daily life is something to be celebrated. Here everyday life is not a ruse of patriarchy but rather a sign of women's grounding in the practical world.

My discussion has shown, I hope, that this ambivalence has a history, that everyday life has long been subject to intense and conflicting emotional investments. Without wishing to deny the new insights generated by feminism, I would suggest that it also continues a tradition of thought that has viewed the everyday as both the most authentic and the most inauthentic of spheres. It is in this context that one can speak of the invention of everyday life. In one sense the phrase sounds paradoxical, precisely because daily life refers to the most mundane, routine, overlooked aspects of human experience - those seemingly beyond the reach of invention, abstraction and theory. Yet I have tried to show that everyday life is not simply a neutral label for a pre-existing reality, but is freighted down with layers of meanings and associations.

One of these associations is, of course, gender. I have explored some of the ways in which everyday life has been connected to women, without simply endorsing the view that women represent daily life. The problem with this view, as the work of Lefebvre makes particularly clear, is that it presents a romantic view of both everyday life and women by associating them with the natural, authentic and primitive. This nostalgia feeds into a long chain of dichotomies - society versus community, modernity versus tradition, public versus private - which do not help us to understand the social organisation of gender and which deny women's contemporaneity, self-consciousness and agency. Furthermore, to affirm women's special grounding in everyday life is to take at face value a mythic ideal of heroic male transcendence and to ignore the fact that men are also embodied, embedded subjects, who live, for the most part, repetitive, familiar and ordinary lives.

What I have found helpful in the phenomenological scholarship is that it takes seriously the ordinariness of everyday life without idealising or demonising it. Within cultural studies, everyday life is often made to carry enormous symbolic weight. Either it is rhapsodically affirmed and painted in glowing colours or it is excoriated as the realm of ultimate alienation and dehumanisation. Yet if the everyday is an indispensable aspect of all human lives, as I have argued, it becomes harder to endow it with an intrinsic political content. The everyday is robbed of much of its portentous symbolic meaning.

Thus it makes more sense to think of the everyday as a way of experiencing the world rather than as a circumscribed set of activities within the world. Everyday life simply is the process of becoming acclimatised to assumptions, behaviours and practices which come to seem self-evident and taken for granted. In other words, everydayness is not an intrinsic quality that magically adheres to particular actions or persons (women, the working class). Rather, it is a lived process of routinisation that all individuals experience. Certain tasks which at first appear awkward or strange - driving is an obvious example - gradually become second nature to us over time. Conversely, the everyday lives of others can seem deeply alien to us, precisely because the quotidian is not an objectively given quality but a lived relationship.

Such routinisation may be politically problematic or even dangerous in some contexts, but it is surely a mistake to see habit as such as intrinsically reactionary. The work of Heller and Schutz is valuable in affirming the pragmatic need for repetition, familiarity and taken-for-grantedness in everyday life, as a necessary precondition for human survival. As Susan Bordo points out in another context, it is an intellectual delusion to think that we can simply abandon our habits, blindspots and assumptions and embrace an infinitely shifting, self-undermining multiplicity of perspectives. This belief is a delusion because such habits form the very basis of who we are.[55] Influenced by modernist ideals of innovation and irony, contemporary theorists have tended either to excoriate the everyday for its routine, mundane qualities, or to celebrate the everyday while pretending that such qualities do not exist. It is time, perhaps, to make peace with the ordinariness of daily life.

55. Susan Bordo, 'Feminism, Postmodernism and Gender-Skepticism', in *Feminism/ Postmodernism*, Linda Nicholson (ed), Routledge, New York 1990.

Thanks to Sara Blair for helpful references and to Allan Megill for stylistic suggestions.

Integuments:
The Scar, The Sheen, The Screen

Steven Connor

INTEGUMENTS: ANZIEU AND THE SKIN EGO

One might say that the language of critical and cultural theory has been full of the presence and pressure of the skin, were it not that the specific compulsion of the skin as a surface disallowed so voluminous a figure. Whether in the concern of Emmanuel Levinas with the exposed skin of the face, as the sign of essential ethical nudity before the other; the ghostly drama of the trace and the drama of its inscriptions on various kinds of surface bequeathed by Levinas to Derrida; the elaborations of the play of bodily surfaces, volumes and membranes in Derrida's concepts of double invagination, the hymen and the sexual dynamics of the pen and the web-sail-paper it punctuates; the concept of the fold or 'pli' in the rethinking of subjective and philosophical depth in the work of Gilles Deleuze; the erotics of texture, tissue and tegument played out through the work of Roland Barthes; the fascination with the intrigues of the surface in the work of Baudrillard; or the abiding presence of skin in the work of Jean-François Lyotard, from the arresting evocation of the opened-out skin of the planar body at the beginning of his *Libidinal Economy* through to the Levinasian emphasis on the annunciatory powers of skin at moments through *The Inhuman*; throughout this work, ubiquitously, the skin *insists*. Perhaps this epidermal insistence relates to that rapt attention to surfaces, as symptom, seduction and defence, which is to be found throughout modernism, from the aestheticism of Wilde, Whistler and Beerbohm, to the emphasis upon hardness, angularity and exteriority in the work of T.E. Hulme and Wyndham Lewis and, finally, the apotheosis of flatness in the critical writing of Clement Greenberg.

The skin insists not only in critical and cultural theory but also in contemporary life. Everywhere, the skin, normally invisible except as the bearer of the messages written upon or displayed through it - of beauty, health, age, status and race - is becoming visible on its own account; not only in the display of its surfaces and forms in cinema and photography, in the concerted efforts to control and manipulate its appearance by means of cosmetics and plastic surgery, and the marked investment in the skin in practices and representations associated with fetishism and sadomasochism, but also in the anxious concern with the abject frailty and vulnerability of the skin, and the destructive rage against it exercised in violent fantasies and representations of all kinds. All of this appears to bear out the judgement of James Joyce - that 'modern man has an epidermis rather than a soul'.[1] It may strike us as a massive act of literalisation, or defiguration; the primary purpose of the skin having always been anyway to put ostension in the place of figure or allegory. This essay enquires into the cultural phenomenology of this ubiquitous ostension of the skin, and the contemporary fascination with the powers of the skin, as substance, vehicle and metaphor.

Nobody can go far in this kind of enquiry without taking account of the remarkable work of Didier Anzieu on the relations between the experience of the skin and the formation and sustaining of the ego. Anzieu underwent analysis with Jacques Lacan between 1949 and 1953 and was a vocal member of Lacan's seminars in the 1960s and 1970s. In his own work from the 1970s onwards, however, he began to turn decisively away from Lacan's influence. In place of Lacan's formulation, 'the unconscious is structured like a language', Anzieu came to prefer the principle that the unconscious is structured like the body; by which, however, he means not the body known to anatomy and physiology, but the imaginary or phantasmal body: 'the body of the phantastic anatomy of hysteria and infantile sexual theories (as Freud clearly showed); and, more fundamentally still, in a more primary and archaic manner, the body as source of the first sensory motor experiences, the first communications and the oppositions that relate to the very basis of perception and thought'.[2] Anzieu has therefore turned away from the textual-interpretative project of realising, or at least unveiling, desire-in-repression, and has mitigated the related Lacanian hostility to the concept of the centring ego, and the centring on the concept of the ego in American psychoanalysis. Anzieu allies himself instead with a psychoanalytic tradition which attempts to understand the formation and functioning of the ego and to develop therapies to repair and sustain it. Anzieu was drawn in particular to the work of Paul Federn on the importance of the experience of the edges and peripheries of the self, and Paul Schilder's related work on the body-image.[3]

These writers, like Anzieu himself, attempt to draw out the implications of a number of tantalisingly undeveloped statements made by Freud in his later work regarding the nature of the ego, and, in particular, the following remarks in *The Ego and the Id*:

> The ego is first and foremost a bodily ego; it is not merely a surface entity, but is itself the projection of a surface. (i.e. the ego is ultimately derived from bodily sensations, chiefly from those springing from the surface of the body. It may thus be regarded as a mental projection of the surface of the body, besides, as we have seen above, representing the superficies of the mental apparatus.)[4]

Anzieu also draws upon interesting work by the English psychoanalysts Frances Tustin and Esther Bick on the formation of defensive shells or carapace-egos in autistic patients as well as some scattered speculations

1. *James Joyce in Padua*, Louis Berrone (ed and trans), Random House, New York 1977, p21.

2. Didier Anzieu, *A Skin for Thought: Interviews With Gilbert Tarrab on Psychology and Psychoanalysis*, Daphne Nash Briggs (trans), Karnac, London 1990, p43.

3. Paul Federn, *Ego Psychology and the Psychoses*, Basic Books, New York 1952; Paul Schilder, *The Image and Appearance of the Human Body*, International Universities Press, New York 1935.

4. Sigmund Freud, 'The Ego and the Id' (1923), *The Standard Edition of the Complete Psychological Works of Sigmund Freud*, James Strachey (trans), Vol XIX, Hogarth Press, London 1953-74, p26 and n1.

5. Bertram Lewin, 'Sleep, the Mouth, and the Dream Screen', *Psychoanalytic Quarterly* 15, 1946, pp419-34; Esther Bick, 'The Experience of the Skin in Early Object Relations', *International Journal of Psycho-Analysis* 49, 1968, pp484-6; Francis Tustin, *Autism and Childhood Psychosis*, Routledge and Kegan Paul, London 1972; J. Guillaumin, 'La peau du centaure, ou le retournement projectif de l'intérieur du corps dans la création littéraire', in J. Guillaumin et al, *Corps-Création - Entre Lettres et Psychanalyse*, Presses Universitaires de Lyon, Lyon 1980; Barrie M. Biven, 'The Role of Skin in Normal and Abnormal Development, With a Note on the Poet Sylvia Plath', *International Review of Psychoanalysis*, 9, 1982, pp205-28; Claudie Cachard, 'Enveloppes de corps, membranes de rêve', *L'Evolution psychiatrique*, 46, 1981, pp847-56.

6. *Le Moi-peau*, Bordas, Paris 1985; *The Skin Ego*, Chris Turner (trans), Yale University Press, New Haven 1989.

7. Anzieu, *A Skin for Thought*, op. cit., p63.

8. Anzieu, *The Skin Ego*, p40. References hereafter in the text, abbreviated to *SE*.

regarding the importance of screens, membranes and envelopes in psychic experience in the work of predecessors such as Bertram Lewin and Barrie Biven and French contemporaries such as J. Guillaumin and Claudie Cachard.[5] The culmination of this work of synthesis and elaboration was his *Le Moi-Peau* of 1985, which was translated into English as *The Skin Ego* (not, as might have been possible, *The Ego Skin*) in 1989.[6]

As a way of understanding the dynamics of self-imagining, Anzieu's model in *The Skin Ego* is both powerfully simple, and yet interpretatively versatile. Anzieu proposes that 'the ego is the projection on the psyche of the surface of the body',[7] and defines the skin ego as 'a mental image of which the Ego of the child makes use during the early phases of its development to represent itself as an Ego containing psychical contents, on the basis of the experience of the surface of the body'.[8] Though Anzieu is attentive to the possibilities of psychosomatic relationships between the mind and the skin, his work goes in the direction specified by Ashley Montagu when he wrote in 1971 that 'the psychosomatic approach to the study of skin may be regarded as centrifugal; that is, it proceeds from the mind outwards to the skin', and recommended 'the opposite approach, namely from the skin to the mind; in other words, the centripetal approach'.[9] The skin fulfils an extraordinarily wide and diverse range of functions with respect both to the body and to the ego. Anzieu distinguishes nine, as follows.

Supporting: In the same way that the skin functions as a support for the skeleton and its muscles, the Skin Ego fulfills a function of *maintaining* the psyche (*SE*, 98).

Containing: To the skin as covering for the entire surface of the body and into which all the external sense organs are inserted, corresponds the *containing* function of the Skin Ego (*SE*, 101).

Shielding: As in Freud, the Ego acts *'as a protective shield against stimulation'* (*SE*, 102).

Individuating: In a similar fashion, the Skin Ego performs a function of *individuating* the Self, thus giving the Self a sense of its own uniqueness (*SE*, 103).

Connecting: The skin is a surface containing pockets and cavities where the sense organs...are located. The Skin Ego is a psychical surface which connects up sensations of various sorts and makes them stand out as forms against the original background formed by the tactile envelope: this is the Skin Ego's function of *intersensoriality* (*SE*, 103).

Sexualizing: The Skin Ego fulfils the function of providing a surface for *supporting sexual excitation*, a surface upon which, in cases of normal development, erogenous zones may be localized (*SE*, 104).

Recharging: The skin's function as a surface receiving permanent stimulation of the sensori-motor tonus from external excitations has its counterpoint in the Skin Ego's function of *libidinal recharging* of the psychical functioning (*SE*, 105).

Signifying: The Skin Ego fulfils a function of registering tactile sensory traces ... Socially an individual's membership of a social group is shown by incisions, scarifications, skin-painting, tattooing, by his make-up and hair-style, and by his clothes, which are another aspect of the same thing. The Skin Ego is the original parchment which preserves, like a palimpsest, the erased, scratched-out, written-over first outlines of an 'original' pre-verbal writing made up of traces upon the skin (*SE*, 105).

Assaulting, Destroying: [T]ransported to the periphery of the Self, these parts [anger, violence, self-destructiveness emanating from the id] have become encysted in the surface layer which is the Skin Ego, where they cut into its continuity, destroy its cohesiveness and impair its function by reversing the goals of those functions. The imaginary skin which covers the Ego thus becomes a poisoned tunic, suffocating, burning, disintegrating. We might therefore speak in this case of a *toxic* function of the Skin Ego (*SE*, 108).

9. Ashley Montagu, *Touching: The Human Significance of the Skin*, 3rd edition., Harper and Row, New York 1986, p19.

It will be seen that the nine functions distinguished by Anzieu do not all co-operate or connect. In the terms of his own metaphor, they do not form a seamless whole or coherent volume, but rather a repertoire of different kinds of metaphorical enactment of skin function. In what follows, I will be drawing in particular upon the eighth and ninth functions, in which the skin becomes the bearer and container of meanings that are not endogenous, deriving from, or serving the purposes of the ego itself, but rather represent a certain kind of ego-reinforcing compromise between the ego and that which threatens to lacerate or destroy its fragile self-enclosure.

Before I do this, I want to try to draw out a striking ambivalence within the conception of the skin ego which, perhaps because it drives much of Anzieu's own diagnostic metaphorology, rarely becomes directly visible within that work. I refer to the structuring contrast between the skin as defining tactile sensation, and the skin as visible shape and form. The skin ego is formed from, and remains powerfully associated with, sensory impressions which are pre-visual or at best weakly visual. The skin ego comes into being in the infant's early attempts to perpetuate or recreate the conditions obtaining in the womb: in which its existence is organised almost wholly in terms of taste, touch and hearing and, in particular, a powerful combination of the last two. And yet, of course, after birth, the sheltering shroud or cocoon of hapto-acoustic sensation is no longer fully available to the infant, precisely because it is no longer wholly within that condition of oceanic oneness with its mother's body. The primal or prenatal ego forms, and is formed by, the experience of the skin as envelope, which is to say, as an atopic interiority without exterior or defining limit. But this fantasy can be constructed only by means of a post-parturitive experience of the skin as a separation. It is only because the skin also comes to be experienced as a membrane, which both divides and connects the self and the world, that the fantasy of the psychic envelope becomes possible. The pre-partum condition of atopic non-differentiation which the experience of the various psychic envelopes - the tactile envelope, the auditory envelope, and so on - preserves and restores, can henceforth be secured only by the differentiation of a fine and private *place* for the ego, which is extopically set apart from an assailing outside.

With birth, then, the skin is born into difference, or the task of differentiating self and world. Indeed, the skin also appears to be biologically implicated in the process of opening the other senses to their exteriors. In mammals, the abrasion experienced by the skin during its passage through the birth canal in vaginal delivery stimulates the action of breathing; in foals, calves and young chimpanzees, this process is prolonged and reinforced by licking immediately after birth, in the absence of which the animals will often fail to survive. Similarly, there is a marked increase in the tendency to apnoea and brachycardia in human babies delivered by caesarean section. This process may even begin before birth, since the rippling contractions of the womb prior to labour known as Braxton-Hicks contractions appear to stimulate the process whereby the foetus inhales and exhales the amniotic fluid. This uterine massage prepares the skin for the abrasions or writing of the world which it will receive upon its surface, and thus come into being *as* a surface. From the very beginning, or perhaps before it, the skin is the surface on which the world is writing the shape that the individual will take.

This birth into difference accomplished in and through the skin is also a birth into vision, or the spatial matrix in which vision will operate, long before the refining of the actual organs of sight. The retreat to the taste-touch-hearing complex of the psychic envelope is necessitated by the irruption into it (except that the spatial conception of irruption is itself evidence that the irruption must already have taken place) of a sense of relative position which has begun to serve the purposes of the eye more than those of the ear and skin. Thus the mirror-stage, which famously marks the accession of differentiated identity for Lacan, is anticipated for Anzieu in a series of as it were 'envelope-mirrors'. Support for such a conception of the skin is offered in a remarkable analysis of the myth of Perseus and the Medusa in a paper of 1971 by Francis Pasche.[10] Pasche focuses on the mythical shield of Perseus, which the hero uses to deflect the petrifying stare of the Medusa, and which allows him ultimately to triumph over it. Pasche identifies the reflective shield given to Perseus by Athena with the excitation-screen of the Pcpt.-Csc system defined by Freud in *Beyond the Pleasure Principle*, seeing it as the vital gift of perspective and differentiated self-perception contained in the mother's look.[11] Ultimately, Pasche declares, 'the shield-mirror is the structure of perception itself'.[12] The shield, or screen against external excitations, is also a mirror, in that it allows the ego to see itself, and to define its position within a world of determinate forms and relations. This imaginary shield derives, not only from the mother's look, says Pasche, but also from her skin: 'The mother is not merely the one who gratifies or

10. Francis Pasche, 'Le Bouclier de Persée, ou psychose et réalité', *Revue française de psychanalyse* 35, 1971, pp859-70.

11. Sigmund Freud, *Beyond the Pleasure Principle, Standard Edition*, Vol. XVIII, p28.

12. Pasche, 'Le Bouclier de Persée, *op. cit.*, p865, my translation.

frustrates, who accords more or less with desires; she is also a concrete reality, a surface, a skin surface, the skin of the world. And it is a piece of this skin, naturalised, which Athena offers to Perseus'.[13] Because it gives him the world's difference, the mother's skin is also a mirror in which the child can see himself. Far from being that undifferentiated plenitude into which the sharp alienation-into-singularity of the mirror stage cuts, the mother's body, and especially her skin, are already 'the first model, as a visible example of unification and bodily differentiation, as a mirror. The mother's body is the first mirror'.[14] The maternal skin-mirror countermands the fantasy of uterine re-assimilation, since it is 'the barrier that separates them, refusing every effort of re-fusion, forbidding the child the path leading back to the mother's belly, preventing the complete re-entry into the maternal structure, the maternal system'.[15]

However, this subordination of the auditory-tactile associations of the skin to the spatialising and differentiating imperatives of vision (and subsequently of language), is never complete. The skin takes its form(s) from the ceaseless iterations of this exchange between the always-to-be-reconstituted archaic plenitude of the hapto-acoustic ensemble and the differentiations imposed upon the skin from the outside. Sight - and the condition of being visible - is the wound of exposure that the egomorphic skin attempts to cure, through the modelling of a protective screen which is also a kind of ulceration of light. I find this conflict between the hapto-acoustic sense of self as envelope and the spatio-visual sense of self as divided membrane in the difference between the active-endogenous functions of supporting, containing and connecting found in functions 1 to 7 of Anzieu's scheme of the nine skin-functions, and those functions which are as it were marked on the skin from the outside, as most dramatically enacted in the last two functions, of signifying and assaulting.

It is a defining conflict which is also to be observed in more contemporary evocations of the skin as metaphor. Because the skin is ubiquitous, because, in its function as a connector of different regions of the self, and the source of a repertoire of different kinds of localising or morphological metaphor for the self (inside/outside, frontal/posterior, up/down), it is also, so to speak, the shape of shape itself, the skin is curiously invisible. The diffuseness of the skin, and its resistance to the localising and fragmenting powers of the eye, make it apt for the kind of erotic or euphoric celebration articulated for example by Rose-Marie Arbour:

> The skin, envelope or membrane, the site of osmosis, cannot be conceived or sensed except as a function of the entire body. It cannot be thought of or sensed in detachable fragments. It is at once interior and exterior; taking in both, it cannot be conceived in terms of an exclusion of one by the other. As the metaphor for this relation of self and world, it includes every movement from one to the other and is a model for thinking of art and eroticism, and for thinking them both at the same time.[16]

13. *Ibid.*, p866.

14. *Ibid.*, p867.

15. *Ibid.*

16. Rose-Marie Arbour, 'La Peau comme dessein', *Revue d'esthétique*, NS 11, 1986, p90.

And yet, precisely because of the omnipresence and unlocalised quality of the skin, it is also uniquely exposed to the operations of the other senses, and particularly those of the eye. As Louise Poissant explains:

> To the long list of cutaneous sensations must be added the most important of the affects connected to the skin: the exposure to looking. The skin, the sense associated with intimacy and proximity, is the only sense which can be the object of all the other senses. Indeed, it has an odour, it has a taste and, when rubbed or torn, a sound; but above all, it has a visual appearance, and is exposed to the eyes of others, to their desires and revulsions, to dangers. Doubtless it is this polyvalence which explains the importance, in both quantity and force, of the taboos and prohibitions imposed upon it. If the other senses have also been subjected to forms of regulation, the regulation of these senses bears more upon the object of the sensation than on the organ itself. If there are indeed things which one knows not to bring to one's lips, with rare exceptions, it is not the eyes, ears or nose which are themselves negated. In different ways in most cultures, the skin is. Its privileged relations with the sexual are perhaps the consequence of these prohibitions.[17]

17. Louise Poissant, 'Carnation', *Revue d'esthétique, op. cit.,* p105.

A similar ambivalence may be at work in the remarkable evocation of the skin which opens Jean-François Lyotard's *Libidinal Economy*. Here, Lyotard asks us to imagine the body, not as a containing and defining volume, but as an opened-out skin, in which the complex articulations of inside and outside, depth and surface are projected into two-dimensional flatness.

> Open the supposed body and spread out all its surfaces; not only the skin with each of its folds, wrinkles, scars, with its great velvety planes, and contiguous with it the scalp and the fleece of hair, the tender pubic fur, nipples, nails, transparent calluses under the heel, the light frill of the eyelids, set with lashes, but also open and spread, make explicit the *labia majora*, the *labia minora* with their blue network bathed in mucus, dilate the diaphragm of the anal sphincter ... [18]

18. Jean-François Lyotard, *Libidinal Economy*, Iain Hamilton Grant (trans), Athlone Press, London 1993.

The seeming reduction of the body to a graphic or even cartographic flatness is in fact intended to enlarge or deterritorialise the body, to dramatise its dynamic libidinal flows, which cannot be fixed, located or organised without repressive violence. The skin evoked metaphorically by Lyotard is designated, not with the word 'peau', but as 'une pellicule', a word evoking not just the epidermal surface, but its metaphorical displacement in photographic or cinematic film. The body that is opened out, or turned inside out for the inspecting gaze of the reader proves to have the form of an infinite unrolling: it is to be understood, not in terms of mapping of the body, but as a Moebius strip, in which the seeming continuity of a single surface in fact leads to the paradoxical exchange of recto and verso, inner and outer. Thus, while seeming to submit to the fixative powers of the eye, along with what Lyotard condemns as the theatricality of Western representational and conceptual thinking, by which he means the enforcement of stable relations of outer and inner, surface and depth, sign and referent, appearance and essence, the skin eludes and impairs these powers. The skin performs the function performed by the notion of the 'hymen' in Derrida's *Dissemination*, in that it is a surface which utopically exceeds every attempt to position or organise the body into a stable volume.

And yet Lyotard cannot entirely countermand the fixative, or defining qualities of the skin ego. The very sentence with which Lyotard achieves this effect, over two pages (and it *is* all one sentence) could be taken as an enactment of Anzieu's audiophonic envelope, which weaves an enclosing structure out of pure mobility or process, and which effects an audio-visual suturing of its movements.

THE SCAR

Recently, my reflections on the question of the meanings of skin have led me to wonder about the concern of children, especially between the ages of about three and six, with scars, scratches and cuts, as well as their intense and abiding preoccupation with the uses of sticking-plaster. One might imagine that, at this early stage in the development of the child's sense of body-image, the lesion, tearing, or perforation of the epidermal envelope can be experienced as the threat of complete collapse, as though the child's skin were sustained by a pressure from within like a balloon and, once punctured, might be transformed into a slack and shapeless rag of flesh. However, children of this age have already learned about the skin's spontaneous capacity to repair itself after it has been damaged. The trick of sticking sellotape over two opposing points of a balloon's surface, to allow one to insert a knitting needle into the balloon and out the other side without bursting it, is experienced with corresponding awe and rapture by children. I believe that these observed physical processes of cutaneous regeneration are accompanied by the development of psychological resources of an equivalent kind. Starting from a consideration of the way a child makes sense of and incorporates into the structure of its own self the processes of cutaneous lesion, scarring and regeneration, I want to move towards a consideration of the relationship between the rent and reconstituted skin in adult experience, most specifically in some practices and fantasies associated with sadomasochism, but also with the cultural generalisation of such image-dynamics. My suggestion, following, but also extending, the work of Anzieu, will be that the rending of the imaginary fabric or envelope of the self staged in such fantasy is both expressed and defended against in the metaphor of writing-on-the-skin: dermographia.

The child sees that the wound sustained by the skin, or through the skin, results in a mark, of abrasion, contusion, inflammation, or incision.

Where 'the skin has been broken' (in that curious English idiom which suggests a desire to see the skin not as a fabric, of which we should say it is torn or ripped, but as a hardened shell or membrane; the equivalent French expression, 'entamer la peau' does not have quite the primary associations of penetration through a hardened surface) the child learns to expect the formation of a scab. This scab is highly ambiguous. It is the perpetuation of the injury, to which the child pays close and repeated attention, each time experiencing a renewal, though with gradually diminishing intensity, of the shock of the injury to the skin, and the accompanying threat to the integrity of the secondary fabric of the ego-skin. But in marking the place of the injury, refusing to let it dissipate, the scab also transforms it. Since the scab is the mark of the injury, and not the injury itself, it transforms the injury *to* the skin into a mark left *on* the skin. A scab is a visual compromise between lesion and healing; it preserves the blemish or disfigurement to the smooth integrity of the skin's surface even as it affirms the skin's successful defence against puncturing or laceration. It is for this reason, surely, that children are unable to resist picking scabs. For the scab offers the pleasure of an averted threat; by reopening the wound, the child may play with and master the symbolic risk to its psychic wholeness. Picking scabs is therefore in part to be understood as a variant of the *fort-da* procedure of playing with danger, absence or negativity in order to bind it into a kind of syntax. This gathering-together of the self is achieved, not in the face of potential loss or trauma, but through it. Such gathering-through-loss can be interpreted in terms also of the Burkean sublime, which reads the dialectic of pain and pleasure in terms of a threatened loss of proportion between the perceiving self and its environment (the loss of a relationship of adequation between the imaginary proprioceptric volume of the individual body and the unencompassable hugeness of the sublime prospect), a potential loss which is responded to, in Burke's version of the sublime at least, by a defensive 'bracing' of the self, a congregation of the energies threatened with dissolution.

Very quickly, the transforming powers of the scab may get transferred to other injurious and non-injurious markings of the skin, and the pleasures of controlling the coming and going of the scab reappear in a more general eroticisation of such markings. This surely explains the pleasures of the sticking-plaster, which allows the play of rending and suture with an artificial surface placed over the surface of a wound, or indeed, over a patch of uninjured skin. The important feature of the sticking plaster is its edge, which both seams and seals the otherwise uninterrupted surface of the skin, marking the skin and then placing it 'under erasure'. It appears that the imaginatively erased wound or mark is more powerfully pleasurable than the merely virgin surface. For the child, as for Yeats's Crazy Jane, 'Nothing can be sole or whole/That has not been rent'.[19] The pleasure in the sticking-plaster makes some of the purposes of deliberate injuries to the skin in adult society intelligible. Among these we could enumerate ritual practices

19. 'Crazy Jane and the Bishop', *Complete Poems of W.B. Yeats*, Macmillan, London and Basingstoke 1979, p295.

or scarification, and their non-ritual equivalents in the practices of self-laceration which seem to be on the increase among both women and men, and body piercing, the point of which is to enable the body to be marked, by a ring, stud, or other material substitute for the scar. It is worth observing how essential it seems to be that what is displayed in, or hung from, the pierced skin should be some hard and inorganic substance, with a preference for metallic objects which recapitulate the act of piercing; few cultures seem very drawn to the use of fabrics or textiles in ear-rings. This is not to say that textiles are not sometimes implicated in the austere play between the organic and the inorganic. In sadomasochistic representations of piercing, both in pornographic images and in performance art like that of Ron Athey, the piercing of sensitive body portions, such as genitals and nipples, is very often supplemented by actions of binding: ringed nipples are drawn together by thread, labia are sewn up, and male genitals are folded inwards and sewn over. The combined action of needle and thread involves a bizarre co-operation of male assault upon the skin, with the puncturing effects of the phallic stylus, and female repair of that surface, the restoration of the skin as web, veil or text. Such practices seem to make it clear that the desire to tear the skin is inseparable from the need to darn it, or make it whole. As we will see, tattooing is a particularly complex form of this interchange between the injury and the mark, since here the marking of the skin takes place through a puncturing of its surface.

The play between openness and closure, the rending and repair of the epidermal surface, is displaced into the dynamics of exposure and concealment in clothing, and Roland Barthes famously derived the pleasure of the text from a further displacement of the gaping and concealment of the garment into the hermeneutic dynamics of disclosure and secrecy in texts.[20] Barthes is one of a number of theorists in the last twenty years who have run the skin-writing analogy backwards; rather than reading the meanings of skin in terms of the erotics of its markings, he reads writing itself in terms of a dermatological dynamic of abrasions, tears, lesions in imaginary veils and surfaces: 'what I enjoy in a narrative is not directly its content or even its structure, but rather the abrasions I impose upon the fine surface ... Which has nothing to do with the deep laceration the text of bliss inflicts upon language itself ... '[21] The relations between the assaulted skin and the metaphorology of writing is also dramatised in Derrida's analysis of the gendered relations between stylus and surface in his *Spurs*.[22]

In all these practices, fantasies and metaphors, the scar and the symbol of the scar are hard to distinguish, since a scar is always anyway a kind of symbol. Symbolism and scarification are never wholly distinct; the symbol of a scab or scar always recapitulates the manner in which scarring is itself already a transformation of injury into visual symbol. At the same time, the infliction of injury to the skin may also be an assault upon the signifying function of the skin. In that the scar signifies that something *real* - some exceeding of mere signification - has taken place, the scar can become the

20. Roland Barthes, *The Pleasure of the Text*, Richard Miller (trans), Basil Blackwell, Oxford 1990, p9.

21. *Ibid.*, pp11-12.

22. Jacques Derrida, *Spurs: Nietzsche's Styles*, Barbara Harlow (trans), University of Chicago Press, Chicago and London 1978.

figure for the violent erasure of the epidermal grounding of figurality.

The examples I have been describing so far are voluntary and controlled forms of auto-inscription. There ought to be an important difference between the eroticisation of the weal, scar or imaginary assault upon the flesh in consensual sadomasochism and the more asymmetrical forms of assault upon the flesh. What of the unwilling victims of the eroticisation of marks? Janet Beizer provides examples of some of these in her *Ventriloquized Bodies*. It was believed by nineteenth-century physicians that there was a close link between hysteria and the tendency to dermographism, which is an extreme sensitivity of the skin to pressure which causes it to flare into long-lasting marks when abraded. The skin of the dermographic person can be written over and, as in some of the photographs from the Salpêtrière archives reproduced by Beizer, may actually be made to announce their diagnosis; her cover-illustration shows a woman's back marked with the words 'démence précoce'. According to Beizer, the literal impressionability of the hysteric-dermographic skin testifies to the morbid, exorbitant expressiveness of the hysteric's body, which is likely at any moment to erupt uncontrollably into meaning. At the same time, the act of writing over that body controls and canalises it. Central to this process is the stilling of sound by sight. As such, the diagnostic photographs of the written-over skins of Charcot's and other hysterical patients are representative of the process of fixing the oral frenzy of hysteria - the incontinent mewing, growling, barking and screaming associated with its visitations - into diagnosis. For Beizer, the two principles are not merely opposed; for the textual spectacle does not merely constrain, but also produces the excess it constrains. 'The potential scandal of the speaking body is neutralized by virtue of its production by an external agent. In fact the body does not speak; it is spoken, ventriloquized by the master text that makes it signify'.[23] For Beizer, the eroticisation of the written-over flesh is an asymmetrical mechanism of control.

Klaus Theweleit suggests a similar motivation for male fantasies directed at the assault upon female flesh; such fantasies are designed both to obliterate the flesh, and to reduce it to the formless condition which it is feared to be in the fascist male imagination.[24] I think that, in their different ways, both Beizer and Theweleit arrest the sado-masochistic dialectic of the skin which, at the level of fantasy, never allows the simple separation of infliction from suffering. The sadistic desire to control/obliterate the other skin is only ever strategically separable from the desire to protect from damage or reintegrate one's own imperfectly formed or contained ego-sense. Insofar as assault is the mechanism of definition, it cannot be reduced to the objectification of the other.

Above all, this self-definition involves the creation of visible signs and guarantees. One of the measures of the mutual implication of sadist and masochist impulses is the polarisation of the visual and the other senses, especially sound. The sadistic impulse is identified with visual command, while the victim of punishment typically is denied the capacity of vision.

23. Janet Beizer, *Ventriloquized Bodies: Narratives of Hysteria in Nineteenth-Century France*, Cornell University Press, Ithaca and London 1994, p26.

24. Klaus Theweleit, *Male Fantasies*, Stephen Conway, Erica Carter and Chris Turner (trans), Polity Press, Cambridge 1987, Vol. I.

Guy Rosolato has pointed to the systematic alignment of sight with exteriority and frontality and of sound with interiority and posteriority.[25] The victim of punishment or assault inhabits the world of sound, and their passivity is emphasised by their subjection to sound-pain. In consensual sadomasochistic scenarios, means are usually employed to give the victim access to sight, allowing them to be the witness to their own visual subjection, through the use of mirrors, photographs or video. Thus the drama of exchanged positions analysed by Freud in 'A Child is Being Beaten' is a fundamentally scopic drama.[26] Here, as in other respects, ambivalence is the point, of course: and the more extreme and paradoxical the ambivalence, the greater the risk, the greater the yield of reintegration experienced by sadist and masochist alike.

But it is by no means necessary for the sadomasochistic victim to be given vision and frontality. In fact an important feature of the dynamics of sadomasochism is the visualisation of sound. Sound is subject to a dialectic of rending and restoration that is very similar to that enacted in the sight of the marked flesh. In a paper of 1958 entitled 'Early Auditory Experiences, Beating Fantasies, and Primal Scene', William Niederland narrated the case histories of patients who derived erotic satisfaction from being subjected to physical and sexual abuse accompanied by violent vocal assault. Niederland suggests that the patients must be understood as attempting to introject and control frightening and traumatic experiences of sound, the 'early fear of bodily extinction by intense, ego-overwhelming auditory sensations', or the threat of impending 'auditory extinction' which Niederland believes may in fact be a feature of all infantile experience.[27] One of Niederland's patients was a homosexual man who was driven to seek masochistic sexual experiences specifically at times when 'the noises of the city - experienced as crude and intensely felt primitive sounds - assail him and threaten to overwhelm his ego'. In doing so, Niederland suggests, 'he *"structures the situation"*, that is, he transforms the threatening unorganised noise into organised meaningful sounds emitted at his own behest'.[28] Niederland draws this analysis from earlier suggestions by Heinz Kohut regarding the psychological process whereby ego-assailing noise is mastered by being structured as music, as well as from a paper by Oskar Isakower which builds on some of Freud's undeveloped insights regarding the relations between audition and ego-formation.[29] Despite differences of emphasis, this psychoanalytic work therefore concurs on the question of the defining contrast between threatening and disorganised noise, which is perhaps to be identified with the conditions of sound itself, and organised sound, or music; it is suggested that it is in the passage from one to the other that the self is formed, in a process in which power and pleasure are intricately interwoven.

Didier Anzieu has also pointed to the close association between sound and the skin. Anzieu suggests that chief among a number of imaginary containing volumes parallel to the skin-ego is the infant's sense of a 'sonorous

25. Guy Rosolato, 'La voix: entre corps et language', *Revue française de psychoanalyse*, 38 1974, p79.

26. Sigmund Freud, 'A Child is Being Beaten', *Standard Edition, op. cit.*, Vol. XVII.

27. William G. Niederland, 'Early Auditory Experiences, Beating Fantasies, and Primal Scene', *Psychoanalytic Study of the Child* 13, 1958, p474.

28. *Ibid.*, p475.

29. Heinz Kohut, 'Observations on the Psychological Functions of Music', *Journal of the American Psychoanalytic Association* 5, 1957; Oskar Isakower, 'On the Exceptional Position of the Auditory Sphere', *International Journal of Psycho-Analysis* 20, 1939, pp340-8.

envelope', in the bath of sounds, especially those of the mother's voice, that surrounds it, soothing, supporting and stabilising. This imaginary envelope is the auditory equivalent of Lacan's mirror-stage, in that it gives the child a unity from the outside; it can be seen, therefore, as a 'sound-mirror or ... audio-phonic skin'.[30] Without the satisfactory experience of this sonorous envelope, the child may fail to develop a coherent sense of self; there will be rents or flaws in the ego, leaving it vulnerable to inward collapse in depression, or invasion from outside, leading to the formation of an over-protective artificial skin in certain forms of autism.

30. Didier Anzieu, 'The Sound-Image of the Self', Monique Meloche (trans), *International Review of Psycho-Analysis* 6, 1979, p23.

Anzieu's analysis has been carried forward recently by Edith Lecourt, who makes more explicit the implication of Anzieu's work that the sonorous binding which a 'good-enough' experience of parental sound provides is in fact a protection against the otherwise diffusive and disintegrating conditions of sound itself. These conditions Lecourt defines as the absence of boundaries in space - 'sound reaches us from everywhere, it surrounds us, goes through us' - and in time - 'there is no respite for sonorous perception, which is active day and night and only stops with death or total deafness' - as well as its disturbing lack of concreteness - 'sound can never be grasped; only its sonorous source can be identified'. All of these qualities are summed up, says Lecourt, in its quality of '*omnipresent simultaneity*'.[31] For both Anzieu and Lecourt, the ego-supporting acoustic envelope is a sonorous defence against sound itself. In turning intensity into shape, noise into sound, the acoustic envelope subordinates hearing and the other proximity senses to sight.

31. Edith Lecourt, 'The Musical Envelope', in *Psychic Envelopes*, Didier Anzieu (ed), Daphne Briggs (trans), Karnac Books, London 1990, p211.

In sadomasochistic fantasies and practices, the wound of hearing yields the scar of organised sound. Just as the punishment inflicted on the flesh is both displayed and contained by its visual form, especially in the fascination with the incision of lines into the skin, so punishment experienced as an auditory phenomenon is equivalently ordered. The sound of sadomasochistic punishment is not undifferentiated, but pulsed, or percussive sound. The formalisation of sound into predictable patterns - the sound of the whip striking flesh that is fetishistically dwelt upon in sadomasochistic representation, or of the imperious voice barking insults or instructions (a favourite masochistic fantasy is of the denunciation that keeps careful time with the delivery of slaps or blows) enables the threat of blind, immeasurable intensity to be predicted and contained by pseudo-visualisation. In sadomasochistic assault, the surface of the body becomes a vast, attentive, vulnerable membrane of hearing. Noise is to wounding as sound is to scarring. The use of recording technologies, which turn noise into a kind of replicable writing, completes the analogy. A common sadomasochistic fantasy is of the victim of a beating being subjected to repeated playing of a tape of his or her punishment; or employing a walkman to play it over to themselves.

THE SHEEN

The libidinisation of the scarified or inscribed skin may be associated with other forms of degradation of the skin. The form that I am interested to explore here is the fantasy of toughened skin, whether in the form of scales, leather or metal, which seems designed to produce a reassuring condition of impenetrability. Central to many of these forms of toughened or impermeable skin is the fascinating, seductive quality of reflectiveness or shine. The shiny skin, whether in the form of the latex or leather that clings tightly to the body of the fetishist, or in the anointed sheen of the bodybuilder, or in the frankly metallic gleam of the body-become-machine, as in films such as the *Terminator* and *Tetsuo* series, is the skin that resists penetration. It is invulnerable because it absorbs nothing, not even light. The fascinating sheen of shining skin, or luminous skin-substitutes reduces the voluminous body to the spill and shimmer of light across a surface and therefore immaterialises it. At the same time, however, the shiny skin mineralises or metallicises the body in such a way as to display it wholly as an object. Epidermal lustre, whether in the form of synthetic second skins, such as latex and rubber, or in the flesh burnished to a semblance of such a second skin, is therefore at once substance and chimera. The shiny skin is skin that is no more than a skin, skin thinned to a sheen. The hardness of the shining skin is constituted out of this impossible compromise between the adamantine and the immaterial.

A corresponding ambivalence results from the shiny skin's enigmatic hesitation between the possibility of moistness or oily lubrication, and the shell-like hardness of high polish. The gleam of the bodybuilder's musculature suggests organic softness and pliability only to countermand it in the display of unyielding hardness; the rubber fetishist's gear suggests the hardness and restraint of the inorganic, while displaying the contrary qualities of elasticity. The hardened skin is in fact a visual as well as a physical shield. Like the modernist building faced in mirror glass, the shining skin is able to hide in plain sight; hardened into pure objectivity, the shining skin eludes its own condition of objectivity by perplexing the act of looking that would make of it an object. The shine of the skin deflects and diffuses the perforative, punctual line of sight across the horizontality of the planar body. The shining body therefore aspires to that abolition of theatrical depth enacted in Lyotard's body spread into infinite, paradoxical surface. The skin becomes a sort of mirror, borrowing the mirror's depthlessness and invisibility (the mirror offers everything to the eye but itself, for you can only ever look *in* a mirror, never *at* it) but declining its perspectival compliance. Like an ordinary mirror, the skin mirror effaces itself in the visibility it returns to the gaze, but also retains a certain opacity. The light of the skin mirror is neither wholly absorbed nor wholly returned to its source, but, as it were, captured, slowed and thickened. (This is surely one reason for the centrality of black in leather and rubber fetishism, for shining black allows the ambivalent exchange of light and its absence, reflection and absorption to an utmost degree.) The skin mirror is, ultimately, narcissistic. On the gleaming surface of the fetishist's second skin, or the burnished armature of the weightlifter, we see an eyeless light that is watching itself, neither accepting nor releasing light, an impossible 'flat depth' of viscous liquidity, a diffulgence that never divulges itself to the eye.

I may so far have seemed to imply that the body reduced to its skin surface is genderless, and it is no doubt important to recognise that the dream of an unfeatured, organless superficiality is to some degree transgendered. But it is also the case that male and female are offered different kinds of access to this shared ideal. Most importantly for present purposes we need to note that one aspect of the condition of shine seems currently to mark it as emphatically masculine, or to evoke a masculinised conception of the body surface. This is its quality of hardness. The shiny skin always involves the suggestion (often, of course, as in latex, leather or rubber, illusory or ambivalent) that the skin has lost its 'organic' qualities of permeability, elasticity and sensitivity. The shining skin suggests a change of biological order - the human become mineral, reptile or mechanical.

Didier Anzieu has suggested that one of the most important characteristics of skin is that it is susceptible to endogenous and exogenous sensation, that is, it can be felt on the inside and the outside; one can feel one's skin as though it were another's, apprehending its softness, moistness, looseness, and so on, from the outside, even as one feels *with* or *through* one's skin (*SE*, 63). You cannot taste your tongue, smell your nose or hear your ears in the same manner. (Though you can, of course, see your eye; this overlap may be involved in some of the insistent links between tactility and sight in the fantasy of shining skin.)

But the hardened skin, the skin that has become no more than the shell of its lustre, represents an exteriorisation of tactility, which is to say, a concentration of sensation on the outside of the skin, with a diminution of sensation on the outside. The armoured skin is anaesthetised, and, in allowing no sensation through, severs that dual directionality characteristic of ordinary skin. In the shining skin, the depth and ambivalence of the skin as epidermis thin and rigidify into tegumental simplicity. The hardened, shining skin is no longer a medium of passage and hymeneal exchange, but of division, separation and cleavage. The uterine fantasy of pure interiority without exterior with which I began here turns inside out - into the display of an exteriority without interior, a container without content. As such, we can perhaps connect the hardness of shining skin to Klaus Theweleit's investigations of male fantasies (along with shared, transferred and diffused fantasies *of* male fantasies) of a kind of hardness that would enclose, canalise or otherwise discipline the threatening fluidity attributed to the female body, or the feminised interior of the male body. The shine of the skin may therefore appear as the mark of its capacity to maintain the divisions between hard and soft, outer and inner, ego and other, masculine and feminine, in that fundamental split which Theweleit's work brings to visibility, a split between 'an inner realm, concealing a "numbly glowing, fluid ocean" and other dangers, and a restraining external shell, the muscle armour, which contains the inner realm the way a cauldron contains boiling soup'.[32] What, then, has the skin-mirror to do with the skin-inscription? Theweleit's account would suggest that they are unquiet opposites; the wounded, lacerated flesh must be kept apart from the rigidified armature of the male phantasmal body, or - not at all the same thing - the phantasmal male body. The scarified skin is the very sign of spoiling and disfigurement, while the shiny skin is perfected and immaculate. The essential feature of shining skin is its quality of uninterrupted surface. The shining skin presents no impediment to the glissando of the eye across the surface; indeed, in enforcing such a movement it converts the body into an imaginary geometry consisting wholly of vectors, planes and trajectories, rather than points and lines. The shining body is phantasmally defended, not only against perforation (from the outside or the inside), but against the dimensionality of the edge, the line, the point in general. It is a kind of visual immune system. It is surface without edge, area without perimeter, connectedness without articulation. This is to say that, curiously, the hardened, armoured, helmeted body of male fantasy, and fantasy of the male, is an aphallic image, in its resistance to the metaphor of the point; indeed, it borrows from an allegedly female metaphorology of flow, movement and surface to enforce its perdurable, phallic impenetrability. The folding-together of male and female topologies is exemplified in the evolution of the heroically mechanical terminating robot in *Terminator* I into the polymorphous robot in *Terminator* II. The Schwarzenegger robot belongs to the world of Newtonian mechanics, in which the concussion of objects separated in space, and the conflict between force (bullets) and resistance (the robot's toughened outer shell and indestructible metallic skeleton) are powerfully operative. The robot is invulnerable because its inside is as tough as its outside. But the next generation terminator against which the Schwarzenegger version is pitted in *Terminator* II is not less, but more superficial than the first, for it is, in a more radical way still, *all* surface, surface all the way through, a surface that never hardens into a permanent distinction between surface and interior, that can reform itself into any shape.

The skin-mirror and the skin-inscription are integrated, by the very function of integration that they both perform. The skin that holds itself together in and through its laceration has as its more than implied ideal the absolute invulnerability of the minero-mechanical integument. The interrelationship of the two modes in fetishistic and sadomasochistic imagery ought therefore to be unsurprising. The ideal of total envelopment indulged by the rubber or latex fetishist is rarely satisfying for long. When it is visualised, such envelopment must be subject to forms of *articulation*, which break into or across the non-differentiation of the shining surface, arresting the lateral skid of sight. Articulation can work in two dimensions: the skin can be written into, its surface penetrated vertically; or it can be written

32. Klaus Theweleit, *Male Fantasies, op. cit.*, Vol. I, p242.

across, gridded, articulated, incised. The articulation of the skin is not simply the opponent of its shine. In fact, it intensifies shine, establishing lines of sight, even as it heightens the sense of the erotic slide or skidding of sight and light across the skin's surface. In extreme cases, it can manifest itself in that desire to cut or mutilate the skin which, as we have seen, far from enacting a violent breakdown of body boundaries, is actually a means 'by which an individual endeavours to maintain body boundaries and self-cohesion'.[33]

33. Barrie M. Biven, 'The Role of Skin in Normal and Abnormal Development, with a Note on the Poet Sylvia Plath', *International Review of Psychoanalysis* 9, 1982, p224.

The shiny skin is therefore articulated with the articulation of the skin associated with the forms of skin-inscription that I began by looking at: in fantasies of flagellation, laceration, incision, marking, as well as, more generally, the erotics of bondage, and the designed alternation of substances and textures in fetishistic clothing and images. This is particularly apparent in particular in the imaging of weightlifting. Male bodybuilders rely on their extreme muscular development and, to use that most telling of bodybuilding terms, 'definition', to bring about the play of surface and articulation across their own flesh. Their bodies are ribbed, ridged and written over with the obstructions to the slide of the eye over the lubricated flesh. Male bodybuilders as it were include the dimension of articulation on the surface of their skins; this kind of body wears its depth on its surface, folding out, in a kind of auto-écorché; the imaginary assaults upon the body, evidenced in the language of bodybuilding which will speak of well-defined muscle groups as 'rips', are turned into the very form of the body's defence. Mass becomes sublimated into the dimensionless play of light and shade: the gleam of the bodybuilder's body allows its symbolic wounding to be converted into the very image of unassailable impenetrability. To borrow and mix up the old footballing joke: the male bodybuilder has got its retaliation in first, on itself.

The skin of the male weightlifter writes its articulation across itself; the skin of the female weightlifter needs to be articulated from outside or above, via the supplementation of clothing, props and lighting. This may connect with another interesting differentiation within bodybuilding images: namely a differentiation in the intensity of *shine*. Take a look at any bodybuilding magazine: in all the photographs, male bodybuilders reflect more light than female ones. The contrast here may be between the body seen as self-sufficient (invulnerable both because of its resistant, excluding shine, and because of its internalised control of its own articulation), and the body which is partial, undefined, dependent.

The ambivalent interchange of surface and articulation of the surface is also, most remarkably, evident in the practice and display of tattooing. The tattoo uniquely combines vertical with horizontal incision, or articulation. It turns the vulnerability of the body, its exposure to penetration, into a flaunted surface. Tattoos often play with the alternation of soft and hard, displaying images of reptiles, shields or metal to suggest a kind of cicatrisation, a toughening through the ordeal of exposure. The tattoo substitutes a surface for the actual surface of the skin: but it does so in a way that plays with the knowledge that the skin has been penetrated, since the technique of tattooing in fact requires pigment to be injected *beneath* the surface of the skin. Thus what appears to lie on top of the skin, in fact lies below it. The body flaunts the surface that it has taken into itself as a secondary interiority. The fact that the tattoo is irremovable involves a similarly ambivalent play between injury and self-defence. Once marked, the skin can never again recapture its infantile immaculacy and clarity. But the very permanence of the blemish-ornament can then make it a guarantee of continuity, or pre-emption of assault from the outside, as well as an imaginary brace against the wearing, sagging and wrinkling of the skin in the process of ageing. A tattoo is for life; indeed it is both a lethal assault upon the skin, and a means of cryogenic survival.

Such ambivalence is expressed also in the larger social symbolism of the tattoo. In tribal or preliterate societies, we are told, the marking of the skin, through scarification and other kinds of modification, effects social cohesion and belonging. In post-literate society, in which law becomes separated from custom and ritual, embodying itself in the more abstract and decorporealised forms of writing, to write upon the body becomes a kind of transgression, and a mark of voluntary or involuntary exclusion.[34] Kafka's 'In the Penal Settlement', in which a machine is employed to incise the details of a crime and sentence in the body of the convict, provides the clearest allegorisation of this process.[35] Jean-François Lyotard reads this story as a dramatisation of the attempt of the law to 'prescribe', to stand before and write in advance the human body which has nevertheless always come before it, and remains irreducible to its operations, as a way of being, or 'touch' which is 'here and now, exposed in space-time and to the space-time of something that touches before any concept and even any representation'.[36] In Kafka's story, the more humane regime introduced by the new Commandant who wishes to do away with the machine is the sign of the continuing distance between the law and the body, a distance which is also the source of the desire for their violent coincidence in the penal writing-machine. In a bizarre, Kafkaesque logic, not marking the body is the same kind of violence as marking the body. The desire for the moment of mystical truth and presence in the integration of law and the body is as strong in the officer as it comes to be in the condemned man; so strong that, when he fails to convince the explorer of the justness of the operation, he submits himself to the machine, which, however, disintegrates in the course of writing on his body the prescription 'Be Just', and balks him of his mystical apprehension of the truth of the law written on the body. For, as with sadomasochistic marking of the skin, this kind of ego-damaging assault is always available for ego-consolidation. When the legal practice of tattooing prisoners in French jails was discontinued late in the nineteenth century, tattooing was adopted almost straight away as a badge of solidary marginality.

There is perhaps enough in what I have already said to indicate that the

34. Louise Poissant, 'Carnation', *op. cit.*, p106.

35. Franz Kafka, 'In the Penal Settlement', in *Metamorphosis and Other Stories*, trans. Willa and Edwin Muir, Penguin, Harmondsworth pp167-199.

36. Jean-François Lyotard, 'Prescription', Christopher Fynsk (trans), *L'Esprit créateur* 31 1991, p18.

intense libidinisation of the skin in contemporary cultural practices and representations is inseparable from a desire for psychic integration through the skin, or, as it might be put, psychic integumentation. (The words *integrity* and *integument* are etymologically less close than one might at first suspect. *Integument* comes from Latin, *tegere*, to cover; *integrity*, meaning the condition of being a singular integer, comes from the Latin *integer*, from *tangere*, to touch, meaning entire in the sense of untouched. But it is hard to resist the notion of a back-formed etymological link between covering, touch and entirety.)

The complex of affects attaching to the marked skin may have a bearing upon contemporary concerns about suntanning. It has proved difficult to persuade inveterate sunbathers in Australia, the US and Europe of the dangers of prolonged exposure to the sun. The reason for this is that the sunbather is wedded to a fantasy of sunbathing as the construction of protective second skin. In English, sunbathing results in a sun 'tan', the word disclosing the association between a change of colour and a change of substance, in the passage from living tissue to the ambivalent rigidity of leather. (In French, in which the word for suntanning is *bronzage*, the fantasised process and outcome is markedly more metallurgical.) The metaphorical association between the change in colour and the change in texture rests upon the larger association between marking, scarification and sheen: the endogenous change of pigmentation and the fantasy of a shield placed over the skin from the outside. The difficulty of persuading people to refrain from sunbathing is that it is experienced as a prophylactic, as a way of making yourself safe from the sun, as well as from light, from eyes, from pain. The suntan is in fact the very best kind of reconstituted skin, in that it is both a scarring - the sign of a secondary shield or integument formed in response to a traumatic assault upon the skin - and a reassertion of the skin's smooth, shining integrity. The association of suntan with sheen completes the reassuring but paradoxical link between exposure and protection.

There are larger dimensions to this - I almost said deeply-rooted, but perhaps ought rather to say stubbornly impermeable - cultural fantasy. The increasing fear of skin cancer consequent upon the dramatic erosion of the ozone layer may be understood partly in the light of a certain doubling of the experience of skin, in its conjoined capacity to contain and to expose, in our relations to the earth itself. The flaying away of the ozone layer - from the inside out, we should note - results in a generalised vulnerability to the harmful rays of the sun, the fragility of the earth's protective shield stripping us all of a vital second skin. The exhortation to 'Practise Safe Sun' offered by one advertisement for sun cream a few years back, trips a switch between openness to infection and vulnerability to sunburn, a switch which perhaps depends at some level on the association between AIDS and Kaposi's sarcoma, the previously rare form of skin cancer to which AIDS sufferers become vulnerable and which was indeed the first form in which the AIDS epidemic manifested itself in the US.[37] It also suggests and supplies a phantasmal identification between sun block and the protective second skin of the condom. The condom protects against the ecstatic passage of bodily fluids, maintaining manageable distinctions between the inside and outside. The phallic, invasive sun is made safe by establishing a quasi-epidermal block or filter against its penetrating rays. No doubt there might be more to be said on the fear of light as sexual violation; such an enquiry would proceed via the myth of the flaying of Marsyas by Apollo, Daniel Schreber's paranoia about the punishing sun and Bataille's exploration of solar erotics. What is new is the actualised fear of a violation of the skin by the light that had previously been believed to nourish and sustain it. The flaying of the body by light and the compensatory fantasy of the body turned into a kind of light via libidinised glow or shine are brought together in the complex of the inscriptive-mirror I have been describing.

THE SCREEN

If we can see an increase in the intensity and frequency of processes designed to promote or supplement the process of psychic integumentation, then it seems appropriate to ask what are the conditions to which this is a response. What, in Didier Anzieu's phrase, might be the terms of 'pathogenic impingement by the environment on the skin ego' to which the development of these second skins is a response?[38] While I am impressed by the implications of psychoanalytic explications of the importance of the supportive and arousing tactile environment provided for the child in early life, I do not find it plausible to derive the sense of the vulnerability of the skin from the mother's or caregiver's failures of caressing technique or monotonousness of voice in early life. I am inclined to ask instead what might be the contemporary conditions of vulnerability to which the investment in the skin might be a response.

One answer might be suggested by a discussion of the aesthetic theory of Walter Benjamin by Susan Buck-Morss, in which she emphasises the close relations in modernity between the aesthetic, the late nineteenth-century cult of neurasthenia and the techniques of anaesthesia. Assailed routinely by shock and sensory discomfiture of every kind, a modern subjectivity comes to be organised around the imperative need to filter, screen and block out excitations.[39] In the light of this, Freud's famous evocation of the origins of the ego in defensiveness may itself be read historically as a response to the same distinctively modern conditions of assault and saturation. To this might be added a prescient remark made by Marshall McLuhan in the course of a more recent discussion of the extending, exteriorising effects of the modern communicative and reproductive media: 'In the electric age', he writes, 'we wear all mankind as our skin'.[40] In the era of what Lewis Mumford calls

37. Randy Shilts, *And the Band Played On: Politics, People, and the AIDS Epidemic*, Penguin, Harmondsworth 1988, pp64-6, 75-8.

38. Anzieu, *A Skin For Thought, op. cit.*, p66.

39. Susan Buck-Morss, 'Aesthetics and Anaesthetics: Walter Benjamin's Artwork Essay Reconsidered', *October* 62, 1992, pp3-41.

40. Marshall McLuhan, *Understanding Media: The Extensions of Man*, Sphere Books, London 1967, p57.

'palaeotechnics', the human body was extended and amplified, mostly for the enlargement of its locomotor apparatus. In the era of neotechnics, it is the nervous system rather than the arm or leg that is enhanced by technology, and therefore in the process transformed. In the epoch of electronic media, the actual skin that bounds us within our individual selves is dissolved away and replaced by a polymorphous, infinitely mobile and extensible skin of secondary simulations and stimulations, which both makes us more versatile by enlarging our psychic surface area, exposing us to more and different kinds of experience, and also numbs us, precisely because of the dazing overload of sensations which this synthetic pseudo-skin conducts.

If the skin is a screen and a filter, it is also the medium of passage and exchange, with the attendant possibility of violent reversal or rupture. The skin is the vulnerable, unreliable boundary between inner and outer conditions and the proof of their frightening, fascinating intimate contiguity. Thus, the threat of 'pathogenic impingement' from the outside is matched, as some have noticed, by a new fear and fascination regarding the interior body, as expressed in fantasies of various kinds of eruption through or perforation of the skin from the inside. The skin has become intensely vulnerable and thoroughly unreliable in its combined incapacity to resist external threats and its tendency to harbour (but then to release) internal threats. In films such as *Videodrome* and the *Alien* series, the skin betrays what is its function to guarantee, the integrity of the distinctions between internal and external, depth and surface, self and other, and the regulation of the passages between these regions. When, in contemporary horror fiction and films, the frail, containing envelope of the skin is torn, dissolved, melted and lacerated, this is perhaps an apprehension in a violent mode of the growing fluidity of relations between the self and its contexts and secondary instruments, a condition in which the skin is no longer primarily a membrane of separation, but a medium of connection or greatly intensified semiotic permeability, of codes, signs, images, forms, desires. In the reforming, infinitely reformable contemporary sensorium, the associations of the skin with transmission, passage and connection become more emphatic than its functions of screening, or separation. We start to learn to live, not so much with the famous body-without-organs of Deleuze and Guattari, but with the transbodily hyperorgan that the skin has become.

Another way of putting this might be to say that the skin becomes recruited to experiences that are more auditory then visual, insofar as the auditory involves the sharing or transmission of impulses rather than their localisation. Indeed, McLuhan's remark may be an instance of an idealising protective response to this condition of permeability and contingency, in its metaphorising of the skin as a visualisable envelope or membrane. Modernity set visuality against the various ecstatic enlargements and invasions of modern auditory technologies, allowing the visual to retain its customary sensory privilege; one defining moment here might be the coming of sound to the movies in 1926, which bound the errant, unlocalised, and permeating voices of electronic technology (telephone, radio) into synchronicity. Not long afterwards, in *Brave New World*, Aldous Huxley was imagining a similar cinematic binding of other kinds of sensory impulse, in the idea of the 'feelies'. Though in one sense the digital technologies of post-modernity offer a mere actualisation of the modern dream of the artificially reconstructed and unified sensorium - the psyche as prosthetic *Gesamtkunstwerk* - in practice the networks of sensory linkage, exchange and mutual transformation mean that the visual is no longer the master sense, providing the stable scene or frame within which auditory, olfactory, and tactile phenomena can be recombined. The immaculate modernist grid of manipulable, permutable possibilities suggested by the Windows operating system belies the fact that the screen has entered the consciousness of its users, and that its function as separating membrane, screening out unwanted stimulus, and marking the point of defining interface between the user and his or her object, is yielding to a much more complex interimplication of the user and the used. The screen was the privileged modernist form of mediated encounter or interface between the self and the world, imagined as these are as surfaces or membranes; the move away from the keyboard to the mouse, the touch screen, the voice command, and even the immediate control of screens by the control of brain impulses, along with the abandonment of the screen altogether implied by such developments as intelligent buildings and the implantation of information and communications technology, makes the screen only one switch in an infinity of possible sensory configurations and reconfigurations.

Though it makes little attempt to connect the psychological and the technological, contemporary psychoanalytic theory and therapy based upon the concept of 'psychic envelopment', such as that evidenced in the work of Didier Anzieu, Claudie Cachard and others, might suggest that the sensory euphoria of postmodernity also gives rise to a sense of exposure and need for defence. But the very idea of exposure implies a certain visual consolation which may not be easily available in the emerging conditions I am evoking. Exposure suggests the condition of being reduced to an object for sight. The objectifying power of sight, which comes from its unique reliance on distance and separation, is capable of separating me from myself, of painfully dissociating the visualisable portion of me from the rest. But this very dissociation is what allows me to dissociate myself in turn from this dissociation of myself, allows recourse to what one can call recursive reparation: as the involvement of the eye in masochistic fantasy suggests, you can always watch yourself being watched. Vision is the most *ironic* sense.

It appears that the other senses, sometimes called the proximity senses because, unlike vision, they require some kind of contact or even intermingling of substance between the senser and the sensed do not allow for such perspectival control. Paul Virilio has spoken of the new era of 'tele-contact', *'tactile perspective'*, in which the old oppositions between the proximate and the remote, the present and the absent, will no longer

41. Paul Virilio, 'Optics on a Grand Scale', in *Open Sky*, Julie Rose (trans), Verso, London 1997, pp35-45.

obtain.[41] This would be an era in which everything distant would be capable of coming close, and the most intimate sensations would be capable of being abstracted and distanced from us.

All these developments leave the body - or the self's relation to its body and its newly dissolving limits - not merely exposed and open to the gaze, but unvisualisable. This is the particular nature of the epidermal jeopardy being mimicked and responded to in so many different contemporary forms of assault upon and reparation of the vanishing skin. The terror of skinlessness evoked by Gilles Deleuze in his characterisation of the schizophrenic seems to match this experience:

> The discovery that *there is no more surface* is familiar to and evidenced by any schizophrenic. The great problem, the first evidence of schizophrenia, is that the surface is punctured. Bodies no longer have a surface. The schizophrenic body appears as a kind of body-sieve. Freud emphasized this schizophrenic aptitude for perceiving the surface and the skin as if each were pierced by an infinite number of little holes. As a result, the entire body is nothing but depth; it snatches and carries off all things in this gaping depth, which represents a fundamental involution. Everything is body and corporeal. Everything is a mixture of bodies and, within the body, telescoping, nesting in and penetrating each other.[42]

42. Gilles Deleuze, 'The Schizophrenic and Language: Surface and Depth in Lewis Carroll and Antonin Artaud', in *Textual Strategies: Perspectives in Post-Structuralist Criticism*, Josué Harari (ed), Methuen, London 1979, p286.

43. *Ibid.*, p287.

There is an odd co-operation between the 'general breakdown of surfaces'[43] evoked in the world of the schizophrenic and the euphoric projection of depth into surface found in Lyotard's *Libidinal Economy* and currently being lived out in the cultivation of fetishism, as practice and obsession in cultural-critical discourse. What is lost in both is what Lyotard calls the 'theatrical' configuration of surface with depth. Both characterise current anxieties about the loss of coherent body-image, or the possibility of effecting a spatio-temporal coincidence between the individual body and the multiple simulation-body of transmitted affects. What both Deleuze and Lyotard miss is the necessity of a compromise between membrane and envelope; between the body-without-organs, or the body-as-infinite surface and the various imaginary enclosures necessary to health and productivity. In this sense the grotesque mingling of masculine assault upon the skin and female repair of it imagined in *The Silence of the Lambs* is a perfect enactment of this contemporary predicament, and an instructive complication of the unilateral model of male violence proposed by Theweleit's account. In the context of the vanishing skin, the forms of dermographic assault upon the skin are essentially attempts at grafting the skin back on. The knife, the needle, the stylus, the pen, the whip, the eye, that perforate the skin, are currently also at work binding it together. We will see if we are going to turn out to be creatures capable of imagining less fetishised, petrifying and toxic forms of self-securing and self-envelopment.

CREATIVE AFFECTS

Mariam Fraser

I sat him down ... and I said, 'Bill, your genes are sensational. Your mother lived to be 92, and was as strong as a rock. Your father lived to 89, your grandmother to 95. So your body's going to last, but your brain is going to go'.[1]

[N]owadays we see movement defined less and less in relation to a point of leverage ... There's no longer an origin as starting point, but a sort of putting-into-orbit'.[2]

Late nineteenth-century psychiatry frequently found in insanity the 'essence', the very 'genesis', of artistic activity 'in its purest form'.[3] The assumption that the artist - and especially the artist who is 'marginal' to social and cultural mores (the artist who is insane, sick, poor, struggling) - is the central element in the production of art persists today, and can be understood as part of what Rosalind Krauss calls the 'discourse of originality'. This discourse binds art, artistic identity and the self of the artist together alongside another holy trinity, that of authenticity, originals, and origins. 'Above all,' Krauss writes, the avant-garde artist 'claims originality as his right - his birthright, so to speak. With his own self as the origin of his work, that production will have the same uniqueness as he; the condition of his own singularity will guarantee the originality of what he makes'.[4]

Although it is the case that 'social marginality' often continues to be coded as 'a wilful act of creative individualism',[5] I want to suggest that disease does not always confer a privileged status on the artist and that it may serve to displace the notion of the artist as the 'origin' or 'source' of authentic art. In order to explore this conjecture, I will consider representations of the Abstract Expressionist Willem de Kooning who, during the last ten years of his creative life, produced a large number of paintings (as many as one a week between 1983 and 1986) at the same time as he was thought to be suffering from Alzheimer's disease. Kay Larson introduces the main areas of contention raised by the artist's late works, asking: 'How much did de Kooning know, and when did he begin to lose it? How "conscious" are the last works, and why do they entrance so many people? Can an artist who is not quite "there" actually produce - as de Kooning seems to have done - paintings that hold their own alongside his other work?'[6]

Notably, de Kooning's condition, and its implications with regards to the (aesthetic and economic) value of his late works, received considerable attention not just from art critics, but also - and this is partly because of the widely publicised trial in which de Kooning's daughter, Lisa, attempted

1. Elaine de Kooning quoted in R. Storr, 'At last light,' in *Willem de Kooning: The Late paintings, The 1980s,* San Francisco Museum of Modern Art, Minneapolis 1995, p41.

2. G. Deleuze, 'Mediators,' in J. Crary and S. Kwinter (eds), *Incorporations,* Zone, New York 1992, p281.

3. M. Réja quoted in A. Bowler, 'Asylum art: The social construction of an aesthetic category,' in V.L. Zolberg and J. M. Cherbo (eds), *Outsider Art: Contesting Boundaries in Contemporary Culture,* Cambridge University Press, Cambridge 1997, p20.

4. R. Krauss, 'The originality of the avant-garde,' in *The Originality of the Avant-Garde and Other Modernist Myths,* MIT Press, Cambridge Mass. and London 1996, p160.

5. J. Cubbs quoted in A. Bowler, 1997, *op. cit.,* p30.

6. K. Larson, 'Alzheimer's Expressionism: The conundrum of de Kooning's last paintings,' *Voice,* 31.5.1994, p41.

(and succeeded) to prove that her father was mentally incapable of managing his estate - from a variety of 'experts' including psychologists and neurologists. These psychological and neurological perspectives on the relation between disease and creativity are especially interesting because they explicitly consider the brain-body-identity conjunction and, sometimes, contest it. This is not to imply that they are preferable to any other model of identity however, or that their dimensions are unproblematic. Scientific notions of identity do not necessarily displace the social categories of 'race', class and gender for example and indeed, Paul Rabinow argues, 'these older cultural classifications will be joined by a vast array of new ones, which will cross-cut, partially supersede and eventually redefine the older categories'.[7] But if it is the case that what Rabinow calls 'biosociality'- unlike sociobiology - introduces notions of identity that are entrenched in actual scientific practice, then I think it is important, as Elizabeth A. Wilson suggests, to 'think the conjunction criticism-science' in ways that unravel the 'interdependent structure of debts and disavowals that constitutes these domains'.[8] One of the things that I want to explore here, for example, is how the discourse of originality described by Krauss is sustained not only by a Euro-American accent on individualisation, but also by particular understandings of the body which posit the brain as the locus of the 'higher' functions, functions which are deemed essential to the production of authentic art. When this specific body-brain formation is called into question, so too is the discourse of originality.

It is not my intention then, to privilege any one or other of these representations as the 'truth', nor is it to claim that they bring us closer to the 'truth' of creativity and/or artistic identity. Instead, I want to examine the *effects* that may follow from particular understandings of disease and how they might dismantle the boundaries that sustain identity in an entangled relation with selfhood and which secure an oppositional relation between 'nature' and 'culture', organic and non-organic, body and brain. In order to think through these effects, and to exploit them still further, I will draw on what John Mullarkey calls Gilles Deleuze's 'ethico-political' analysis of force'.[9] This analysis has rarely been applied to the subject position 'artist', although it is frequently mobilised in relation to art, and in relation to subjectivity more generally. With regards the latter, Deleuze's debt to Foucault must be acknowledged: in *Foucault*,[10] Deleuze calls attention to the distribution of forces in diagrammatic power/knowledge relations. While the axes of power and knowledge form/alise force, Foucault's third axis, the axis of ethics, constitutes subjectivity. Here too, an analysis of force is central: the interiority of the subject is understood as folded force, a doubling movement, whereby the fold relates 'back to itself'. It is in this folding back that a relation to the self emerges: processes of subjectivation are shown to be constitutive of interiority.

For my purposes, what is significant about this analysis is that it allows Deleuze to argue that, even if flows of forces may be folded into molar

7. P. Rabinow, 'Artificiality and enlightenment: From sociobiology to biosociality', in J. Crary and S. Kwinter (eds), *Incorporations*, *op. cit.*, p245.

8. E.A. Wilson, *Neural Geographies: Feminism and the Microstructure of Cognition*, Routledge, New York and London 1998, p206.

9. J. Mullarkey, 'Deleuze and materialism: One or several matters?', *The South Atlantic Quarterly*, Vol. 96 No 3. Here, Mullarkey points to some of the problems raised by the use of force in Deleuze's ethics.

10. G. Deleuze, *Foucault*, S. Hand (trans), University of Minnesota Press, Minneapolis and London 1988.

entities (such as 'artist' or 'mentally ill'), these entities are only a *temporary* and *contingent* coagulation. In other words, it is not inevitable that forces will cohere in the form of a 'unified' self and, equally, it is not inevitable that the 'source' of creativity will necessarily be 'bounded by the enclosure formed by the human skin or carried in a stable form in the interior of an individual'.[11] Alternative understandings might locate 'creativity' not only in the figure of the artist, but in the relations between artist, art market, critic, canvas and paint. My aim therefore is not to illustrate the total *erasure* of the notion of artistic identity, but rather, as Judith Butler puts it, to 'exploit and restage [the term], [to] subject [it] to abuse so that [it] can no longer do [its] usual work'.[12] And I want to do this alongside critics who themselves exploit and abuse neurological conceptions of the brain and of the body.

THE SOVEREIGN ARTIST AND THE SOVEREIGN BRAIN

Lawrence Alloway argues that since the 1960s in particular the art world has been saturated with information, information which is 'new in its scale and intensity' and 'endlessly generative of signs'.[13] Although himself in favour of this general expansion, Alloway is disappointed by much art criticism which, he claims, in response to this abundance of information, relies on a crude notion of the 'survival of the fittest': 'In terms of art, the idea takes the form that artists and their movements displace one another in competitive succession, thus obligingly thinning the total field'.[14] Art critics, 'when faced with great amounts of data … opt for the deceptive neatness of causal models'.[15]

The reliance of art critics on neat causal models forecloses discussion around de Kooning in two respects. Firstly, as Alloway anticipates, the artist's reappearance on the art scene during the 1980s was perceived to disrupt the 'evolutionary' sequence frequently imposed on art. Peter Schjeldahl suggests that a 'subtle embarrassment … attends de Kooning's standing in just about every sector of the art culture. Here is someone who ought to be safely historical, long since pensioned off with a ceremonial epithet: Last of the So-Called Geniuses'.[16] There is a second sense in which the use of causal models closes down discussion of de Kooning's late work however, and one which is of more interest here because it raises questions about the subject position 'artist'. In this context, de Kooning's day is said to be done not because 'new' art has overtaken him, but because illness has overcome his ability to produce 'authentic' and 'original' work. Referring to 'expert' knowledges, and in particular to the expertise of those who are wont to pinpoint precisely the sources of creativity, a number of critics draw on a linear model of cause and effect where Alzheimer's (cause) = an inability to paint (effect). *Art and Antiques* cite Serge Gauthier, for example, director of the McGill Centre for Studies on Ageing in Montreal, who suggests that as Alzheimer's disease progresses, de Kooning will increasingly be unable to produce new material because '[i]nitiative would be lost.' Initiative, Gauthier

11. N. Rose, 'Identity, genealogy, history', in S. Hall and P. Du Gay (eds), *Questions of Cultural Identity*, Sage, London 1997, p144.

12. J. Butler in I.C. Meijer and B. Prins, 'How bodies come to matter: An interview with Judith Butler', *Signs: Journal of Women in Culture and Society*, Vol. 23 No 21, p279.

13. L. Alloway, *Network: Art and the Complex Present*, UMI Research Press, Michigan 1983, p29.

14. *Ibid.*, p18.

15. *Ibid.*, p29.

16. P. Schjeldahl, 'Different strokes – The late work of Willem de Kooning', *Artforum*, January 1997, p55.

claims, is 'found in the front part of the brain ... The front part of the brain is what allows you to change pattern; without it you just reproduce the same pattern over and over again'.[17] This point is further supported by Antonio Damasio, head of neurology at the University of Iowa College of Medicine. For him, 'there's a big difference between being able to do something and knowing what that something is ... De Kooning might be resorting to a certain type of gesture that has to do with the way he manipulates his hand and the brush on the canvas'.[18]

The implicit assumptions here are, firstly, that the ability to produce 'original' art is dependent on the effective operation of the 'higher' functions of the brain (functions which pertain, for example, to initiative) and that, secondly, if the brain is somehow damaged then artistic ability, too, will be radically altered - altered to such a degree, perhaps, that work produced under these conditions no longer constitutes authentic art. In a debate that implicitly assesses the 'crucial independence of instinct and intent',[19] the conclusion here seems to be that de Kooning is relying on some kind of instinct but, in this context, instinct is closely aligned to habit. The psychologist Howard Gardner writes: 'One thing that happens over the course of a long life is that highly elaborate skills and habits are developed and it is often difficult to break those skills down. The habits of the studio can be overlearned'.[20] The notion of a painter relying on the 'overlearned' habits of a lifetime or 'resorting', as Damasio puts it, to a 'certain type of gesture', troubles the traditional image of the artist and calls into question the originality of the work. As Robert Storr notes: 'in the absence of the signs of struggle long thought to be the artist's hallmark, [some] refused to credit [de Kooning's late works] with an authoritative intention'.[21] De Kooning, he adds dryly, appears to be an Action Painter literally 'captivated by the act'.[22]

Jeffrey Cummings, director of UCLA's Alzheimer Disease Research Centre, claims that Alzheimer's 'has a specific profile of deficits,' one which affects declarative memory, but spares procedural memory: 'It would be completely consistent that the brushstrokes would be maintained ... but the abstract concept would be impaired ... Because introspection is one of the highest human abilities, it is lost early'.[23] It is notable that the pinpointing of specific functions in particular parts of the brain brings with it its own developmental narrative: while the 'lower' functions, such as complex motor acts (acts which are clearly embodied), may be maintained throughout much of the disease, abstraction and introspection, perceived as two of the 'highest' human abilities (abilities which are usually associated with the mind), are, according to Cummings, lost soon after the onset of Alzheimer's. As Wilson notes, this mapping of the brain is not 'simply inscriptive over an otherwise innocent organ,' rather, it is constitutive of the brain itself and, moreover, it constitutes it along the lines of the classic Cartesian division of head from body: 'In the same way that Cartesian dualism becomes embodied through a division and hierarchization of the body and the head, so too a dualism is

17. Quoted in C. Barnett, 'The conundrum of Willem de Kooning', *Arts and Antiques*, Vol. 6 No. 9, p73.

18. *Ibid.*, p72.

19. R. Storr, 1995, *op. cit.*, p69. For more details of this debate, and in particular its role not only in the construction of the subject position 'artist' but also of the category 'human', see M. Fraser, '"The face-off between will and fate": Artistic identity and neurological style in de Kooning's late works', *Body and Society*, Vol. 4 No 4. 1998.

20. Quoted in C. Barnett, *op. cit.*, p72.

21. R. Storr, 1995, *op. cit.*, p.53.

22. *Ibid.*, p58.

23. Quoted in K. Larson, 1994, *op. cit.*, p42.

located in … the brain … The higher one moves up the brain stem and the evolutionary ladder, and the further away from the rest of the body, the less embodied and more cerebral … the cognitive processes become'.[24]

The loss of introspection that de Kooning is said to suffer is a loss which pertains to the self. As one psychologist puts it: 'When de Kooning steps back to look at what he's just painted … we may imagine that this is him looking at something he's just done and trying to find some semblance of self there … If he's disappointed when he looks at the canvas, it's because he doesn't see de Kooning … he is struggling to regain de Kooning'.[25] This image - of an artist stepping back to look at the canvas - is a particularly evocative one, perhaps because it is so familiar. In an atmospheric analysis of de Kooning's early work for example, Storr compares de Kooning to Picasso, and has them both wholly absorbed in contemplation of their art: 'Picasso's isolation and concentration - and the sense these convey that, outside this visual circuit between the painter and his painting, there is no world - closely match the impression made by photographs of de Kooning sitting in a heavy rocker facing his easel in a state of remoteness and total absorption'.[26] Such an image, whether written or visual, contributes to the authority and authenticity of the artist in question.[27] Yet, in the *Sunday Telegraph's* description of de Kooning cited above, it is an authenticity which is at once invoked and disputed: de Kooning may 'look' (for some semblance of self), but he does not 'see' (his self). Informed by the discourse of originality, the analysis rests on the presupposition that it is the *self* of the artist that the artist seeks (but in this instance fails) to find in (his) art. This serves to confirm the relation between art and artist, and at the same time hints that because de Kooning's 'self' is under threat, so too is the authenticity of his work.

Indeed, one of the issues at stake here is the financial and aesthetic value of de Kooning's abstract art specifically, and of non-representational art more generally. While the debate around Alzheimer's continued, *Esquire* noted that too long an 'absence of new de Koonings from the marketplace would cause collectors to loose interest' and that hence 'the value of the artist's assets [would] decline.[28] Larson too, writing before de Kooning's death, claimed that: 'There is a fear for what his illness would do to his market, which is readying itself for his death'.[29] Crudely put, de Kooning is either perceived *not* to have Alzheimer's, in which case he can continue to produce authentic art - one neuropsychologist claims that 'if de Kooning is painting as well as reported, "it's unlikely that he is suffering from Alzheimer's disease"'[30] - or the artist *does* have Alzheimer's, in which case his work can no longer be considered Abstract in its legitimated sense. Michael Gazzaniga, a neuroscientist cited in *Art and Antiques*, argues that: 'The visual engines can't work without the parts of the brain that are really involved with thinking … *If nonrepresentational art takes the same conceptual powers as representational art*, de Kooning's continued ability to paint "masterpieces" would be impossible'.[31]

24. E. A. Wilson, 1998, *op. cit.*, p131.

25. H. Gruber quoted in M. Collings, 'Who gains from a senile old genius?', *Sunday Telegraph* 22.12.1991, p111.

26. R. Storr, 1995, *op. cit.*, p71.

27. Which may be especially significant in the context of Abstract art, since it goes some way to forestall the suspicion that *'anyone* could have done that!', B. Selsky, 'I dream of genius … ', in J. Doyle et al. (eds), *Pop Out: Queer Andy Warhol,* Duke University Press, Durham and London 1996, p185. Thanks to Angela McRobbie for pointing this out to me.

28. R. Katz, 'Not a pretty picture', *Esquire*, April 1991, p114.

29. K. Larson, 1994, *op. cit.*, p43.

30. Quoted in R. Katz, 1991, *op. cit.*, p116.

31. Quoted in K. Larson, 1994, *op. cit.*, p73, my emphasis.

The critics and commentators that I have cited so far close down the debate around de Kooning by insisting on a linear and causal relation between disease and creativity. Notably, this causal relation is premised on the notion of disease as 'loss'. For these commentators, to explore the effects of Alzheimer's is to explore the effects of a deficit; their concern is with the kind of artistic contribution that de Kooning can continue to make without 'the front part of the brain,' without 'a sense of self' or without, as another writer summarises it, 'the powers of speech, organisation or judgment, or the ability to recognise his own past work'.[32] Further, work produced in the assumed absence of memory, judgement, organisation and/or selfhood stretches the definition of the abstract beyond the boundaries of legitimacy. The gesture that calls de Kooning's artistic status *specifically* into question, at the same time ensures that the definition of what *does* constitute this identity (more generally) is produced and regulated. What is interesting here is that the discourse of originality is sustained not only through authoritative interpretations of the Abstract, through particular representations of the artist at work, and through presuppositions about the relation between artistic identity and the singular self of the artist. It is also maintained through the harnessing of a particular conception of the body, a conception that is informed by neurology and psychology, and which suggests that 'genuine' creativity is dependent on the 'higher' functions which are to be found in the brain. In this respect, the discourse of originality is supported not only by social and cultural expectations, but also by scientific analyses of the body. The sovereignty of the artist finds its parallel in the sovereign brain.

32. M. Collings, 1991, *op. cit.*

These, then, are some of the effects of the folding force, as Deleuze might put it, into an 'intelligible' human corporeality, endowed with an origin, interiority and depth from which creativity is perceived to spring. In the face of the progression of Alzheimer's disease, de Kooning's self, assumed to be the principle source of creativity, is recast as a self 'lost' - lost to the artist, and also, therefore, lost to 'his' art. The evolutionist stance described by Alloway appears, in this context, to be not so much about natural *selection* as about natural *destruction*: the erasure of the so-called - and in de Kooning's case rather literally - *ill*-adapted.

For Deleuze, however, 'there is no diagram that does not also include, besides the points which it connects up, certain relatively free or unbound points, points of creativity, change and resistance, and it is perhaps with these that we ought to begin'.[33] It is to these relatively 'unbound' points that I want now to turn. I want to suggest that it is the opacity which characterises Alzheimer's that loosens the linear and causal connection between disease and de Kooning's assumed inability to produce art, and from which follows a disruption to the discourse that preserves the status of the artist, reinscribes the body-brain duality and contracts and limits notions of creativity.

33. G. Deleuze, 1988, *op. cit.*, p44.

NEURONAL ACTIVITY AND ARTISTIC IDENTITY

The claim to any *singular* and *linear* causality between Alzheimer's disease and an inability to paint may at the very least be precarious given, firstly, that the possible causes of Alzheimer's are numerous and in dispute; secondly, that there is no single diagnostic test for the disease; and finally, because there are more than sixty neurological disorders that mimic its symptoms.[34] De Kooning's final condition is further complicated by the artist's alcoholism, depression and possibly deafness. Thus it is that the neurologist Oliver Sacks urges commentators to hesitate before 'disallow[ing] the possibility of a continuing creativity in de Kooning. We need to know more, to be open to wonder. His latest works *could* be as rich as anything he has done'.[35]

Sacks's interest in de Kooning's condition is not especially surprising in the light of his long-term concern, as Julian Evans puts it, 'with the bridge between neurology and identity that becomes visible in the dawn of illness'.[36] In the introduction to *An Anthropologist on Mars* Sacks argues that '[d]efects, disorders, diseases ... can play a paradoxical role, by bringing out latent powers, developments, evolutions, forms of life, that might never be seen, or even be imaginable, in their absence. It is the paradox of disease, in this sense, its "creative" potential, that forms the central theme of this book'.[37] This emphasis on the unexpected consequences that may emerge from disease renders Sacks's work attractive to those commentators who seek to explore all the possible implications of de Kooning's condition. For example: in a lengthy catalogue essay which accompanied an exhibition of the artist's late works at the San Francisco Museum of Modern Art, Robert Storr draws on an interview he conducted with Sacks in order to claim that the effects of Alzheimer's on de Kooning's ability to paint cannot necessarily be anticipated in advance: 'It is not so much that miracles happen,' he writes, 'as that the infirmities that inevitably betray us are not always so simple or complete as their onset and symptoms portend'.[38]

I do not want to suggest that Sacks's account of the brain, which I will explore in some detail below, is entirely different from the ones that were referred to in the first half of this paper (in many ways, as I will illustrate, it is not). Nor am I concerned either with the scientific accuracy of Sacks's model of the brain, or with how it 'really works'. Instead, I want to suggest that, partly because of its openness, Sacks's explanation can be exploited by commentators (including myself) such that conventional notions of artistic identity are dismantled. In short, my focus lies not on what Sacks's account of the brain *is* but on what it can *do* in terms of manipulating understandings of creativity. Later, I will suggest that art critics and commentators, who (I am assuming) have relatively little scientific knowledge, are willing to push the implications of de Kooning's condition further than Sacks is able.

During the course of his interview with Storr and, in his typically literary manner,[39] Sacks harnesses a neurological understanding of the brain to an analysis of (artistic) identity. He says: 'Personal (and artistic) identity is forged

34. H.E. Hamilton, *Conversations with an Alzheimer's Patient: An Interactional Sociolinguistic Study*, Cambridge University Press, Cambridge 1994.

35. O. Sacks, 'Alzheimer's and creativity', letter to *Art and Antiques*, January 1990, p20.

36. J. Evans, 'Journey to the centre of the psyche', *Guardian Weekend*, 19.10.1996, p36.

37. O. Sacks, *An Anthropologist on Mars*, Picador, Basingstoke 1995, pxii.

38. R. Storr, 1995, *op. cit.*, p51.

39. Indeed, Sacks has been described as 'the man who mistook his patients for a literary career', in T. Shakespeare, book review, *Disability and Society*, Vol. 11 No. 1, p137.

40. O. Sacks in R. Storr, 1995, *op. cit.*, p51.

41. *Ibid.* Sacks' model of the brain appears to be almost entirely 'flat'. He makes no reference, as perhaps one might expect in a discussion of that which is 'deeper' than consciousness, to the *unconscious* as it is commonly understood. Like Freud's analysis of memory and perception written 'while he was still primarily a neurologist', Sacks' 'neurological style' appears to be unconscious not 'in the sense that [it is] part of some entity in the psyche, merely unconscious in the sense that [it has] not passed through the filter of consciousness because [it is] *before* consciousness', F.P. Cilliers, 'The brain, the mental apparatus and the text: A post-structural neuropsychology', *South African Journal of Philosophy*, Vol. 9 No. 1, p2).

42. C. Lury, *Prosthetic Culture: Photography, Memory and Identity*, Routledge, London 1997, p167.

43. M. Valverde, 'Governing out of habit', paper presented at Lancaster University, 1996, p7.

44. *Ibid.*, p5.

45. However, where Sacks's model of neuronal activity posits an

throughout life, becoming richer and richer as one experiences and thinks. It seems to be determined ... by ever changing 'global mappings' of neuronal activity, which involve every part of the brain, and are unique to each individual'.[40] The claim that artistic identity 'grows richer and richer as one experiences and thinks' suggests that Sacks's understanding of identity includes that which is determined, as well as that which is unique. Identity is determined insofar as neuronal activity is a characteristic of all brains, and unique insofar as the *distribution* of this activity is 'unique to each individual'. Put crudely, while the essence of the brain (neuronal activity) never changes, its 'outward manifestation', what Sacks calls *style*, does. '"Style", neurologically, is the deepest part of one's being, and may be preserved, almost to the last, in dementia'.[41] Artistic identity is thus, for Sacks, neither a naturalised 'gift of the individual',[42] nor is it entirely acquired. One might say instead that it lies somewhere in the shadowy twilight zone, as Marianna Valverde puts it, between freedom and necessity, will and determination, 'social' and 'natural'.[43] As Valverde argues in relation to habits, so Sacks seems to imply that: '[t]here is no deeper truth [of the self] ... there is just a groove, or rather, a series of grooves'.[44] In this respect, like Valverde, he offers a 'decentralised' or 'detotalising' notion of the self and (artistic) identity.[45]

Sacks's accent on neuronal activity differs from the models of the brain outlined above which assume, firstly, that creativity rests upon specific functions located in specific parts of the brain and, secondly, that when these parts are 'damaged' by Alzheimer's the artist is no longer in a position to produce original, or even 'intelligible', art. In a letter to *Art and Antiques* Sacks writes: 'I doubt if one can think in the simplistic terms of left and right brain or frontal vs occipital lobes, etc. But even in the face of widespread brain damage there can be sudden, remarkable if transient "restitutions" of function'.[46] Sacks's emphasis on neuronal activity then, enables him to argue that the onset of Alzheimer's, even if it causes *widespread* brain damage, does not necessarily erase all artistic ability. Implicit here is the claim that because specific functions are not locatable *as such*, neither is the ability to produce art. This is an ability, therefore, that cannot be wholly 'damaged' as such either.

In displacing the emphasis on site in favour of an emphasis on activity, Sacks goes some way to contest the assumption that artistic identity is inextricably bound to the self of the artist.[47] As I have already noted, for some commentators creativity is perceived to be dependent on the so-called 'higher' functions of abstraction, introspection, judgement, etc. These faculties are also assumed to be necessary to selfhood: witness the artist who, bereft of these capacities, looks at the canvas but does not see his 'self' there.[48] Without self-reflexivity (at least), the only 'choice' available to de Kooning, from this perspective, is to rely on, or rather 'resort' to, the habits or gestures learned over a lifetime of painting. For Sacks, by contrast, the works produced by those with Alzheimer's 'are not mere mechanical facsimiles of previous work, but can show real feeling and freshness of thought'.[49] This is possible because artistic identity does not depend on a coherent self, so much as 'emerge' out of a particular (and changing) pattern of neuronal pathways. To extend this analysis further than Sacks might choose: as in a connectionist network,[50] the brain can be understood as 'a machine that appears to function on its own'.[51] Insofar as the system's network constitution ensures that global co-operation emerges *spontaneously*, there is no 'self' or a central governor here, who, in 'possession' of artistic identity, 'initiates' the creative process.

Thus, while some commentators reinforce the identity-selfhood relation (a relation which is laid bare in Krauss' analysis of the discourse of originality), claiming that without selfhood there can be no authentic artistic expression, Sacks's understanding of the brain displaces the significance of the relation between artistic identity and the self of the artist. It is this, in its turn, which enables him to argue - to repeat - that de Kooning's 'latest works *could* be as rich as anything he has done'. For him, a work of art may be 'authentic' and 'original' whether the artist is mentally incapacitated or not, capable of self-reflexivity or not, and even if the self of the artist is in abeyance.

What is notable about Sacks's analysis, and in this respect it is similar to the representations outlined above, is that it does not contest the assumption that creativity resides in the 'head' of the artist or, more specifically, in the brain. Indeed, the relation between creativity and the brain remains axiomatic: artistic identity is 'determined' by neuronal activity which is holistically distributed *throughout* the brain, but which nevertheless remains, for the most part, confined *within* the brain. This is problematic because, as Wilson argues, although '[i]t has become a popular and scientific orthodoxy that thinking can be located in the head',[52] this is an orthodoxy that continues to find resonance with the Cartesian mind/body distinction. Contemporary neuropsychology, Wilson persuasively argues:

> rescues only the central nervous system (and then only a small part of that) from Cartesianism; the rest of the body is readily abandoned to brute, noncognitive mechanization ... The extraneurological body that is implied in contemporary neuropsychology, but never explicitly discussed, is the same degraded, unthinking, unknowing body that is to be found in Descartes's philosophy of the mind, and on which that philosophy is founded.[53]

Although some commentators seek to lift the brain out of the head and to deposit it in a different part of the body - Thomas Hess for example argues that de Kooning has a 'brain in the hand which, while drawing, will criticize, improvise, invent, erase - think new thoughts'[54] - I would argue that this does not challenge so much as simply relocate the site of the mind/body dualism. Furthermore, this shift of creativity from head to hand confirms, rather than contests, the significance of the artist in the production of art.

authoritative (scientific and 'expert') reading of the brain, as Valverde notes, 'there is no central committee with privileged authority over the application of the category "habit"', *ibid.*, p2.

46. O. Sacks in *Art and Antiques*, 1990, *op. cit.*, p20. Elsewhere, Sacks acknowledges his debt to Alexander Luria, who championed antilocalisation views of brain function.

47. Although see M. Fraser, *op. cit.*

48. A view which is not confined to commentaries on de Kooning. See for example D. Webb, 'A "revenge" on modern times: Notes on traumatic brain injury', *Sociology*, Vol. 32 No. 3.

49. O. Sacks in *Art and Antiques*, 1990, *op. cit.*, p19.

50. My intentions here are neither to suggest that Sacks's model of identity is connectionist (it is not), nor that connectionist models of the brain offer a more adequate way of theorising identity or creativity than any other. If it is possible to find in his short account some *resonance* with connectionist theories of cognition however, this might be because, although connectionist theories and models have been deployed in a variety of contexts (from computer

science to linguistics), neurology remains, broadly speaking, 'the yardstick of connectionism's credibility and potential', E.A. Wilson, 1998, *op. cit.*, p11.

51. *Ibid.*, p160.

52. *Ibid.*, p121.

53. *Ibid.*, p123-4.

54. Quoted in R. Storr, 1995, *op. cit.*, p69.

55. R. Cooper, 'Assemblage notes', in R. Cooper (ed), *Organized Worlds: Explorations in Technology and Organization with Robert Cooper*, Routledge, London and New York 1998, p131.

56. E. Grosz, 'A thousand tiny sexes: Feminism and rhizomatics', in C.V. Boundas and D. Olkowski (eds), *Gilles Deleuze and the Theater of Philosophy*, Routledge, New York 1994, p197-198, my emphasis.

57. R. Bogue, 'Gilles Deleuze: The aesthetics of force', in P. Patton (ed), *Deleuze: A Critical Reader*, Blackwell, Oxford 1996, p263.

58. G. Deleuze and C. Parnet, *Dialogues*, Athlone Press, New York 1987, p60.

59. E. Grosz, 1994, *op. cit.*, p200.

60. G. Deleuze, 'Ethology: Spinoza

Artistic identity remains confined to the body of the artist (once in the head, now in the hand) in a static, inert and self-contained location. There is movement here, but 'of a kind: the simple movement of definite things from one definite place to another … it's a form of movement which denies the restlessness of transformation, deformation and reformation'.[55] In the final part of this paper I want to focus on some of the representations of de Kooning which seem to me to sit well alongside another conception of creativity, one which does not privilege any single body part (such as the brain), which displaces the accent on the individual as the 'source' of artistic creativity, and in which an analysis of movement is central.

CREATIVE AFFECTS

As I noted briefly in the introduction and illustrated in the first section of this paper, Deleuze's account of forces aids in an analysis of the territorialising effects of the three strata of organism, significance and subjectification. At the same time however, it is an account that allows for the possibility that the subject, conceptualised 'as a series of flows, energies, movements, and capacities, a series of fragments or segments [is] capable of being linked together in ways *other than those that congeal it into an identity*'.[56] The subject is a 'body', but a body in a 'special sense of the word',[57] defined, that is, not by its forms or functions (although it may be formed, and be functional sometimes), but as forces or affects distributed on a plane of immanence. For Deleuze, the definition of a body will no longer reside in what it *is*, but in what it can *do*, in the affects of which it is capable.[58] To define a body in this way, by the play of its forces, is to suggest that all things, 'regardless of their type, have the same ontological status'.[59] A body 'can be an animal, a body of sounds, a mind or an idea'.[60] With respect to the argument being developed here, this account of forces and affects is useful not only because it enables particular formations of artistic identity to be addressed - so for example, the habits, gestures and brains referred to in the first parts of this paper can be understood to be contingent stratifications which may have the effect, in specific contexts, of contracting or extending the affective capacities of a body - but also because it suggests that these formations are neither given nor inevitable. More importantly still, a body may be extended beyond the narrow confines of a (human) corporeal and anthropomorphic solipsism. It can cut across the boundaries which are assumed to divide organic from inorganic, human from non-human.

Just as Deleuze asks not what a body is, but what it can do, so he addresses his questions to art by asking not '"What does it mean?" (interpretation) but rather "How does it work?" (experimentation)'.[61] Again, the question 'how does it work?' pertains to forces, that is, to the specific way in which art mobilises forces: 'Different art forms have different affective capacities, so they harness forces in distinctive ways'.[62] Twentieth-century painting, for example: 'aimed not at the reproduction of visible forms but the presentation of the non-visible forces that act behind or beneath these forms'.[63] Francis Bacon's paintings are exemplary in this regard: where imitative and figurative art renders *the* visible, Bacon, by contrast, renders visible intensive forces. Instead of painting the *sensational*, the horror that produces the scream for instance, Bacon attempts to paint the *sensation* - the scream itself. The former paints a story; the latter captures 'an invisible force'.[64]

This analysis of forces - both in relation to art, and in relation to the subject more generally - clearly has implications for the subject position 'artist'. For Deleuze, the question 'what can it do?', or, 'of what affects is it capable?' applies as much to artist as it does to art (as well as to the relation between them). It is notable that nowhere in *Francis Bacon: The Logic of Sensation* does Deleuze refer to 'the biographical details which often characterise the popular psychological readings of Bacon as the suffering artist, bestial homosexual, or religious pervert'.[65] Rather than pathologise the artist and 'interpret Bacon's paintings as the expressions of a tortured artist', Deleuze 'enters the habitat as an apprentice and performs a clinical diagnosis of how the paintings function to harness forces':

> *Logique de la Sensation* is itself a habitat or body composed of image and text, theory and paint, philosophy and artist interviews. It is a modulating arrangement distributed around an encounter between Deleuze and Bacon ... Carried along in the struggle between forces, the meaning of all bodies is unfolded through continuous sign-chains which are open to ever new interpretations and adaptations, contractions and extensions.[66]

I want to draw on Deleuze to illustrate that, in some of the commentaries on de Kooning, creativity is neither solely confined to nor located within (the self and/or body of) the artist. Instead, it appears to emerge in the encounter between artist, canvas, paint ... And secondly - relatedly - I want to suggest that when creative processes are understood in this way, the status of Alzheimer's changes, such that it no longer signifies a deficit, lack, or loss.

Rackstraw Downes's commentary, for example, can itself be understood as a body which cuts through and across the assumption that de Kooning and the canvas on which he paints are discrete entities. In doing this, the Downes-body, in its encounter with techniques of painting, has the effect of destratifying the notion of the artist as the singular origin of the work of art. 'De Koonings,' he writes, 'have the thinking-aloud quality of good jazz improvisation. "I see the canvas and I begin" ... not "I see the model ..." or "I foresee the end."'[67] Deflecting attention away from a traditional portrait of the artist (the isolated and self-contained subject), away from the 'model' (clearly defined object to be represented) and away from the 'end' (the final outcome or product), the emphasis here lies instead on the symbiotic relation between de Kooning and canvas. Creativity emerges in the relation *between* de Kooning and canvas; there is no sole source or origin of creativity here,

and us', in J. Crary and S Kwinter (eds) *Incorporations*, 1992, *op. cit.*, p629.

61. D.W. Smith, 'Deleuze's theory of sensation: Overcoming the Kantian duality', in P. Patton, 1996, *op. cit.*, p47.

62. S. O'Connell, *Drawing on Deleuze and Guattari*, Major thesis, Department of Visual Arts, Monash University 1996, p59.

63. D. W. Smith, *op. cit.*, p40.

64. *Ibid.*, p42.

65. S. O'Connell, 1996, *op. cit.*, p57.

66. *Ibid.*

67. R. Downes, 'De Kooning's attitude', *Art Journal*, Vol. 48 No 3, p241.

68. N. Millet, 'The fugitive body', *Journal of Philosophy and the Visual Arts*, 1993, p44.

69. M. Stevens, 'De Kooning's master strokes', *Vanity Fair*, May 1994, p124.

70. I. Lassaw quoted in S. Wick, 'De Kooning's art isn't ailing', *Newsday*, 235.1989, p3.

71. T. Ferrara quoted in R. Storr, 1995, *op. cit.*, p53.

72. R. Bogue, 'Gilles Deleuze: The aesthetics of force', in P. Patton, 1996, *op. cit.*, p262.

73. G. Deleuze and F. Guattari, *A Thousand Plateaus: Capitalism and Schizophrenia*, Athlone Press, London 1988, p158.

74. R. Bogue, 1996, *op. cit.*

75. R. Downes, *op. cit.*

76. M. Gatens, 'Through a Spinozist lens: Ethology, difference, power', in P. Patton, 1996, *op. cit.*, p170.

77. G. Deleuze quoted in M. Gatens, *ibid.*, p171.

since creativity is a process which would not occur without de Kooning *and* canvas. The artist is 'circuited, immanent to the production process' and, so, it becomes impossible to trace the 'art-work ... back to an original unity'.[68]

If a number of commentators, alongside Downes, appear to be at ease with this notion of the artist as immanent to the creative process, it is an ease which is most notable after de Kooning's Alzheimer's is made public. Where de Kooning's *Women* emerged, in the 1950s, from 'an indeterminate space in which figure and ground never seem fully distinct',[69] by the late 1980s it is the *artist* who is no longer a distinct entity. De Kooning, one commentator claims, 'greets the canvas as if it were a part of his anatomy, like an arm or a leg'.[70] Painting undergoes a process of becoming lung: de Kooning 'just breathed [paintings] out'.[71] In these encounters (which include the critic), organic and inorganic, human and non-human are conjoined in a zone of undecidability: arm, leg, canvas, breath are all bodies in 'an affective dimension of becoming, one in which no entities as such may be recognised, but only vectors of force-matter and currents of affects'.[72]

While the accounts of the brain outlined above *organise* de Kooning's body parts into 'that organization of the organs called the organism',[73] here, there are 'only provisional organs that emerge and disappear, or unspecified organs with multiple and contradictory functions'.[74] Downes argues that in de Kooning's final years: 'The head that conceives and the hand that executes were never so indistinguishable, nor has the hand ever "talked back" so much and the head "listened" so well'.[75] Head and hand are not confined to the roles of conceiving and executing, and creativity is located *neither* in the head *nor* in the hand. Instead, it emerges in the interchange between a talking hand (which is provisional), and a listening head (which is contingent). There is no 'mental' and 'physical' here, no 'mind' (that thinks) and 'body' (that acts) since the interchange itself renders these organs indistinguishable. This is Deleuze's 'ethology', which 'maps connections between bodies - without regard to their designated form or function'.[76] In ethology, hand and head will be bodies which are capable of affects (and are capable of being affected), rather than *body parts* which refer back to a monadic and possessive unity.

This conception of creativity is above all dynamic; the encounter between critic, artist, canvas, breath, hand, head *and* disease is productive of a mobile assemblage, formed by connections that shift and multiply. In this context, disease does not function as the *cause* of a lack or a loss, but is rather an additional player in the encounter, a body with affective capacities that alters that encounter without necessarily diminishing it. Or to put that another way: Alzheimer's is one of 'the most varied components (biochemical, behavioural, perceptive, hereditary, acquired, improvised, social, etc.) [that] can crystallise in assemblages that respect neither the distinction between orders nor the hierarchy between forms'.[77]

Throughout this paper I have been contesting the various assumptions that sustain the figure of the artist in a privileged position with regards to creativity. In order to do this, I have drawn on Deleuze's analysis of forces and affects. Brian Massumi argues that there is a liability that often accompanies such an analysis however, in that it may be mistaken for an appeal 'to a pre-reflexive, romantically raw domain of primitive experiential richness - that nature in our culture'.[78] Because of this liability, I think it is important to underline, briefly, how this latter view - which does make its appearance, on occasion, in representations of de Kooning - only serves to reinforce the very stratifications that this paper has sought to deterritorialise.

78. B. Massumi, 'The Autonomy of affect', in P. Patton, 1996, op. cit., p223.

Consider, for instance, the claim that de Kooning 'worked before in an immediacy, without too much reflection ... now you get a feeling of meditation, of deep reflection. His knowledge is so inbred in him that he can't make a mistake'.[79] The narrative construction here (and in the following extract) of a before and after Alzheimer's implicitly suggests that the disease has enabled de Kooning to arrive at - or perhaps more accurately, to *recover* - an 'unsullied' immediacy that he had been unable to properly grasp prior to the loss of his self (or at the very least, prior to the loss of self-reflexivity). Similarly, it is said that 'neurological change may even have *enhanced* a master for whom "painting is as natural as walking or reading"'.[80] Arguably, in these representations, Alzheimer's confers on the artist an authenticity that - in the late nineteenth and early twentieth centuries in particular - was the domain of children, the insane and the 'primitive'. All these figures, in their different ways, were believed to have access to an 'unspoiled' creativity, to an origin of some sort, whether that be the origin of art, of the psyche, or of civilisation.[81]

79. C. Herman quoted in S. Wick, op. cit.

80. J. Warren, 'Alzheimer's and art', Chicago Tribune, 16.11.1989, p2, references omitted, my emphasis.

81. A. Bowler, 1997, op. cit., p26.

Hal Foster's work suggests that the attribution of 'authenticity' to the other is not confined to turn of the century art, medicine and psychiatry but continues to have considerable purchase today. The other, he argues, 'usually assumed to be of color,' is seen to have 'special access to primary psychic and social processes from which the white subject is somehow blocked'[82]:

82. H. Foster, The Return of the Real, MIT Press, Cambridge Mass. and London 1996, p175.

> discourses like psychoanalysis and disciplines like art history ... still often assume a connection between the (ontogenetic) development of the individual and the (phylogenetic) development of the species ... In this association the primitive is first projected by the Western white subject as a primal stage in *cultural* history and then reabsorbed as a primal stage in *individual* history ... this association of the primitive and the prehistoric and/or the pre-Oedipal, the other and the unconscious, *is* the primitivist fantasy.[83]

83. Ibid., p177-178.

To suggest that Alzheimer's has lent de Kooning access to an unmediated sensory world is to reinscribe the body/brain duality once again and, also, to reconfirm the authoritative status of artist in the creative process. In the first instance, the accent on brain - 'the materialization of certain masculinist and ethnocentric desires about the mind and their attendant anxieties about

84. E. A. Wilson, 1998, op. cit., p132.

85. C. N. Serematakis, 'Implications', in C.N. Serematakis (ed), The Sense Still: Perception and Memory as Material Culture in Modernity, University of Chicago Press, Chicago and London 1994, p124.

86. Ibid.

87. H. Foster, 1996, op. cit., p168.

88. G. Deleuze, 'Ethology', 1992, op. cit., p625-626. As Gatens notes, this is an immanent rather than a taxonomic means of evaluation, M. Gatens, 1996, op. cit., p168.

89. R. Storr, 1995, op. cit., p50.

the (psychologically and culturally) primitive body'[84] - is now replaced by an accent on the body, specifically the body of the (diseased) other who becomes a reified deposit for, and site of, a 'primal and original sensory experience'.[85] The body/brain dyad is not displaced then, only the values associated with each side of the equation are reversed. Secondly, and relatedly, the notion that Alzheimer's has 'cleared' de Kooning's head (leaving his body in a transparent immediacy) reconfirms the privileged position of the artist: de Kooning is again in a unique relation to creativity, this time because he is perceived to be in possession (even if he does not 'know' it) of some kind of 'a generic sensory expertise'.[86] This puts de Kooning, as Foster evocatively says in relation to the trauma subject, in the 'paradoxical condition of absentee authority'.[87]

In the analysis of forces and affects that I have deployed above, Alzheimer's disease is to be understood not as a vehicle through which a 'primal creativity' can be accessed, but rather as one part of a machinic assemblage which generates particular formations of art and artist. I would include among this assemblage not only the figure of the artist, the critic and the canvas, but also art markets, their financial and aesthetic constraints and/or possibilities, as well as contemporary understandings of disease, brain and body. This assemblage will be distinguished and evaluated not by its degree of *authenticity*, but according to its relations of movement or rest, its power to affect or be affected. Drawing on Spinoza, Deleuze refers to two axes against which bodies may be individuated and appraised: the kinetic axis, which refers to speed and slowness, and the dynamic axis, which relates to power and affectability.[88] Thus, the understanding of creativity that I prefer - where creativity emerges out of encounters which may include, but do not privilege, the individual artist - is not more 'authentic' than, nor is it situated *in opposition to*, that installed by the discourse of originality (which, whether or not it includes some reference to a 'raw domain of experiential richness,' is usually supported by assumptions which confirm the individual unique-ness of the artist as the well-spring of inspiration). Instead, it is an understanding which, in emphasising no single and discrete creative entity, is more likely to enhance its affective capacities than one which confines creativity to a specific location, where it resides in stasis, vulnerable to disease.

It is clearly the case, as I outlined at the start of this paper, that not all commentators are open to the interpretations that I have just offered. For example: it is precisely the ambiguous implications of Alzheimer's, which I have claimed *disrupts* the subject position 'artist', that can also be exploited to further *bolster* de Kooning's status as a creative 'genius'. Robert Storr reminds his readers that not only is there 'little agreement on the medical etiology of the disease,' but it is also unclear 'how its development would affect a person of de Kooning's special talents'.[89] This suggests that de Kooning, because he has 'special talents' is more likely than an 'ordinary' person to be able to respond favourably to the changing conditions to which his body is subject. This is a commonplace, if not banal, representation of an Artist. Donald Kuspit writes: 'Because he is able to experience himself in a way that is impossible for other people, he is one of those heroes we are supposed to worship, for he has overcome fate through creativity'.[90] For some commentators, de Kooning's artistic identity enables him to overcome not just fate, but a *fatal disease*. Emilie Kilgore, one of de Kooning's friends, claims that the effects of Alzheimer's on de Kooning are not predictable because: 'We're dealing with a genius'.[91] This is the artist as hero and 'super-subject'.

Yet it is also the case that the notion of 'artistic identity' moves from zone to zone; from artist to art critic, neurologist to psychologist to sociologist and back again (no doubt via other encounters). And it is in this exchange that the term is un-formed, de-formed and re-formed. How these new formations might be cast, of what affects they might be capable, or what forces they might harness, cannot be anticipated (this is characteristic of the modesty that accompanies Deleuze's ethology). To take Sacks's model of neuronal activity for example: at first glance, one might expect a model of the brain, one which confirms the brain/body duality, and which draws on the authority and 'expertise' of science, to support the discourse of originality. And yet somewhat unexpectedly, in its encounter with de Kooning and Alzheimer's, and in the context of this paper, it is a body which gives rise to joyful affects: it begins to destratify and disentangle the identity-selfhood relation on which the subject position 'artist' depends. This example - which illustrates that (even) the intensive capacities of a body of science cannot be forecast - returns me to a point that I raised in the introduction: that is, that it is not necessarily to the advantage of criticism to too quickly reject 'science' out of hand. What I have tried to do in this paper, then, is to contribute to these alternative formations, with a mind not necessarily to replace, but certainly to loosen the connections that sustain restrictive notions of artistic identity and creativity.

90. Quoted in T. Osborne, 'The aesthetic problematic', *Economy and Society*, Vol. 26 No. 1, p141.

91. Quoted in C. Barnett, *op. cit.*, p70.

On Homo-Sex, Or Is Homosexuality a Curable Vice?

Guy Hocquenghem

'Homosexual liberation is imagined according to the model of national liberations of the 1970s, that is as a gradual and invincible process founded on the progressive revelation of a pre-existing and irrepressible reality. This is an illusion of hindsight. Homosexuality, the fruit of the coupling of psychiatry and political progressivism, is a provisional solution. Its days may well be numbered, not only for the person embodying it, but as a blip or aberration within an already ephemeral modernity'. I wrote these lines in *Race d'Ep* five years ago.[1] The passage of time has made this malaise around the definition and existence of homosexuality only more explicit. When we consider the transition from the traditional 'queen' (*folle*) to the 'clone',[2] from the sexual imperative to the monogamous couple, from cruising to affection, it is difficult to believe that a single, constant explanatory principle, a concept of homosexuality, underlies such different, heterogeneous and changing attitudes.

It is because they 'are' never enough, that they overdo it. This formula can be adapted to designate the homosexual: there is a difference and there is not, since the ultimate goal is to be treated 'as if there were no difference', given the difference's capacity for imperceptibility. There is no essential difference: therefore - just look at history - homosexuality is not an enduring essence with immutable characteristics. Homosexuality exists only as a problem, and is lived only as a problematic. In 1972 I began *Homosexual Desire* with these words: 'The problem is not so much homosexual desire as the fear of homosexuality'.[3] I've come a long way since then! It was perfect for the time (the *Front homosexuel d'action revolutionnaire* (FHAR), the first 'radical' gay movement in France), but the formula is very deceptive. I heard it reproduced more or less word for word in the mouths of guests on a *Dossier de l'écran* in 1984.[4] It sounded false. At the time of the collapse of 'liberationist' values, of AIDS, and of renewed outbursts of anti- 'paedophile' hatred, it seemed blinkered and arrogant. There exists an ossified, vulgar, self-confident homosexual assertion which is no longer a response to an onslaught of anxiety which concerns us all, or to a world that has seen so much come and go anyway. I have never believed in a homosexual essence. But I believed for a time that 'anti-homosexual paranoia', caused by repressed homosexuality, could explain the main causes of repression. Things have turned out to be more complex.

Does this mean that the heterosexual is right, that homosexuality, which might not exist, ought to disappear, and be brought back to the theory of a

1. Hocquenghem, *Race d'Ep: Un siècle d'images de l'homosexualité*, Libres-Hallier, Paris 1979, p14. 'Race d'Ep' is backslang for 'pédéraste'.

2. Hocquenghem writes, 'the macho-moustache style'.

3. *Homosexual Desire*, D. Dangoor (trans), Duke University Press, Durham N.C. 1993, p49.

4. *Les Dossiers de l'écran* was a long-running primetime programme (1967-1991) on the second French television channel, consisting of a film followed by a debate. Hocquenghem is no doubt referring to that broadcast on 4.9.1984, 'To Be Gay Today'.

curable vice or an avoidable social disability? No. The 'problem' has to be posed differently: yes, homosexuality is 'a problem', this is even its sole constant mode of existence. It is probably a redundant category. There is nothing fixed about it. It does not exist because it is 'more real' than the self-repressive phantasms of normative heterosexuals. The problem is neither that of the homosexual nor of the homophobe, but between the two, in the unpredictable and provisional emergence (*surgissement*) of a homosexuality that is recognised or confessed.

'And if we constantly need to repeat that there is no difference between homosexuals and heterosexuals, that both are divisible into rich and poor, male and female, good and bad, then this is precisely because there is a distance, because there is a repeatedly unsuccessful attempt to draw homosexuality back into normality, an unsurmountable chasm which keeps opening up. Homosexuality exists and does not exist, at one and the same time; indeed, its very mode of existence questions again and again the certainty of existence'.[5] I still think this. There is therefore no positive, defined principle that can be called 'homosexuality', understood, not just as sexual relations between two people of the same sex, but as everything bound up with it socially and personally.

The most efficient model for thinking about homosexuality, if the term is to be retained in order to express a certain 'attitude towards life' rather than an 'identity', would be that of the hidden god associated with Gnosticism, or the Romantic notion of 'witz'. This is a negative super-essence, expressed in striking shorthand (the instant of the word), utopian in the real sense of 'no place'. In *Race d'Ep* I explored with Lionel Soukaz the history of homosexuality through its cycle of appearance and disappearance. We took as starting points two silences: that preceding the 'homosexual movement' and the word itself, in other words the nineteenth century, and that following the crushing of the German movement in 1930 which lasted until our own period, the second emergence. Homosexuality is nourished not by existing - through open and unrestrained confession - but also by not being, that is by appearing (and disappearing only to reappear). Homosexuality is baroque, dramatic, it is an 'effect', not a principle. This does not mean that it is inferior to the concept; rather, it undermines the concept's assurance.

It is because they 'are' never enough that they overdo it. They are not themselves when they are 'out', they are boring and tiresome. The only metaphysical status homosexuality might possess is that of excess: a cyclothymia,[6] a vibration (*battement*), a coming and going between extremes, including between being and not being. If homosexuality exists, it is only as a problem, as a utopian figure, an anti-hero of modernity (in Baudelaire's sense). What it reveals is the very excess of nature (its exuberance and mortality), as in the baroque and its use of the vegetal, and 'physics' whose (anti-physical) mirror it is. Despite what many English dictionaries say, 'gay' does not come from the Old French *gai*. 'Gay' is derived from an anglo-

5. *Homosexual Desire*, 1993, *op. cit.*, p53.

6. From *kuklos* ('circle') and *thumos* ('state of mind' or 'temper'). In both French and English this is a psychiatric term denoting swings of mood between depression and elation.

saxon word, *gāl*, meaning 'merry', 'proud', and 'lascivious'. Ultimately, it comes from an Indo-European word, *ghoilo-s*, meaning 'to effervesce, ferment, froth', which we find in contemporary Germanic languages: the Dutch *gijlen* 'to ferment' and Norwegian *gil* 'fermenting beer'. Cognates in Slavic and Balto-Slavic languages contain words within the same semantic field, such as Old Slavic *dzelo* and Old Czech *zielo* 'very', Lithuanian *gailas* 'violent'. Modern German *geil* means 'sexually aroused, horny, lascivious, its originally positive meaning changing to a negative one.[7] Minority excess, as in the Anglo-Saxon 'gay' for 'homosexual', inherits the dionysian excess represented by the alcoholic fermentation of beer, in which humanity sees the symbol of sexual excess and of drunkenness. It is interesting to discover that a text attributed to Aristotle, the *Problemata,* devoted to the subject of melancholy, that is to the brilliant insanity of exceptional people and great geniuses, makes the comparison with the 'wine bubbles' of the Greek champagne of the time after discussing the fact that men of genius are hypersexed (overflow with *physis*, with natural forces).

Out of this cyclothymia between being-too-much and disappearing, between melancholy and hysteria, what I call 'homosexual sense'[8] goes from tears to laughter, dances between sexual ferment and death (see the examples of Pasolini, backrooms and criminality, and of AIDS and hypersexuality). 'Homosexual sense' is not simply putting desire into practice, satisfying a particular object-choice (of the same sex, which just happens to be forbidden). 'Homosexual sense' is not a concept nor something constant outside its particular manifestations, it is a sexual tension, an overabundant expression of appetite or of the tragic effort of being. This 'homosexual sense', this sixth sense, makes one aware that existence consists of a striving to be. And that fundamentally the real world is just, as in Leibniz, the intersection of the efforts that each point, each monad, makes in order to exist. This is a world of tensions rather than satisfactions: the revolutionary assertion of the FHAR and the new tweeness of loving domesticity have at least one thing in common. In neither case is the 'sexual' lived as a simple and positive satisfaction (which does not mean there is any hidden frustration). In these cases what is sensual is not the repression or sublimation of the sexual. 'Homosexual sense' is oriented more towards a 'sublime body' which avoids physiology and sexology as much as it avoids Puritanism (such as the photographic body, or the body of the lover in Genet, etc.).

'The term "sexual minorities" is now widely accepted. The use of the plural spontaneously establishes a parallel with racial or national minorities, and suggests that the existence of a factual diversity is obvious. In fact, there are no "sexual minorities", and none have ever existed. What this all-inclusive term designates is a sexual majority (women, considered to be the oppressed people of History), and a sexual minority discovered last century and which served as the model for any possible sexual minority, namely homosexuality'.[9] Even the 'sexual minority' of childhood and adolescence can be thought about only in relation to the notion of perverse archetypes,

7. In this linguistic passage, Hocquenghem is freely translating from R. Aman, 'On the Etymology of Gay', *Maledicta*, 3, no. 2, 1979, pp257-8.

8. As well as 'sense' or 'meaning', *sens* can also mean 'direction' or 'tendency'.

9. *Race d'Ep*, 1979, *op. cit.*, p15.

those of incitement to corruption, and more precisely the archetype of homosexuality. The homosexual is the archetype of the social pervert. Like the fetishist in the analyst's office, it is he who, for the past century, has allowed sex to be conceived in concrete terms as perversity, through the conjoined assumption of power by notions of sexuality, sexual categories, and perversions (in the medical and legal senses), which he inaugurates, symbolises, and takes pleasure in playing with (it is this dramatic aspect which characterises his 'identity').[10]

'Homosexual sense' sails on the troubled waters of the perverse. The great game of shame and pride, the vibration (*battement*) between protest slogans, 'glad to be gay', and the disturbing contemporary (or 1950s) desire for conformism, make the message of a dominant, self-confident homosexuality look terribly dated. This is a good thing. I have personally put up with enough with the censorship of a pseudo gay militancy (in the USA as well as in France), and their stupid dictates (such as never taking the risk of giving straight people a negative image of gays), that I can repeat without reservations what I said in my first book: 'By becoming passionate propagandists of homosexuality, referring … to a homosexual "nature" as opposed to the heterosexual one',[11] in other words to be proud of not being ashamed to be homosexual, is indeed the trap set by the overabundant gay journalistic literature of that period and ours. The trap (which Gilles Deleuze had characterised as the 'double bind' of compulsory transgression, and Michel Foucault as the 'will to know') is that of compulsory confession, and also of any kind of visibility.

Unlike these two philosophers, I would posit another homosexuality, more exactly a 'homosexual sense', against a regime whose interdictions are so strong that they create in return the centring of desire on that which is forbidden (and through this process designated and classified). I would 'musicalise' the idea of homosexuality: it exists only in its rhythm, its intervals and its pauses, it exists only through its (dramatic) movement. It conjugates invisibility and visibility in this rhythm of emergence and disappearance, of 'repetition' in the full and strong Kierkegaardian sense. Pure philosophers, such as Deleuze and Foucault, remained relatively indifferent to the French gay movement. It so happened I was in the midst of it, hence my need, which they did not share, to find a meaning (*sens*) for it. Today I would basically retain only the form of that experience, in the way in which that meaning gathered and was born, that form of evaporation and condensation that Sartre admirably summarised in relation to Genet: 'Genet's femininity is an evanescent being, the pure challenging of virility'.[12] But at the same time, Deleuze and Foucault were right philosophically: unlike Greek love, for example, the categorising notions of homosexuality and of 'gay culture' are unacceptable, even inquisitorial. This is particularly the case, and I will go into no further detail in order to avoid controversy, when those notions, in the background, serve to legitimise journalistic sermons and condemnations made in the name of a gay 'positive image'.

10. In French, the expression *jouer de*, translated here as 'play with', means to make skilful use of something, as in, especially, playing a musical instrument.

11. *Homosexual Desire*, 1993, *op. cit.*, p143.

12. J.-P.Sartre, *Saint Genet Actor and Martyr*, B.Frechtman (trans), W.H.Allen, London 1964, pp291-2.

'Visibility' is the faculty of 'saying oneself', of being adequate to the idea of oneself, it implies frankness, constancy of meaning, the unequivocal content of the message (gay and proud to be so). I was for visibility when it was emergence (*apparition*). Today, like many younger than myself, I find myself wishing for its disappearance. Without a play with invisibility, visibility is no more than pointless foolishness, a false problem, second-rate psychology. Visibility is not an aim in itself. I have been sufficiently visible to wish often I were a bit less (but I wish to point out that I will take no lessons from militant latecomers comfortably ensconced in publishing, the press and business). It is what Deleuze understood by 'pervert'. An official pervert. I understand it differently: perversities of languages and of intellectual concepts, 'innocent' or playful perversity.

In the alternating flight and constitution of the 'homosexual sense', and in its (sexual, familial, public) situations, 'talking about oneself' or even 'shouting about oneself', as we did in 1971, is less a confession than an aggression, and the desire to 'blend in' that many share with me today is less a desire to hide than to be undifferentiated. This has always been the aim. I wrote somewhere, 'It is often said that the Nazis' hatred towards the Jew, even stronger than that towards the Arab or the Black, was nourished by the near imperceptibility of the Jew's difference from the Aryan. It was as if racism increased the more its object resembled its proponent. The fact that it is impossible to found homosexuality, in any lasting way, in something organic, and to recognise the gay man in an unequivocal way, is perhaps the source of homophobia, with the homosexual seen as a degenerate fellow creature rather than belonging to another race or species.'[13] On the contrary, perhaps, through this subtle lack of differentiation we could arrive at the point where the 'homosexual sense', independently of its content, would be purified of anything confessional, or of anything to do with 'truth'. It would have become a pure 'problem', not a psychological, social or political problem, but a problem of the indiscernibles, in the sense of the baroque philosophy of monadology: no two identical beings exist in the world, since their mere appearance side by side, inviting comparison, makes of them two distinct objects. No two points, subjects or persons are truly similar, for the space in which a comparison might be made is but the pattern woven between monads striving to be.

13. *Race d'Ep*, 1979, *op. cit.*, p13.

COMMENTARY: 'ON HOMO-SEX'

Bill Marshall

This late article appeared a year before Guy Hocquenghem's death, from an AIDS-related illness in 1988, in the then best-selling French weekly gay magazine, *Gai Pied Hebdo*.[1] According to Hocquenghem's friend and collaborator René Schérer, it was given as a lecture to students in Yugoslavia in 1985 under the title 'De l'Homo-sexe'.[2] That title is combined in this version with its more eye-catching but unrepresentative equivalent from 1987.

While Hocquenghem's output of fiction and theory has received more sustained attention in the Anglo-Saxon world in the 1990s, it is only in 1999, with the republication of his short stories[3] and especially the attention given to him in Didier Eribon's massive *Réflexions sur la question gay* (Paris, Fayard 1999) , that he may be being rediscovered in France. His seminal theoretical work from 1972, *Le Désir homosexuel*, remains out of print there, as is a prescient and caustic essay from 1979 on French nationalism, *La Beauté du métis: réflexions d'un francophobe*. The reception of Hocquenghem's work needs to be traced across differences between French and Anglo-Saxon cultural histories and political traditions, in particular, the supposed lack of receptiveness in France to notions of identity politics and of 'communities' because of the weight of the republican tradition which emphasises the relationship between individual citizen and state. However, this explanation, which runs the risk of cliché with its binary oppositions between 'France' and 'America' that bedevil much current political and cultural debate on both sides of the Atlantic, contains several paradoxes. While much official discourse in France is still allergic to notions of multiculturalism which would unsettle the abstract notion of the French republican citizen as universal template of humanity, the reality is that a civil society consisting of networks of interest groups and associations - what the French call *la vie associative* - has proliferated over the past quarter century. This has included gay and AIDS-related organisations, even if they developed later than in the Anglo-Saxon world (ACT-UP Paris was founded in 1989). Moreover, it seems that French society is discovering identity politics just when much theoretical work elsewhere is calling it into question, along with the notion of 'identity' itself. This has been one possible direction for queer theory to take. However, much discussion of non-identity, of hybridity, of the cyborg, in turn owes a great deal to a certain French theory which demonises both the state and totality, in for example the pluralising and historicising work of Foucault, or Deleuze's emphasis on becoming rather than being. Hocquenghem would have enjoyed these spiralling paradoxes and transnational exchanges.

Both Judith Butler and Jeffrey Weeks have written of, respectively, the

1. *Gai Pied Hebdo*, Nos. 278-9, 11.8.1987, pp64-5.

2. Afterword to Hocquenghem, *L'Amphithéâtre des morts*, Gallimard, Paris 1994, pp133-5.

3. *Oiseau de la nuit*, Albin Michel, Paris 1999.

4. J. Butler, *Gender Trouble: Feminism and the Subversion of Identity*, Routledge, London 1990, p15; J. Weeks, 'The Idea of a Sexual Community', *Soundings*, no.2, Lawrence and Wishart, London 1996, p83.

'provisional unities' and 'necessary fictions' involved in the elaboration of an emancipatory sexual politics.[4] 'On Homo-Sex' represents a voyage into the 'provisional' and 'fictitious' sides of these formulae. However, Hocquenghem is not in the business of a dispersal of the self or of a dissolution of 'the homosexual' in the wider society and world. Indeed, he keeps the term 'homosexual', but aligned with *sens*. The 'homosexual sense' represents an attempt to hold in relation, tension and play that stabilised assembly of meanings around 'homosexual' or 'gay' which enables agency and intervention, and that element of questioning and movement which would prevent the provisional stabilisation turning into fixity and complacency. It is always situated, *en situation* in the Sartrean sense of the social, historical, even personal contexts in which choices are made and actions entered into.

As he makes clear, his formulations grow out of his experience of the gay movement in the 1970s and 1980s. In a sense, his life illustrates that relation of stability and subversion, visibility and invisibility, around the notion of 'gay', in that it combined periods of militancy (as one of the founders of the FHAR) and, not only of highly questioning theoretical work, but of a 'non-coming out' about his illness. His disillusion with French society and politics of the 1980s was a result of the way in which the radicalism of the post-1968 period had been transformed into a Socialist hegemony dominated by nationalism (the Rainbow Warrior affair), an acceptance of liberal consumerism, and a general celebration of the status quo. Both French intellectuals and the 'gay community' had thus been complicit with the new orderings of French society and capitalism. As in Foucault, there was no straightforward progression from 'repression' to 'liberation'; rather, French society had witnessed the creation of new dispositions, orthodoxies and interdictions.

Influenced by the first volume of *History of Sexuality* and impelled by his work on the film and book of *Race d'Ep*, Hocquenghem in the 1980s was interested in pushing what we might call the 'social constructionist' approach to gay identity as far as it could go. This approach for him emphasised civilisational rather than political analyses, in that it encouraged the investigation of ways of thinking ourselves out of modernity, with its cohort of notions of the self, the subject, identity, reason and the nation. His two major novelistic achievements of the decade are a response to this need. *L'Amour en relief*[5] challenges the image-dominated society of the West, with its cult of the visual and of visibility, by constructing a philosophical tale around the intercontinental adventures of a blind Tunisian. *La Colère de l'agneau* is a life of St John which provides a sweeping portrayal of the Mediterranean world of the first century AD.[6] As for his theoretical work, even this short article illustrates an astonishing density and eclecticism. On the hunt for traditions antagonistic to notions of the plenitude of identity and assertive of provisionality, he alights upon the negative theology of Gnosticism

5. Albin Michel, Paris, 1982, *Love in Relief*, M.Whisler (trans), preface by G. Stambolian, SeaHorse Press, New York 1986.

6. Albin Michel, *La Colère de l'agneau*, Paris, 1985.

and on Schlegel's Romantic irony. In perhaps the first encounter between Kierkegaard's thought and what might loosely be called gay or queer theory, the notion of repetition helps to formulate the relationship between constancy and motion. In *Repetition* (1843), Kierkegaard is interested in the ways in which, as opposed to mere habit, what is repeated can in fact, raised to a second power, contain the new: 'that which is repeated has been - otherwise it could not be repeated - but the very fact that it has been makes the repetition into something new'. If life is not to dissolve 'into an empty, meaningless noise',[7] we need the categories of recollection or of repetition. Whereas the Platonic 'past eternity' involves a facing backward, repetition offers a facing forward, with meaning radiating from the future, not the past. In this way, it represents a receptivity, a future-oriented move towards God (as when Abraham and Job have their lives bestowed on them anew, in the strongest sense) or the Good of open possibilities, not fixed finalities.

However, it is the notion of the baroque which provides perhaps the most sustained underpinning of Hocquenghem's procedure. In this, he was of course not alone in the 1980s. Deleuze in *The Fold*, originally published in 1988, had disinterred Leibniz for contemporary theory in order to offer alternative mappings of the self. Indeed, the notion of the self in this world is not one of autonomous identity but of a certain collection or concentration of singularities within the infinite, convergent series that is the world. The relationship between self and world, that of the world in the self and the self for the world, as expressed in the famous category of the monad, is thus to be seen in terms of tension rather than repose. This description of Leibniz' thought was of interest to anyone dissatisfied with the plenitudes of identity politics on the grounds that they failed both to let in enough of the outer world and to embrace the variety within: in Deleuze's formula, 'No philosophy has ever pushed to such an extreme the affirmation of a one and same world, and of an infinite difference or variety in this world'.[8] Christine Buci-Glucksmann's *Baroque Reason*, originally published in 1984, had concentrated on the nineteenth century and argued for the baroque as an alternative resource to the instrumentalist thought of modernity. Indeed, she had attempted to appropriate it for feminism, linking it, like Hocquenghem in 'On Homo-Sex', to negative theologies such as Taoism.[9] Hocquenghem himself had written on the Belvedere palace in Vienna, emphasising the baroque's proliferating play of absence and presence, its tension between form and movement, empty infinity and density of images.[10] In *L'Ame atomique*, co-written with René Schérer in 1986, the baroque, and in particular its notion of allegory, is used to provide a purchase on the so-called postmodern spectacle. The baroque is capable of injecting a sense of (non-linear) history back into society, and also a belief in the world back into the world, according to Kierkegaard's notion of repetition and Nietzsche's eternal recurrence:

7. S.Kierkegaard, *Fear and Trembling; Repetition*, H.V. and E.H. Hong (eds and trans), Princeton University Press, Princeton 1983, p149.

8. G. Deleuze, *The Fold: Leibniz and the Baroque*, T. Conley (trans), Athlone Press, London 1993, p25.

9. C. Buci-Glucksmann, *Baroque Reason: The Aesthetics of Modernity*, P. Camiller (trans), Sage, London 1994.

10. *L'Europe des villes révées: Vienne*, Autrement, Paris 1986.

Faced with the return to the self, with the falling back on and contraction of identity, allegory widens the field, distends the world, brings in some air, detaching itself, like some animated shadow, from the messages, myths and master narratives it was supposed to convey. It does not reduce all signs to incoherence and insignificance, but defers meaning in an experience that is always unique and always to be renewed, unpredictable, reiterated, eternally transitory.[11]

11. *L'Ame atomique: pour une esthétique d'ère nucléaire*, Albin Michel, Paris 1986, p178.

The baroque and Kierkegaard are also the main sources in 'On Homo-Sex' for the striking and beautiful image 'musicalising' 'the idea of homosexuality'. In *The Fold*, Deleuze argues for the ways in which baroque music corresponds to a wider cultural and philosophical moment, in the relationships between harmony (multiplicity and unity) and the infinite lines of individual melody, and in the preparation and resolution of dissonance. In an essay on Mozart's opera, Kierkegaard sees the figure of Don Giovanni as an embodiment of the 'sensual' appropriate to the abstractions of music: 'Don Giovanni constantly hovers between being idea - that is to say, energy, life - and individual. But this hovering is the vibrating of music … Similarly, Don Giovanni is an image that constantly appears but gains neither form nor substance, an individual who is constantly being formed but not finished'.[12]

12. 'The Immediate Erotic Stages or The Musical Erotic', in *Either/Or: A Fragment of Life*, A. Hannay (trans), Penguin, Harmondsworth 1992, pp98-9.

I write these words on the weekend following the bomb attack on a gay pub in London's Soho on 30 April 1999. At first sight, Hocquenghem's arguments about visibility and invisibility seem inappropriate to a moment when identities are interpellated by aggression and need to be responded to defiantly and urgently. This renders all the more problematic those passages in 'On Homo-Sex' when Hocquenghem leaps from visibility/ invisibility, as played out in an individual's biography or in the history of the term 'homosexuality', to a quasi-essentialising reading of gay lifestyles, and of AIDS, as somehow illustrating this 'cyclothymia'. However, it must be remembered that Hocquenghem's own practice, and indeed his theoretical arguments, are perfectly consistent with an emphasis on the relationship between tactics and context. He is favouring a problematising **play** of visibility and invisibility, not a perpetual renunciation of visibility. The idea is to render oneself invisible in order to intensify the antagonism towards homophobic violence, not to hide from it. Was it altogether an accident that the bombing of the 'gay' venue was the most devastating of the fortnight, with the bomb placed in a confined space so as to maximise maiming and loss of life? 'Not being able to tell', as Hocquenghem points out in relation to the Jews and Nazis, is the most unsettling position of all, and it can be assumed that the bomber's hatred was prompted by both visibility and invisibility. Furthermore, the bomber was able to place the device more easily there than in a mostly Black or Asian venue: he could 'pass' as 'gay'. The result, of course, was a slaughter that failed to discriminate on the grounds of sexual orientation.

This raises important questions for both gay identity politics and for the current state of capitalist modernity/postmodernity. As Eve Sedgwick pointed out in *Epistemology of the Closet*, there is no ultimate arbitration to be made between 'universalising' and 'minoritising' discourses on and of homosexuality, be they homophobic or anti-homophobic.[13] In Britain at the turn of the twentieth and twenty-first centuries, the 'gay community' is being assimilated to the status of an ethnic community on the multiculturalist model. This obviously has advantages, but the disadvantage is that the 'universalising' potential of homosexuality, the generalised challenge it offers to all gender and sexual norms and stabilities (including its own manifestations), is downplayed. Hocquenghem's writings are a reminder of that potential. In addition, in their eschewal of the identity/non-identity, inside/outside, Self/Other binarisms, the theoretical traditions in which he is operating, including his massive debt to Deleuze (and Guattari), promise, if we are to follow Foucault's hyperbole in the English preface to the *Anti-Oedipus*, nothing less than ways of living in a non-fascist way in a century which, Foucault also predicts, will be Deleuzean.[14]

13. *Epistemology of the Closet*, University of California Press, Berkeley 1990, pp1-2.

14. G.Deleuze and F.Guattari, *Anti-Oedipus: Capitalism and Schizophrenia*, R. Hurley, M. Seem and H. Lane (trans), Viking Press, New York 1977, ppxi-xiv, especially ppxiii-xiv.

THE ART OF SMOKING IN AN AGE OF TECHNO-MORAL CONSUMPTION

Fred Botting

A cigarette is the perfect type of a perfect pleasure.
It is exquisite, and it leaves one unsatisfied. What more can one want?
(Oscar Wilde, *A Picture of Dorian Gray*)

'Could I get some tobacco and a pipe?'
'Of course,' said he, 'what was I thinking of, not
asking you before? Well, Bob is always telling me that
we non-smokers are a selfish lot, and I'm afraid he is right!'
(William Morris, *News from Nowhere*)

Do you mind if I speak, using up communal air and exhaling sounds, noxious fumes for aural inhalation? Do you mind if I write, clouding clear sheets with dirty marks, traces of a less visible process of respiration, inspiration and expiration? Do you mind if I smoke, sucking on nothing, appropriating and expelling nothing but vile gases in an idle indulgence?

Smoking, once a sublime and sovereign gesture of idle and wasteful consumption, has become an antisocial menace, a repellent instance of perverse and pathological enjoyment. But within the modernity that invented it - 'the only new pleasure that modern man has invented in eighteen hundred years'- smoking has been seen simultaneously as a universal panacea for ills of mind and body and a diabolical weed, source of corruption and evil.[1] As one of the few luxuries of bourgeois consumption, tobacco constitutes an affront to the morality and cleanliness of domestic order and a poetic pleasure of inestimable value. In a collection of essays published in nineteenth-century America, the ambivalence of tobacco is set out in the form of a contest: a bachelor gambles his pleasure and the money expended on it in an attempt to convince his matronly aunt about the value of smoking as a 'soother of disturbing feelings' and an aid to meditation and romantic contemplation. The aunt, a voice of bourgeois domestic morality, considers the habit a 'filthy abomination'. The bachelor, however, makes a case for the cigar as a symbol of love, matrimony and life in a series of elaborate, poetic reflections: as in love, new smoke has a freshness and fragrance about it, a rapture that 'fills up all the craving of your soul', 'roseate clouds' separating one 'from the chill atmosphere of mere worldly companionship' to make 'a gorgeous firmament for your fancy to riot in'; as in marriage, smoking begins with fire that uses itself up; as in life, the start is 'fresh and odorous' but soon ends 'in a withered cinder, that is only

1. Pierre Louÿs, 1896, cited in Richard Klein, *Cigarettes Are Sublime*, Duke University Press, Durham and London 1993, p28.

fit for the ground'.[2] Smoking encourages romantic reveries, a metaphor embracing love, life, death in a poetic effervescence of imagination. Though a little excessive the strange pleasure of smoking was tolerated by bourgeois morality as a fairly harmless masculine indulgence, while for women it possessed more transgressive connotations. These days, however, the ambivalence is erased: the world concurs with the judgement on the 'filthy abomination'. The shift in perceptions of and reactions to smoking suggests that a personal indulgence has become an object of general concern, a strange symptom of post-, or hyper-, modernity, an excess at odds with the imperatives of a liberal humanity absorbed in the machines of a technological, corporate and consumer capitalism.

SUBLIMITY, POETRY, ECONOMY

Cigarettes are Sublime, both an elegy and ode to the delights of tobacco, contends that smoking forms 'a crucial integer of our modernity'.[3] Bound up with the culture, freedom and aesthetic experience of modernity, smoking once occupied a symbolic and almost sacred position, a status mourned by Richard Klein as a sign of modernity's decline. Though mass-produced commodities cigarettes were associated with a realm apart from the ordered, repetitive temporality of industrial production and useful labour. Smoking displayed an indifference to practical bourgeois values in that 'the smoker adopts an aesthetic standpoint, outside the realm of utility or ethics, that kills the time of work or responsibility in order to bear witness to the time, the music, of pure passing'.[4] Here, a 'poetic sensibility' is evinced.[5] Indeed, an activity associated with nineteenth-century dandyism becomes 'the luxury of billions of people':[6] 'all that is left of Baudelaire's high romantic ecstasy is available in cigarettes, at the small price of a pack and eventual death'.[7] The aura that disappears in the age of mechanical reproduction smouldered in the habitual gestures of billions: not only did celebrities gloss their decline into mere two-dimensional celluloid 'personalities' with the mysterious charms and magical allure of cigarettes, millions of smokers partook daily in the small sacrificial act of transcending the mundane to embrace all that is evanescent in desire.[8] The sublimity of the experience as an aesthetic and financially wasteful gesture comes from its rejection of economically productive considerations: it is a sublime 'negative pleasure' that makes no sense in terms of health, utility or the pleasure principle, defying them and exasperating desire by inflaming 'what it presumes to extinguish' and refusing the equilibrium pleasure attempts to sustain. Smoking's 'perversity' arises from its antipathy to pleasure and harmonious gratification, in its arousal of desires in excess of utility and calculations of profit and loss.[9]

Within modernity's rational, useful, and moral modes of production and social organisation, the art of smoking introduces an excessive and heterogeneous element associated with the sacred and the profane, luxury and poverty, sovereignty and abjection, habit and freedom, *jouissance* and

2. I. Marvel, *Reveries of a Bachelor*, Dent, London 1894, pp82-7.

3. Richard Klein, 1993, *op. cit.*, pxi.

4. *Ibid.*, p118.

5. *Ibid.*, p8.

6. *Ibid.*, pp48-9.

7. *Ibid.*, p62.

8. Walter Benjamin, *Illuminations*, Harry Zohn (trans), Fontana, London 1970, p233.

9. Klein, 1993, *op. cit.*, p45.

death. Conjoining extremes in a way that makes no sense to homogeneous social practices, smoking pertains to what Bataille calls a 'general economy': outside the world of work, useful production and morally sanctioned consumption, smoking wastes time and expends resources without making a profitable return. Like alcohol, cigarettes retain a trace of sovereign excess. Commenting on the worker who takes a drink of wine after the day's labour, Bataille writes: 'into the wine he swallows there enters a *miraculous* element of savor, which is precisely the essence of sovereignty'.[10] Cigarettes, whether or not they come in packs of Sovereign, Regal or Royals, also offer their consumer a moment of savour. Useless consumption, directed only by an intensity of pleasure rather than being administered according to need, opens on to a 'life *beyond utility*', to a glimpse of a sacred realm that is 'impossible' but 'nonetheless there'.[11] At this point, too, bourgeois servility is cast off: the sacrifice of the commodities so important to an economy of accumulation and conservation discloses sovereign values in excess of property, wealth and production. As forms of 'creation by means of loss', poetry and the arts also manifest an element of sacred heterogeneity, though their sovereign expenditures are somewhat diminished in bourgeois society.[12] Great art, notes Lyotard, citing Adorno, should be pyrotechnical and 'simulate perfectly the sterile consumption of energies in *jouissance*'.[13] True art goes up in smoke, consuming images and meanings in a wasteful expenditure that returns nothing. Nothing, perhaps, but an aesthetic value.

The relationship between a restricted economy of production and a general economy is not one of simple opposition, but underlies a movement in which things are turned into values, the sacrifice, destruction and loss of commodities inaugurating a symbolic exchange. And smoking, an activity of consumption linked to aesthetic values rather than material goods, occupies a juncture between restricted and general economies. For Jacques Derrida, tobacco is linked to the 'aneconomic' status of the gift. In a reading of Baudelaire's 'Counterfeit Money', a short story framed by acts of apparently useless consumption, Derrida resists the temptation to regard smoking as a purely unproductive expenditure. Tobacco exhibits fantasmatic, political, economic and symbolic functions:

> the reinscription of tobacco in the economic cycle of exchange - contract, gift/countergift, alliance - necessarily follows the incessant movement of *reappropriation of excess* in relation to the system of simple natural need and to the circular equivalence between so-called natural need and the labour or production that corresponds to it. But this excess in relation to so-called natural need does not mean that the passage to the symbolic suspends the economic movement. Tobacco is a symbol of the symbolic, in other words, of the agreement [*engagement*], of the sworn faith, or the alliance that commits the two parties when they share the two fragments of a *symbolon*, when they must give, exchange and obligate themselves one to the other. Tobacco symbolises the symbolic: it seems to consist at

10. Georges Bataille, *The Accursed Share*, Vols II and III, Robert Hurley (trans), Zone Books, New York 1991, p199.

11. *Ibid.*, p198, 214.

12. Georges Bataille, *The Bataille Reader*, Fred Botting and Scott Wilson (eds), Blackwell, Oxford 1997, p171.

13. Jean-Francois Lyotard, *The Lyotard Reader*, Andrew Benjamin (ed), Blackwell, Oxford, 1997, p171.

once in a consumption (ingestion) and a purely sumptuary expenditure of which nothing natural remains. But the fact that nothing natural remains does not mean, on the contrary, that nothing symbolic remains. The annihilation of the remainder, as ashes can sometimes testify, recalls a pact and performs the role of memory.[14]

14. Jacques Derrida, *Given Time: I, Counterfeit Money*, Peggy Kamuf (trans), University of Chicago Press, Chicago and London 1992, pp111-12.

In sacrifice, a thing or commodity is consumed, its destruction the occasion for the constitution of a community around a value. In the negation of nature what appears, on another level, is the symbolic ordering of meanings rather than things. As Klein observes of the 'potlatch' or 'sacrificial ceremony' of smoking, one sacrifices a commodity in a process of symbolic destruction and appropriation: 'the disappearance of something solid, tobacco, is infinitely compensated by the symbolic gain I acquire in appropriating to myself the world around me'.[15] Smoking situates smokers in a network of unwritten rules surrounding the offer, acceptance and exchange of cigarettes: 'the gesture of offering and accepting the light establishes a *socius*, a bond or contract … '[16] In this way, tobacco establishes the possibility for civilised exchange.

15. Klein, 1993, *op. cit.*, p38.

16. *Ibid.*, p119.

Tobacco symbolises the symbolic: what returns after tobacco goes up in smoke, instituting itself in place of the destroyed or negated remainder, is the signifying surplus of economic value. In his discussion of Poe's 'The Purloined Letter' , Derrida notes that Dupin's 'sole luxury' - smoking - is affordable through 'a *remnant* of paternal inheritance': drawing income from 'the surplus-value of a capital which works by itself' this remnant 'is relocated' and 'cuts across the space of the restricted economy like a gift without return'.[17] Tobacco articulates monetary and symbolic economies, a differential site at which restricted circulation is opened to a more general movement: 'the symbolic opens and constitutes the order of exchange and of debt, the law or the order of circulation in which the gift gets annulled'.[18] Excess, the effect of a remnant which appears at the same time as the signifier, a gift and its annulment, is transformed into the surplus-value which, as a little piece of heterogeneity, guarantees the continued circulation and capitalisation of the symbolic economy as an all but entirely restricted system. The restricted economy is supplemented by *differance*, the gift that is no longer a gift manifests 'the restricted economy of differance, a calculable temporisation or deferral'.[19] Tobacco operates aneconomically, both inside and outside circulation, as the condition and excess of modernity's symbolic economy.

17. Derrida, 1992, *op. cit.*, p105.

18. *Ibid.*, p13.

19. *Ibid.*, p147.

The tobacco that for Derrida symbolises the symbolic and, when burnt, turns from commodity to value, is thus the site of Klein's extended mourning: a poetic, sublime and infinitely symbolic gesture ephemerally central to modernity will vanish, smouldering on the point of extinction. What Klein's poetic recovery of the value of smoking mourns, then, is the disappearance of a sovereign, sublime value, a value internalised and generated everywhere in liberal culture as the sacred excess of commercialism associated with poetry.

In Derrida's economic reading of Kant's *Third Critique* poetry is seen as the value of values: a gift, artistic production establishes the role of the liberal, free man 'capable of pure, that is non-exchangeable productivity', a 'pure productivity of the inexchangeable' which, Derrida observes, 'liberates a sort of immaculate commerce'.[20] The poetic gift inaugurates a divine 'plus-law'(*un plus-de-loi*), sacralising poetry as 'the universal analogical equivalent, and the value of values'.[21] But the closure of Kant's sacred system of immaculate commerce, Derrida notes, emerges at the expense of a profane and inassimilable thing, alien to the circuit of Kantian law and pleasure. Vomit is the 'single "thing"' that is unassimilable. It remains, 'in-sensible', 'un-intelligible', 'irrepresentable', 'the absolute other of the system …Vomit, is related to enjoyment (jouissance), if not to pleasure. It even *represents* the very thing that forces us to enjoy - in spite of ourselves … '; it is 'absolutely heterogeneous' in that, force-feeding enjoyment, 'it suspends the suspense of non-consummation' underpinning pleasure, even the highest pleasure of poetry, and gives 'too much enjoyment (*trop a jouir*)', 'and burns up all work as mourning work'.[22] If tobacco, poetically, symbolically, works within a restricted economy of difference as the remnant on which the paternal surplus is established, it also drags with it an unassimilable aspect associated with vile and useless consumption.

ABJECTION, CONSUMPTION, DESIRE

'The abject is edged with the sublime'.[23] In celebrating the sublimity of smoking, Klein minimises all that is foul, abject and disgusting in the consumption of cigarettes. In the general economy, however, sovereign and abject, luxurious and miserable forms of consumption are linked in their heterogeneity, whether sacred or profane. Smoking occupies this ambivalent position, at once the pinnacle, the sacred apex, of bourgeois modernity, symbolising the symbolic as its valuable surplus, a small piece of which everyone can consume in acts of apparently unproductive enjoyment, and also a base, abject and unbearable *jouissance*, an impossible consumption that can never completely be expectorated from the system. Smoking makes one sick, induces feelings of nausea and anxiety. But this negative pleasure is no longer either individual or sovereign, no longer a glamorous aesthetic transcendence of mortality and anxiety. Cigarettes make everyone sick, the individual pathological symptom becoming a general cultural sinthome and site of nausea. Gone are the days when every movie star smoked on and off screen, when untold luxuries and dreams wafted smokily from television commercials. From being a pervasively visible cinematic activity, replete with its own repertoire of significant gestures, smoking, if shown at all, must signal only aberrance and villainy. Censorious tones extend beyond the abhorrence of advertising tobacco to motions to ban its production in Europe and to the litigious pursuit of rich tobacco conglomerates. Most public and corporate institutions ban smoking on their premises. Smoking is now

20. Jacques Derrida, 'Economimesis', *Diacritics*, 11, 1981, pp8-9.

21. *Ibid.*, p18.

22. *Ibid.*, p22.

23. Julia Kristeva, *Powers of Horror: an Essay in Abjection*, Leon Roudiez (trans), Columbia University Press, New York 1982, p11.

represented in images of abjection: beggarly figures, solitary or in groups, huddle, cold and sodden, outside buildings, coughing and choking on foul clouds of smoke amid the detritus of soggy ash, crushed tobacco and butt-ends. Their lot is that of the miserable and the wretched, their fate best represented by the horrible images shown to children as part of their education: the picture of a pair of smoker's lungs, ragged, rotten, tar-ridden sacks. The filthy butts, clinging, malodorous smoke and expectorating gasps signal abject smokers to be more than simple objects of pitiful self-abuse: they are carriers of disease, symbolically infectious consumers who pathologically persist in debilitating pleasures while contaminating others in real and imagined ways with their irresponsible, incomprehensible and uncontrolled enjoyment. The loathsome fumes stain clothes with invisible residues and penetrate innocent lungs with noxious smoke, thereby flagrantly encroaching on the precious borders of individual identity, an invasive attack on personal space.

The current abjection of smoking, however, is an effect of the same cultural and economic forces bearing upon Klein's hymn to the poetry of cigarettes: it raises similar questions concerning liberalism, freedom and tolerance, and suggests, furthermore, that not only smoking and its symbolic and poetic value have gone up in smoke, but that the very modernity sustaining the surplus enjoyment of cigarettes is also disappearing. The shift in emphasis from poetic to abject smoking, then, highlights the cultural and economic movements that are commonly described as a move from modernity to post- or hypermodernity, a shift from the priority of production to patterns of accelerated consumption. A major transformation in the relation between restricted and general economies manifests itself, an upheaval which, as Jean-Joseph Goux argues, means that bourgeois notions of useful and moral consumption and rational production no longer apply when superfluous, non-productive expenditure assumes economic predominance. Wasting resources, that is, spending beyond the requirements of rationalised need, becomes the rule: 'in the capitalism of abundance the distinction between luxury and non-luxury has become indeterminable'.[24] Postmodern capitalism erases distinctions between sacred and profane, useful and useless: 'the difference between need and desire, between "useful use" and "wasteful use", between vital necessity and symbolic consumption, has absolutely no bearing on the logic of capitalist political economy'.[25] What has happened, Goux argues, is the generalisation of Jean-Baptiste Say's rule that *supply creates its own demand*'.[26] Where rational economic theories founder on 'a metaphysical uncertainty regarding the object of human desire' - stressing the priority of need and demand, Say's law, and postmodern capitalism, thrives on this uncertainty: supplying first, with demand coming later, capitalism's object is to create desire and consumption and then, maybe, make a profitable return. Capitalism 'must create this desire through the invention of the new, the production of the unpredictable'.[27] Hence capitalism is irrational, but also generous, innovative and beneficial; it

24. Jean-Joseph Goux, 'General economics and postmodern capitalism', *Yale French Studies*, 78, 1990a, p214.

25. *Ibid*., p208.

26. *Ibid*., p211.

27. *Ibid*., p212.

operates without a notion of predetermined need or an idea of the greedy individual at its centre. Instead, according to the American right-wing economist, George Gilder, it involves *potlatch*, a giving without assurance of return. The model of the capitalist is that of the gambler, risking a fortune on fortune itself, sacrificing in order to supply what consumers may want. The ethos is not that of the bourgeois, sober, calculating, predictable investor, but the aesthetics of the speculator and the entrepreneur.

The massive transformation of the relationship between the restricted and general economies, particularly in the manner that desire comes to the fore, also involves unprecedented changes in the aesthetic, social and cultural systems articulating subjectivity, sexuality and symbols. In bourgeois economic models the circulation of money and signification depended on a heterogeneous figure of general equivalence articulating contracts, bonds and desires, exchanges, meanings, bodies and subjects. As money takes the form of tokens, 'signifiers of an abstract and wholly *virtual* reality', the investment in the paternal metaphor, its function as law and meaning binding subjects together, is weakened so that the 'dominant relations of production cease to be inter-subjective, becoming rather relations between *positions* - whence the segregation of the economic sector as a separate agency, as an autonomized machinery to which semantic investment fails to give meaning'.[28] When applied to banking, new technology discloses a different symbolic order, an 'order of the *mechanical* symbol', of '*abstract operational symbolization*'.[29] The result is that subjects, separated from the order which once established the conditions of identification and meaning 'come to have only an operational relation to substitution and exchange'.[30] The subject, in an enlightenment and humanist sense, vanishes: organisations and machinery 'supplant the decisions of autocentred individualities'.[31] For Goux, 'imaginary signifiers of *paternity* are called into question at a time when the sociohistorical meaning of "creativity" is overturned, when metasocial guarantees, now defunct, yield to a new mode of historicity.'[32]

The 'metaphysical uncertainty' in respect of human desire which perplexed classical economics and becomes central to postmodern capitalism turns into an integral condition of a technologised capital: unanchored, desire and lack are generalised and cast off from a symbolic framework with humans at its apex and centre. For Slavoj Zizek, what emerges with the disappearance of metaphysics is the '*inherent structural imbalance*' of capitalism, its 'innermost agonistic character' of 'constant crisis, the constant revolutionizing of its conditions of existence', the absence of a 'balanced state' and 'the permanent production of excess'.[33] The link between capitalism and the Freudian superego means that, with the latter, 'the more we obey its command, the more we feel guilty'; with the former an imperative to 'enjoy!' demands that the more we consume, the more we must consume in a 'vicious circle of a desire whose apparent satisfaction only widens the gap of its dissatisfaction'.[34] There is, it seems, no escape from the vicious cycle of desire and excess, no transcendent prohibition with which to regulate

28. Jean-Joseph Goux, *Symbolic Economies: After Marx and Freud*, Jennifer Curtiss Gage (trans), Cornell University Press, Ithaca and London 1990b, p117, 129.

29. *Ibid.*, p130.

30. *Ibid.*, p131.

31. *Ibid.*, p196.

32. *Ibid.*, p194.

33. Slavoj Zizek, *Tarrying with the Negative*, Duke University Press, Durham 1993, p209.

34. *Ibid.*, pp209-10.

desire. Paternity, agency and creativity are called into question as part of a general economic transformation to the extent that their place, and the investment of their human subject, are no longer external to systems of exchange:

> In the particular type of society that we are entering (dominated by technoscientific production) the productivity principle, *poiesis*, and demiurgy are no longer projected *above* the process of social activity - in a religious heaven or a state sun or the providential dictates of a pre-charted history. They are carried out and absorbed in the workings of an atheological and ateleological society.[35]

35. Goux, 1990b, *op. cit.*, p195.

The absorption of heterogeneous elements like providential divinity or the determined agency involved in social planning and progress constitutes part, Goux goes on, of the 'overall capitalist market strategy, which consists of dropping into the magnetic field of the political economy (of market exchange-value) everything "sacred" and "transcendent" that might appear to escape it - including desire'.[36]

36. *Ibid.*, p202.

The space that is evacuated in the incredulity towards the paternal metaphor forms the locus or void of collapse, reconfiguration, multiplication and dissemination of desire to excess. In the flattening attendant on the transformation of the relationship between restricted and general economies, desire disperses, dissipates and escalates, without limit or transcendence: in the absence of paternal figures of reason, morality or utility, the generalisation of desire informs the criteria of performance, optimisation, maximisation. In postmodern capitalism where luxury and sumptuous expenditure become the rule, desire is the motor of uninhibited consumption, consumption without object. It is a little misleading, however, to assume the dominance of forms previously associated with the general economy. Though notions of gift and luxurious consumption reach greater economic importance in the absence of a bourgeois morality or rationality, there remains an underlying imperative to accumulate wealth accompanying more conspicuous forms of spending. A generalisation of restricted economic practice results from the absorption of previously heterogeneous forms: the aim of uninhibited accumulation, of freeing the market in order to make money, is not a sign of sovereignty except in the way that it burns up older moral, utilitarian restrictions. Instead of a sovereign contempt for wealth, an overriding servility appears towards it, manifested in the celebration of the lives of the rich and, more abjectly, in the servile gambling of popular consumption, the minimal risks and chances of lottery tickets generating disproportionate dreams of entering the hallowed portals of a wealthy lifestyle.

The generalisation of restricted economy can be identified in the fate of poetry. What was, for Kant, the value of values, the sacred, transcendent excess of mercantile and monetary exchange, is absorbed as the rule of postmodern economy. Poetry, as an 'immaculate commerce', as the luxury of language and sacred surplus of symbolic exchange, is incorporated as the working principle of postmodern economy: 'Money is a kind of poetry'. J. Hillis Miller elaborates on Wallace Stevens' suggestion: 'if money is a kind of poetry, "poetry", in the broad sense of cultural forms generally in various media, is also a kind of money'.[37] The reversible equation of money and poetry locates them as equivalent informational commodities. Indeed, in the romanticisation of new technologies, all production is creative, innovative and poetic: worlds are created from nothing and in nowhere, in the virtual nonspaces of hard drives and databanks. The entrepreneur, too, has a new image: shedding the skin of the fat, greedy, cigar-smoking capitalist, he is an artist, a visionary speculator, a gambling, buccaneering hero, romanticised by Gilder as a pioneer in the 'realm of dark transcendence', the locus of 'all true light and creativity'.[38] The interimplication of aesthetic and economic discourses creates these new roles: 'precisely at the moment when the entrepreneur must think himself into the model of the most advanced artistic genius, at the moment when the avant-gardist strategy of innovation at any price becomes the paradigm of dominant economic practice, that the artistic avant-garde necessarily loses its difference, its marginality, its deviance-value'.[39] Aesthetic experimentation, social critique and innovation, become the norm of the consumptive economy, to the extent that the poet cannot distinguish himself from the grocer, nor the surrealist from the 'dishevelled manager'.[40] Indeed, in the 1980s, the aesthetics of the entrepreneur were celebrated in the curious heroism of the successful tycoon, investor and speculator and the alluring villainy of Wall Street bond dealers and corporate raiders like Gordon Gecko.

While the entrepreneur assumes the mantle of avant-garde aesthetic experimenter, the consumer also becomes something of an artistic connoisseur. The proximity between the high cultural aesthete and contemporary consumption is underlined in Rachel Bowlby's reading of *The Picture of Dorian Gray* where the cigarette again assumes significance: 'one of the most ubiquitous and widely advertised commodities of the twentieth century, it nonetheless occupies a prominent and honourable position in the work of an avowed critic of vulgarity'.[41] Though strange, Bowlby observes, that so popular a commodity should be praised by a noted critic of the commonplace and banal, the brief and unfulfilling pleasures of the cigarette have, she argues, something of the aphorism about them. The aphoristic mode comes close to the style of the advertising slogan. The ephemeral pleasures of cigarettes also exemplify the 'untenability' of sustaining a fixed relation of subjects and objects, exhibiting instead, the elusive and captivating movements of representation celebrated by Wildean aesthetics: 'the cigarette, again, is an apt illustration. It could connote the indolence of the beautiful life of the dandy but also, in another context, the sexually transgressive associations of the "New Woman" of the period'.[42] While the aesthetic dandy exemplified by Dorian Gray is a 'walking

37. J. Hillis Miller, 'The University of Dissensus', *Oxford Literary Review*, 17, 1995, p125.

38. Goux, 1990a, *op. cit.*, p218.

39. *Ibid.*

40. *Ibid.*

41. Rachel Bowlby, 'Promoting Dorian Gray', *Oxford Literary Review*, 9, 1987, p147.

42. *Ibid.*, p148.

advertisement' of the undying pleasures of youth and beauty, Lord Henry's 'new Hedonism' advances novelty and sensation over moral restraint so that experience and commodities come to be seen as 'sources of gratification' and lead 'to a (new) focus on expenditure as opposed to accumulation'.[43] In economic texts of the time consumption begins to assume a quite contemporary meaning: 'in its basic sense of wastage or using up, the expenditure involved in consumption acquired all the dissolute connotations of Victorian "spending": the throwing away of a finite and precious substance on a solitary and debilitating pleasure'.[44] The sexual associations of the term, as evinced in the French 'consommation', too, are never far away. In the work of aesthetes, like Wilde and Walter Pater, the term suggests a positive resistance to the 'puritanical deferral of gratification', the immediate indulgence in diverse sensations valorised so that life's brief interval before death can be enjoyed as fully as possible: in this way, the aesthete becomes 'a consumer or recipient of impressions'.[45] Art is replaced by advertising to mark what Bowlby calls the 'beginning of consumer culture'.[46]

The gratification of multiple and diverse fleeting pleasures also defines the pluralistic lifestyle of the aesthetic and consumeristic subject of postmodern culture as described by Lyotard: 'eclecticism is the degree zero of contemporary general culture: one listens to reggae, watches a western, eats McDonald's food for lunch and local cuisine for dinner, wears Paris perfume in Tokyo and "retro" clothes in Hong Kong'.[47] Art becomes kitsch and 'artists, gallery owners, critics, and the public wallow together in the "anything goes", and the epoch is one of slackening. But this realism of the "anything goes" is in fact that of money'.[48] As the aesthete establishes the ideal form of the consumer, the cigarette describes the paradigmatic form of consumer pleasure: 'It is exquisite, and it leaves one unsatisfied. What more can one want?'[49] The unsatisfactory gratification offered by smoking as it furnishes desire with an object only to enjoy and waste it, sustains desire at the expense of the object. Desire, of course, 'is avid not to be satisfied', its object is 'what's impossible. Otherwise desire would be quenched, desire would die'.[50] What more could one want than wanting itself? The perfect object of desire, pleasure and consumption, then, is the cigarette since it remains ultimately inappropriable, an object of consumption that is used up and enjoyed while never fully satisfisfying, or stabilising, the organism, thereby leaving it in a state of desire. The subject never completes itself in the appropriation of objects, though the fantasy of plenitude sustaining desire persists. Instead, desiring comes to the fore, its agency prior to that of subject or object. The subject of desire, always becoming, always in search of the ultimate object while expending energy and resources on a variety of unsatisfactory commodities, finds perfected form in the contemporary consumer. A culture of consumption depends upon it: 'contemporary consumer culture not only includes but openly affirms and commands non-productive expenditure'.[51] However, the link between smoking and shopping, for Klein, involves both desire and anxiety:

43. *Ibid.*, p152.

44. *Ibid.*, p153.

45. *Ibid.*

46. *Ibid.*, p163.

47. Jean-Francois Lyotard, *The Postmodern Condition*, Geoff Bennington and Brian Massumi (trans), Manchester University Press, Manchester 1984, p76.

48. *Ibid.*

49. Oscar Wilde, *The Picture of Dorian Gray*, in *The Writings of Oscar Wilde*, Isobel Murray (ed), Oxford University Press, Oxford 1989, p107.

50. Georges Bataille, *Guilty*, Bruce Boone (trans), The Lapis Press, San Francisco 1988, pp151-2.

51. Rhonda Lieberman, 'Shopping Disorders', in *The Politics of Everyday Fear*, Brian Massumi (ed), University of Minnesota Press, Minneapolis and London 1993, p259.

52. Klein, 1993, *op. cit.*, p52.

'The passion to appropriate what is inherently inappropriable, under the illusion that it will give some secure ground to one's sense of self, motivates all the pathologies of consumerism. Shopping, like rolling your own, thinks Sartre, offers illusory protection against the anxiety of radical freedom'.[52]

The fantasy - and the horror - of being able to do anything one wants to do, be anything one wants to be, go anywhere one wants to go, is assuaged when the wanting to do, be and go is fixed on a particular object and used to sell a single commodity. But every object of desire must ultimately be unsatisfactory so that desire is not extinguished, and rolls mechanically on. Which, of course, is why the cigarette mirrors consumption as well as desire, so perfect a figure for the wanting underlying technologised, postmodern capitalism:

> The obsolete psychological category of 'greed' privatizes and moralizes addiction, as if the profit-seeking tropism of a transnational capitalism propagating itself through epidemic consumerism were intelligible in terms of personal subjective traits. Wanting more is the index of interlock with cyberpositive machinic processes, and not the expression of private idiosyncrasy. What could be more impersonal - disinterested - than a *haut bourgeois* capital expansion servo-mechanism striving to double $10 billion? And even these creatures are disappearing into silicon viro-finance automatisms, where massively distributed and anonymized human ownership has become as vacuously nominal as democratic sovereignty.[53]

53. Nick Land, 'Machinic desire', *Textual Practice*, 7:3, 1993, p478.

54. Lieberman, 1993, *op. cit.*, p245.

55. *Ibid.*, p255.

56. Poetry similarly provokes a dissolution and consumption of meaningful language in the unanchored flights of metaphor, a 'perversion', according to Bataille, 1988, *op. cit.*, p78.

57. Lieberman, 1993, *op. cit.*, p253.

Wanting more denotes the generalisation of desire underlying consumptive capitalist economy. But desire, exceeding the restrictions of morality, rationality and utility, also drags lack with it: the generalisation of desire is simultaneously the generalisation of lack. In incorporating the symbolic, poetic, sacred surplus of enjoyment, economy also absorbs the supplementary *jouissance* beyond the phallus that was once associated with the heterogeneous excess of female sexuality: the supplement supplants what it once seemed merely to support, and *jouissance* becomes a rule of consumption. Indeed, as the realm of aesthetics and luxury once associated with the insubstantiality of a feminine masquerade becomes a dominant condition, the cry of 'encore' rings from the panting mouths of every consumer, every aestheticised subject of postmodern plurality. Wanting more is the norm and rule of consumption so that 'under consumer culture "lack" is not only circulated but is actively sought out and produced by any body, masculine or feminine identified ...'[54] All consumers are subject to a demand once associated with feminine desire, wanting 'to *be* the object of capital's desire, not only to *have* it'.[55] The effect of generalising want discloses a general perversity, a perversity evinced as precisely the norm of sexuality, language and consumption.[56] The useless economic expenditure of shopping 'exposes the constitutional perversity of all desire mediated by capital'.[57]

Indeed, the commodity discloses both a perverse answer to and exacerbation of the question of subjective desire, since the object functions to define the symbolic subject by occupying the site of internal lack, allowing the subject's perverse refusal of 'all recognition of his own lack'.[58] Thus, the commodity disavows lack while perpetuating it.

Smoking, it appears, delineates the dominant form of desire in a consumer economy: a product of the production of consumable objects that leave the consumer wanting, it provides a model of the capitalisation of uncertain desire as an infinitely exploitable resource. Billions of mass-produced cigarettes are made and sold in order to be used up wastefully, a luxury becoming an addiction on which everyone can afford to squander money. By selling nothing but commodities that go up in smoke, goods that do no discernible good, tobacco conglomerates can accumulate billions for no apparently useful end. It may thus appear strange, even ironic, that in an era of unbridled consumer activity so perfect a mode of consumption finds itself under increasing censure, with the tobacco industry under moral, legal and medical assault and smoking banned in many public places, or every public space if one lives in California, the most liberated state on the planet. The lavish expenditure so characteristic of the 1980s, a decade when consumption was never so conspicuous or so wasteful, is also the period when the onslaught against one of the few tolerated luxuries of bourgeois life gained pace. It is strange that a period which saw the erasure of distinctions between need and luxury and an unprecedented escalation in spectacularly wasteful expenditure also generated a discharge of intense negative energies at smokers and smoking.

The strange exclusion of smoking has a paradoxical cause: the unbearable excess of an economy of excess must be suppressed precisely because it is the ideal mode of consumption. As the perfect form of consumer desire, it takes the pleasures and gratifications of consumption to their impossible limit, disclosing the unfillable void at their centre, marking an excess internal to consumption that must be excluded, expelled beyond its borders. Abjected, smoking discloses the generalised abjection of the contemporary consumer: 'the abjection of self would be the culminating form of that experience of the subject to which it is revealed that all its objects are based merely on the inaugural *loss* that laid the foundations of its own being'.[59] In abjection desire meets its limit in horror: 'apprehensive, desire turns aside; sickened, it rejects'.[60] Disclosing loss and an unbearable limit, abjection is not an object but a vacuole at the centre of a spinning symbolic system whose gaping uncertainty causes only a vicious superegoic cycle of desiring.

In comparison with smoking, then, shopping is not wasteful enough: the luxurious expenditure that wastes time and money on the accumulation of unnecessary goods both attempts to fill a lack and discloses it as unfillable. Instead of wasting without thought of material gain, shopping accumulates things: within the fragile protection of anticipated wealth in the form of credit, the consumer assumes the subjectivity central to an economy in which

58. Joan Copjec, *Read My Desire: Lacan Against the Historicists*, MIT Press, Cambridge Mass. and London 1994, p109.

59. Kristeva, 1982, *op. cit.*, p5.

60. *Ibid.*, p1.

wealth is accumulated through desiring to the point that wealth is the only sign of prestige and value, symbolic meaning reduced to things, confused with commodities, everything orchestrated on an index-linked electronic exchange of prices. This is not to mourn, as Lieberman does, the passing of an age when waste had symbolic significance. But the devaluation of a sense of the sacred through the safeties of credit schemes and consumer accumulation implies, she acutely notes, a major shift in the meaning of waste and the actuality of loss and destruction. Without the risk of loss and the threat of destruction, however, expenditure loses its meaning and its value. Ideological interpellation cedes to what Lieberman calls 'commodity interpellation' in which the question of the Other's desire is answered with an imperative to enjoy: what should I buy? Buy anything you want, is the reply. With every commodity calling out to be consumed, the consumer is hysterrorised. Shopping's imagined plenitude cedes to an unavowable abjection: the 'disordered shopper' is a pathological being who consumes beyond the dictates of reason, utility and life itself, a fragmented body writhing in 'discontent, chronic unrest and stimulation' caught in the vicious impasse of alienated identity and fantasised fulfillment, double bound by an insatiable demand and a frustrating and frustrated desire.[61] In a culture dominated by subjects of this kind, it is little wonder that smoking assumes a negative charge. Smoking appears as the destiny of the shopper, the abjection signalling consumption's baseless basis: while the smoker sucks in more of a drug that heightens unrest and anxious stimulation, s/he blows smoke in the face of a fuming and disordered consumer, an excess of the excess of the same.

61. Lieberman, 1993, *op. cit.*, p246.

ENJOYMENT, MORALITY, MACHINE

Abjection tends to serve as a prelude to a rediscovery of sacred values: it 'accompanies all religious structurings and reappears, to be worked out in a new guise, at the time of their collapse'.[62] Though difficult to discern in an age in which transcendent or metaphysical values have been absorbed in an immanent and exchangeable procession of luxurious commodities, the restructuring of a quasi-sacred or moral order which follows the collapse and attendant abjection of subjects of older economic and symbolic formations can be seen in relation to the unbearable limit of consumer culture. Smoking, in the unreserved condemnation and almost universal disgust it elicits, is marked out as a locus of abjection and thereby the site for the erection of a new order of exclusion. The energies discharged in the direction of smoking, unproductive expenditures themselves, manifest an enjoyment that feeds off a desire to extinguish, renounce and destroy a useless consumptive act. The expenditures of money and energy campaigning against the promotion of smoking in advertising, the circulation of educational warnings, the prohibitions in public buildings, the omnipresent 'No Smoking' signs and the general social disapproval

62. Kristeva, *op. cit.*, p17.

that ranges from the polite to the overtly hostile enjoy smoking in an entirely different manner to the smoker: the pleasures of uttering a paternal no, conscious of rectitude and authority, gloss the prohibitive chorus with a righteous enjoyment exercised in the name of morality.[63]

The imagined or desired destruction of smoking sacrifices a material commodity and renounces a pleasure for what appears to be a sacred symbolic value at the core of liberal and democratic societies: the promotion of general health calls up rights to life, liberty and happiness central to the utilitarian, democratic humanist imperative. As Foucault notes, modernity's progress, its social and political organisation, its disciplines and liberties and physical and economic functioning operate in the interests of life, the life of individuals as well as populations: where sovereigns exercised the right to take life, modern states acted to ensure everyone's existence, operating as 'managers of life and survival' to the extent that even wars could be fought in the name of the life of the population as a whole.[64]

Currently, the imperatives of morality and economy dictate that one ought to renounce smoking because it debilitates health and foreshortens one's own life and the life of others. 'Healthism' becomes 'part of the dominant ideology of America'.[65] The term 'healthism' suggests that, though partaking of what seems to be a thoroughly liberal and utilitarian discourse, the general insistence on health is an effect of a different and complex arrangement of forces which, in the manner of the unrestricted postmodern economy, combine a morality, or rather an imperative, that places desire rather than life at the centre of production, consumption, corporeal well-being and corporate efficiency. Paul Virilio argues that current enamorations with sporting performance, exercise and health are not concerned with the preservation and improvement of the well-being of a nation or its individuals but incursions of a technoscientific order aiming to turn the body into a machine, to speed up its workings so that it can keep up with the pace set by the machine.[66] Healthism, however, is more than a supplement to economic production and performance. It is also commodity, 'a product that is sold': 'It has become one of the most profitable businesses of all - on the way to becoming this country's principal economic activity - in the form of what is called 'health services'.[67] Bound up with consumer culture, the moralistic energy healthism expends on denouncing unhealthy modes of living and abjecting certain practices and lifestyles does not simply arrest the unanchored flows of desire with a resounding 'no!', it augurates new directions for desire and consumption, establishing new mores and codes separating good consumption from bad.

The abjection of smoking, then, feeds health culture, the negative charge activating a repulsion that re-orientates desire from an explicitly unproductive and useless expenditure to one that appears valuable. But health is just another 'advertised commodity'[68]: the energies invested in it are not positive affirmations of a founding need, but are created as a movement away from bad habits. In choosing 'health' or 'eco-friendliness' or 'ethical consumerism'

63. Discussing science fiction and horror films, Susan Sontag notes the satisfaction that comes from 'extreme moral simplification', 'a morally acceptable fantasy where one can give outlet to cruel or at least amoral feelings': 'This is the undeniable pleasure we derive from looking at freaks, beings excluded from the category of the human. The sense of superiority over the freak conjoined in varying proportions with the titillation of fear and aversion makes it possible for moral scruples to be lifted, for cruelty to be enjoyed'. Susan Sontag, 'The Imagination of Disaster', in *Film Theory and Criticism*, G. Mast and M.Green (eds), OUP, New York and London 1974, pp427-8.

64. Michel Foucault, *The History of Sexuality: Vol. I An Introduction*, Robert Hurley (trans), Penguin, Harmondsworth 1981, p137.

65. Klein, 1993, *op. cit.*, p185.

66. Paul Virilio, *The Art of the Motor*, Julie Rose (trans), University of Minnesota Press, Minneapolis 1995.

67. Klein, 1993, *op. cit.*, p99.

68. *Ibid.*, p186.

one renounces the commodities associated with an industrial capitalism callously indifferent to the welfare of individuals, races or the planet itself. This movement opens new markets for medical and insurance packages, for health studios, gym equipment, sportswear, for fitness and diet magazines selling a range of exercise programmes and nutritional regimes. New markets are created, but they still sell desire, the desire to be desirable, to be 'fit' meaning to be both healthy and attractive. 'Live life to the max', advertising slogans for a low-calorie cola declared. The healthy consumer is being sold life in all its plenitude, a life whose potential is maximised and enjoyed to the fullest extent. The subject of desire, the want-to-be, is sold being itself, the market apparently pouting and puckering around the lack/desire integral to the subject. The injunction to live life to the full doubles as the imperative to consume as much as possible with a single caution: one must only consume what is good for you, that is, commodities and services that keep one in a healthy enough state to keep on living/consuming. All expenditures are tolerated and no expense is spared so that one can accumulate as much life as possible, living at all costs. Apart, of course, from the ultimate expenditure, death, which must be avoided, held in check, staved off. The fullest life remains in constant and disavowed proximity to the familiars of misery, corporeal decay and death, until the resources poured into genetic research liberate desire from even that uncertain foundation.

While the abjection of smoking occasions the erection of a new moral order of healthy living, the virulent loathing of smoking suggests another level of concern. The 'passionate excess of zeal with which cigarettes are everywhere stigmatised', Klein suggests, conceals 'some other more pervasive subterranean, and dangerous passions that directly threaten our freedom'.[69]

69. *Ibid.*, p15.

The threat to freedom appears as a contradiction and antagonism internal to liberalism itself: the freedom to smoke is attacked in the name of other liberal freedoms like the right to life, a right become synonymous with the right of free consumption. The liberal impasse which places freedom against freedom is drawn out by smoking's unbearable proximity to consumption, in which the desire to own is never one's own, and the rights centred on the particularity of an autonomous individual diverge from those universal rights in which particularity ought to be reflected and recognised. Passive smoking is symptomatic of the anxieties of individual freedom, bespeaking, Frances Ferguson argues, a 'social annoyance' with the space taken up by so many other free individuals: it precedes from a wish to 'free ourselves from claustrophobia', from the invasive presence of others threatening individual space and freedom, a desire to be free from the 'pressures of intersubjectivity'.[70] The concern with others, as manifested in reactions to smoking, are as much to do with their imagined invasiveness as their actual presence. Contesting Ferguson's assumptions, Joan Copjec identifies the phobia of crowds and the fear of passive smoking as effects of 'the historic deterioration of the symbolic relation' which mean that the world and those around are forced 'to carry the burden the modern subject will not internally

70. Frances Ferguson, 'The Nuclear Sublime', *Diacritics*, 14, 1984, p9.

bear'.[71] The burden is the 'interior lack' that defines subjectivity while being eliminated in liberal humanist discourse's assumption of a useful and full being able to affirm itself. It is not actual bodies, not crowds of people, not clouds of smoke, but the proximity of the neighbour prescribed by moral law, the super-egoic imperative instituted in the place of lack, whom the subject guiltily flees.[72]

In condemning the self-evident harmfulness of smoking, then, the liberal moral subject appears free from the guilt internal to its constitution, projecting it onto the smoker who assumes its full weight. No wonder there is so much enjoyment in not smoking. The place of the smoker is thus 'other' in the sense of both object (of condemnation) and abject of one's own disgust, a pathological and recalcitrant activity eliciting a pathological, overzealous reaction. The place allotted to the smoker becomes a site of extimacy, a locus for the delimitation of a moral law whose object remains alien. Without an 'Other of the Other', a metalanguage, the ground of alterity is problematic: the signifier alone is not adequate since one signifier 'can always be substituted for the other and vice versa'.[73] Law, then, is established in the relation of the signifier and the Thing, 'founded on what one imagines about the Other's *jouissance*; it is hatred of the particular way, of the Other's way of experiencing *jouissance*'.[74] Law depends on an excess, on an element heterogeneous to its stated principles, reasons and values. Miller offers the example of racism: 'racist stories are always about the way in which the Other obtains a "*plus-de-jouir*": either he does not work enough, or he is useless or a little too useful ... '[75] In terms of race and nation, as Zizek develops the argument, the Thing occupies the obscure core of the subject's fantasmatic organisation, impenetrable to reason, persuasion or argument, as incontestable as it is ambivalent and contradictory: 'We always impute to the 'other' an excessive enjoyment: he wants to steal our enjoyment (by ruining our way of life) and/or he has access to some secret, perverse enjoyment'.[76] The fantasmatic relation to the Thing moreover, requires no recourse to empirical evidence since the 'theft of enjoyment' is not an effect of 'immediate social reality' and the presence of others, but occupies the locus of the *'inner antagonism inherent in those communities'*.[77] Not only a site of expulsion, other enjoyment torments the subject with the problem of an inaccessible *jouissance* at its own core: *'the hatred of the Other is the hatred of our own excessive enjoyment'*.[78]

A locus of expulsion, of moral expenditure and enjoyment, smoking also prompts a horrified fascination about its pathological persistence in the face of all reason. As an excessive and recalcitrant pleasure, however, the continued existence of smoking appears as a defiant gesture the *jouissance* of which remains beyond the grasp of the non-smoker whose consumptions and expenditures nonetheless follow an all-too familiar pattern. Smoking elicits what Zizek, writing on the 'PC problematic', calls an 'ambivalence toward the other's fantasmatic enjoyment'.[79] In PC there is a 'compulsive effort to uncover ever new, ever more refined forms of racial and/or sexual

71. Copjec, 1994, *op. cit.*, p106.

72. *Ibid.*, p99.

73. Jacques-Alain Miller, 'Extimité', *Prose Studies*, 11: 3, 1988, p125.

74. *Ibid.*

75. *Ibid.*

76. Zizek, 1993, *op. cit.*, p203.

77. *Ibid.*, p205.

78. *Ibid.*, p206.

79. *Ibid.*, p213.

violence and domination' while maintaining one position as a negative but necessary counterpoint: 'all other positions can affirm their specificity, their specific mode of enjoyment, only the white-male-heterosexual position must remain empty, must sacrifice its enjoyment'.[80] Zizek's analysis raises serious questions about the assumptions underlying particular deployments of political correctness: PC is not severe enough in that, while appearing to require important sacrifices for the other, it fails to renounce 'the very gesture of self-sacrifice'. Moreover, while emptying out the position of the dead white male, that position is maintained 'as a universal form of subjectivity' by providing 'newer and newer answers, *in order to keep the problem alive*'. Political correctness is thus a last-ditch gesture, serving as the 'protective shield' of bourgeois liberalism and, in perpetuating concerns about others' independent enjoyment, fuelling its internal horror of excessive enjoyment.[81]

80. *Ibid.*

81. *Ibid.*, p214.

Smoking, despite medical evidence and general condemnation, confounds the questions of renunciation and self-sacrifice: in not giving up, the smoker performs a kind of extenuated sacrifice of self. The good consumer gives up cigarettes or fatty foods, thereby avoiding the renunciation of his/her consumerist enjoyment, to participate in newer modes of consumption supplied by the health services: more and more money, time and energy can be expended on 'lite' foods, exercise programmes, diets etc. The gesture of giving up is not therefore a gesture of loss or sacrifice, it merely enables other pleasures and a fuller life devoted to consumption. The wasteful expenditure and refusal to give up the desire for a cigarette perversely mirrors the consumer's refusal to sacrifice consumption: the object which never satisfies desire or fills the place of the lost object displays the vapidity of the illusion fostered by the supply of and desire for ever more and newer commodities, health regimes and lifestyles, the fantasy that one can find fulfilment at the expense of so many objects, that lack is but a prelude to plenitude. Here, again, the enjoyment of a cigarette in all its pathological recalcitrance appears to know something about consumption that the consumer does not.

If the smoker occupies a position in excess of consumerist excess, within and alien to patterns of postmodern consumption, there is another sense in which s/he holds up a disconcerting mirror: a mirror reflecting that subject's steady vanishing, if not absence, and the appearance of another subject for whom the question of lack has been foreclosed. The shift from a restricted economy based on production, utility and moral regulation involving the renunciation and conservation of desire to an economy of luxurious consumption, wasteful expenditure and uninhibited, libertarian desire signals the emergence of a figure Zizek defines as the postmodern subject:

In her article 'Nuclear Sublime', Frances Ferguson registered the growing claustrophobia displayed by a series of features in our everyday life: from the awareness of how smoking endangers not just smokers themselves but non-smokers in their company, through the obsession with child abuse, up to the revival of the theory of seduction in (the critique of) psychoanalysis (Masson's *The Assault on Truth*). What lurks in the background of these features is the Spinozist idea that, imperceptibly, at a pre-subjective level, we are entangled in a network by way of which others encroach upon us: ultimately the very presence of others as such is perceived as violence. However, in order for this enhanced awareness of how others threaten us, of how we are totally 'exposed' to them, to emerge, a certain solipsistic shift had to occur which defines the 'postmodern' subject: this subject has withdrawn from the big Other, maintaining a protopsychotic distance toward the Other; i.e., this subject perceives himself as an out-law, lacking the common ground shared with others. And for this reason, every contact with others is perceived and experienced as a violent encroachment.[82]

82. *Ibid.*, p218.

Where postmodernism signals the aesthetic, cultural and subjective fragmentation of liberalism, it has nothing to substitute for it other than dispersed and embattled groupings at odds with each other: the insistence on increasingly particular rights sustains the empty form of liberal democracy and breeds the psychotic foreclosure of otherness.

The end of history, and its subject, cedes to a hyper-liberal and hyper-moral mode of social and political organisation. As Zizek notes, following Hegel, liberal democracy 'cannot be universalised' since its victory would also be the occasion of its fragmentation. What appears in the wake of an impossible universalisation of liberalism provides the basis for a new world order unimaginable in liberal terms while reiterating its rhetoric. For Zizek, 'the triumphant liberal-democratic "new world order" is more and more marked by a frontier separating its "inside" from its "outside" - a frontier between those who manage to remain "within" (the "developed", those to whom the rules of human rights, social security, etc., apply) and the others, the excluded (the main concern of the "developed" apropos of them is to contain their explosive potential, even if the price paid for such containment is the neglect of elementary democratic principles)'.[83] Though the major division of this new order of inclusion and exclusion can be seen in the geopolitical divisions between 'First' and 'Third' worlds, the modes of incorporation and evacuation operate along boundaries quite different from those established by nationalism, colonialism and imperialism. The boundaries separating the 'inside' and 'outside' of the new world order can just as well be maintained by interests operating irrespective of national or cultural identity and delineated by modes of consumption. To be 'inside' means that one has consumed the appropriate vocational commodities and invested in successful brands and corporate logos: not only does one wear appropriately branded clothing, one also buys suitable technical skills, software packages and health insurance. All this because one works for a renowned corporation. One's life, its pleasures and expenditures, depends on whether one has a career, that is, one has speculated successfully on the opportunity to devote oneself to a

83. *Ibid.*, p222.

particular corporate logo, or, in an age of downsizing, become a small business, a logo, oneself. To be otherwise is to find oneself 'outside' in the detritus of what was once called society, dependent on a shrinking State rigorously policing its resources. The 'outside' may exist close by: on the street or in a shopping centre, in a neighbouring part of town, or breaking in at the rear window of one's home. The unemployed, the sick, the elderly, the homeless, the travellers and beggars, exist as constant reminders of this 'outside'.

Smokers, it seems, are among this abject and wretched morass of humanity expelled from the delights of a new corporate order. Their perverse, excessive and wasteful consumption is alien to a world whose hygienic morality and luxurious expenditures are directed towards another plane, a plane of optimal performance and maximised life. The general abjection of smoking, however, also announces an excess at the heart of corporate, virtual, consumer culture, it manifests something altogether human, but a humanity divested of the noble identity sustained by the attribution of value and dignity to the life of a particular being. An object of recoil, horror and disgust, the position of the smoker is also the abject intimation of a destiny, a fate that will befall all that is left of humanity. In the abject and slightly sovereign gesture of smoking, then, there is a hint of prophecy, a threat and a promise binding smokers within the lumpen mass of dejected and abject humanity. In the world described in Michel Serres's *Angels*, all bodies are messengers, communicational vehicles, especially the wretched and utterly destitute of the earth who 'risk seeing even the seeds of humanity destroyed in them and around them by the horror of this assault'. Yet these figures of abject destitution are 'so primally human' they become 'archangels' whose message announces that 'we are all born from poverty, and to it we shall return'.[84] The message is not simply sent from a distant outside (the Third or Fourth world) to an inside that looks away, it also haunts the inside with the approach of something unknown, ghosts from a barely determinable future rending the fragile surfaces of the present: 'the wretched of the earth are messengers of an extraordinary state which is unknown to us. They roam the streets, they keep a low profile, they don't say much, they reach out a hand, they disappear ... and then suddenly re-appear on a street corner: they are phantoms but they are real, in the sense that they pierce through our illusory realities'.[85] The ghostly presence of the unemployed, the homeless, the beggars, heralds a future that is to come while emerging from a past that has gone, beings in transition, messengers of change. Ejected from older forms of work and an industrial base that has itself become wasteful, polluting and dangerous, the archangels of destitution gesture towards the imminent arrival of the new city of light and electronic information steadily growing above the ruins of an old world. Puncturing the security of older, and virtual, symbolic constructions of reality, the arrival of telecommunicational angels not only supersedes traditional liberal models of humanity, but erases their physical traces, obliterating even the corporeal remnants that currently stand among the ruins as ghostly prophets of divine

84. Michel Serres, *Angels: a Modern Myth*, F. Cowper (trans), Flammarion, Paris 1993, p17.

85. *Ibid.*, p20.

states to come. The wretched, as unbearable limit and prophetic destiny, a site of horror and fantasy, signal both an avoidable end of humanity as it has been known and the locus of a re-pulsion that directs a panic-stricken flight from the human, a winged disappearance into the divinity of technology.

Take a long reflective drag. Breathe out. Cough a little. Enjoy an act of senseless human consumption too excessive and irrational for the technocorporate machine. There may well be virtual cigarettes in the realm of digital divinity, but they will carry no health warnings. Nor will they have a bad taste and foul smell and any pleasure they may bring will be wholly divested of the negativity that comes of a tiny touch of death. As a human pathology, an activity that defines the human as a fundamentally pathological entity, smoking intangibly embodies the lack and excess inimical to the advertised goods of hypermodernity. Indeed, to smoke is to forsake the good of life, health and, these days, a long career of (virtual) consumption, a sacrifice of goods for nothing, for no positive purpose and no tangible gain. The horror of so useless an act establishes a limit from which incorporated humanity flees; it also holds up a hideous mirror that discloses, beyond the fantasy of fullness, a drive towards death. Like the phantoms of smoking destitution, cigarettes glow with a little bit of horror that can no longer be countenanced and promise a beggarly and abject existence to come. The abjected rabble, excreted by the technological orders of existence as lumpen flesh and inane drives, expectorate the lack and excess of humanity in a manner that resonates with more than the sighs of passive stupefaction. For Virilio, 'the passivity of individuals made useless, hence supernumerary, becomes a social menace because of the strong component of boredom and discontent'.[86] The rumblings of a negativity too obscure to be identified lurks among the wretched, the superfluous bodies of hypermodernity retaining an element of excess in them and more than them. It is not a positive condition, but a sovereignty beyond the orders of technocapitalistic consumption: 'the true luxury and real potlatch of our times falls to the poverty-stricken, that is to the individual who lies down and scoffs. A genuine luxury requires the complete contempt for riches, the sombre indifference of the individual who refuses to work and makes his life on the one hand an infinitely ruined splendour, and on the other, a silent insult to the laborious lie of the rich'.[87] A different kind of expenditure emerges in Bataille's account of sovereignty and the impossible, an ethics of horror braving a glance at an unthinkable limit and dissolution. In the negativity, in the contempt for accumulation, an acephalic figure arises, cigarette in one hand, match in the other. And in the manifestation of the burning, headless drive, the cigarette presents a vain, impossible resistance to incorporation, a point of blockage and negativity gesturing in the direction of a different path to death. A different life.

86. Virilio, 1995, *op. cit.*, p129.

87. Bataille, 1997, *op. cit.*, p208.

AVON'S CALLING: GLOBAL CONSUMPTION AND MICROCULTURAL PRACTICE IN A LATIN AMERICAN FRAME

Anny Brooksbank Jones

In a fascinating paper on popular culture in São Paulo, Geert Banck asks why 'an international cosmetic firm - Avon - goes to the *favelas* to sell its products'.[1] The question is prompted by an encounter with a *favela* resident who keeps a tin of Avon face powder hidden in a drawer in the only table in her shack. Banck does not direct his question to her, and offers no answer himself. This essay situates Avon's strategy and that of its secretive consumer in global and local frames, linked in each case to different ways of thinking about the relations of consumption and identity, culture and politics in Latin America.

Throughout the nineteenth and early twentieth century debates around Latin American cultural identity were restricted almost entirely to élite groups. However recent years have seen a broader questioning of once rigorously-imposed national identities. This questioning has been linked with and refracted through international communications and academic networks which have made the local identity claims and circumstances of certain non-élite groups (Mayan indigenist activists, for example, or the Chiapas-based Zapatistas) increasingly visible. Brazilian cultural sociologist Renato Ortiz is one of a number of influential theorists in the region to highlight the processes by which the development of these globalising networks is tending to create new hybrid cultural forms and identities. His analysis of the factors which he sees as implicated in these processes will be used to explore the popularity, availability and wider possibilities of products like Avon's in Latin America. Recent work by critical anthropologist and fellow hybridity-theorist Néstor García Canclini will then be used to examine consumption's role in identity politics as it relates to the specific micro-practice of Banck's *favela* resident.

In Latin America, questions of national and continental identity have frequently been associated with a certain ontological obsession, focussing on notions of authentic core or essence. As Ortiz notes, the continent has been represented as alienated to the extent that this core or essence, that which has determined Latin America's historical trajectory, has for so long been seen as located outside of it.[2] He contrasts this view with Levi-Strauss's notion of identity as 'una especie de lugar virtual' (a kind of virtual space) indispensable for thinking about certain questions but with no real existence: 'la identidad [es] una construcción simbólica que se hace en relación con un referente' (identity is a symbolic construction made in relation to a

1. Geert Banck, 'Mass consumption and urban protest in Brazil: some reflections on lifestyle and class', *Bulletin of Latin American Research*, Vol.13:1, 1994, pp45-60, p59.

2. Renato Ortiz, *Otros territorios*, Universidad Nacional de Quilmes, Buenos Aires 1996.

referent).[3] This referential frame may be cultural, national, ethnic or generic, but it is always a product of history. Ortiz's analysis plots the decline of certain, once dominant, referents and the emergence of some powerful new ones. Above all he is concerned with what he sees as the weakening of national identity as a result of the globalising of culture. In *Mundializaçao e cultura* (Mundialisation and Culture) and *Otros territorios* (Other Territories)[4] he makes a fundamental distinction between 'globalizaçao' (globalisation), which he sees as driven by economic and technological phenomena, and 'mundializaçao' (mundialisation),[5] the process by which these phenomena produce cultural effects. This mundialising process is not restricted to 'developed' high-consuming nations; Ortiz claims that capitals in the poorest nations on earth have their globalised zones where the same international goods are bought and sold as in Paris or New York. Away from the Benetton and Dior outlets in downtown Buenos Aires or Rio, however, *favela* residents too are accessible to 'global' marketing, via national and foreign films and TV programmes but also via sales teams, like Avon's, which work in clients' own locales. Wherever it occurs, Ortiz insists, mundialisation changes the particular cultural circumstances in which it operates. The result is not simply homogenisation, however, because the mundialising process works on and in local contexts which are themselves complexly different, giving rise in each case to specific views of the world or symbolic universes. To this extent, he claims, modernity has material, symbolic, and ideological dimensions which have brought in their train a new way of being in the world, and one which entails new values and new forms of cultural legitimation.

Although Ortiz avoids the more sweeping generalisations of euphoric or cataclysmic globalisers, a lot more could be said here about precisely how these processes work, the complex interrelations and the levels of specificity involved. With one exception, however, these are not his concerns here. The exception is deterritorialisation which, in his view and that of Canclini, is one of the most powerful features of world modernity. This term (with which he refers to Canclini's cultural hybridisation rather than Felix Guattari's micro-politics) is used to designate the process whereby messages, symbols, and culture in general all circulate freely in networks disconnected from this or that specific place, and which may emanate from within or outside of national borders.[6] Its primary motors are transnational and multinational business and international communications networks, through which we may 'know' more about an indigenous community in Chiapas than we do about an elderly neighbour. Ortiz does not explore the status and limits of this virtual solidarity. Like Canclini he is more immediately interested in how indigenous artefacts may be removed from the local place of production and displayed in a metropolitan folklore museum, for example, or may be mass-produced in distant cities for tourist consumption. In each case their cultural significance is transformed: in the first a local ritual object becomes a symbol of national cultural richness; in the second it becomes a marketable and infinitely replicable token of cultural

3. *Ibid.*, p77.

4. Renato Ortiz, *Mundializaçao e Cultura*, Brasilense, São Paulo 1994.

5. In a personal communication Ortiz has confirmed that he prefers this neologism to 'worlding', which carries post-colonial and other connotations not intended here.

6. Ortiz, *Otros territorios*, 1996, *op. cit.*

difference. Through these deterritorialisation and partial reterritorialisation processes, Ortiz contends, world modernity helps shape cultures from within the nation state. At the same time it colludes with transnational and multinational corporations to destabilise the (never wholly stable) relations between what he terms centre and periphery, external and internal, the indigenous and the foreign. The resulting weakening of the nation state (which can no longer rely on the support of the forces that once colluded in its legitimation) and of centralised notions of identity means that neither is any longer able to neutralise subaltern, local or regional identity movements within the national borders.

For Ortiz, this does not necessarily mean that the nation state is in terminal decline. But it does mean that socio-cultural relations and identities are being realigned, in some cases at planetary level, to produce new configurations. People from the Bolivian Altiplano and the Hebridean Islands may now find themselves sitting side by side in international indigenous forums. Meanwhile, he suggests, world modernity is (gradually and patchily) opening up and reconfiguring the local spaces traditionally associated with our daily lives, with presence, authenticity, rootedness and difference from other locales. Products like Avon's, for example, have no 'home' territory, because their marketing organisation and strategies are global, but also because their sales teams know customers' locales and circumstances intimately: they are usually sisters, mothers or neighbours. The deterritorialising processes Ortiz describes mean that individuals can no longer be conceived as geographically rooted in the traditional sense but rather as possessing certain referents. This new mobility does not mean that individuals today experience total rootlessness. Instead they live out what he refers to as 'una territorialidad desarraigada' (a rootless territoriality) in places traversed by a range of forces.[7] Cosmopolitans and certain academics apart, world modernity is thus, in his view, rarely experienced as such but lived out by individuals in its local manifestations, where it gives particular meanings to individual practices.

Once again, Ortiz offers no examples of this particularity. As Canclini demonstrates, however, Latin American cultural production offers some striking ones. Around five years ago, for example, in a tiny village outside the town of Oaxaca in Southern Mexico, Josefina Aguilar and her three sisters began making clay figures based on the paintings of Frida Kahlo. As Eli Bartra has observed, at the time they did not know she was a metropolitan middle-class Mexican artist of mixed European and Mexican descent who appropriated aspects of pre-Columbian and popular iconography for her élite artistic work: they thought she was North American.[8] In fact her perceived exoticism, the fact that she was precisely *not* North American, has been a major factor in the popularity and replication of her images in the US and elsewhere, and thus in their availability as potential models for non-élite artistic production in southern Mexico. The sisters' unironically irreverent re-appropriations of Kahlo's images qualify as 'arte popular'

7. *Ibid.*, p68.

8. Professor Bartra of the Universidad Autónoma Metropolitana, Xochimilco (Mexico) brought the sisters to wider attention in a fascinating paper presented at the 1997 Conference of the Society for Latin American Studies, St Andrews University, Scotland. I am grateful to her for furnishing me with information and material which I was able to develop in an interview with Aguilar in Ocotlán, Mexico, in July 1997.

(popular art) on the basis of the materials and techniques used and, above all, their limited objectives. But for those familiar with Kahlo's work and reputation - and those concerned with cultural hybridisation - each clay model is much more than a naively decorative object. The appeal of this excess to élite tourists has made the sisters' work known and marketable in places as apparently alien to it as Germany - where Kahlo's father was born. This illustrates the extent to which deterritorialisation is loosening the links between identity and place on the one hand while on the other making a new set of referents available for ethnic, regional, artisanal and other collectivities to appropriate in different ways. However, such appropriations do not fail to reflect the power and legitimacy invested in particular actors. They have brought Josefina Aguilar to the attention of certain Mexican and European academics, for example, but (as lamented in a framed press cutting on her wall) in the process she has accumulated more cultural than economic capital.

As the worlding of culture recasts the rootedness of local communities and identities we become closer to more distant things and (particularly where they are out of synch with modernity) more distant from some local ones. A young *favela* resident may identify more closely with aspects of a Hollywood blockbuster, Ortiz notes, than with a home-produced soap or local religious festival. At the same time, however, world modernity offers new possibilities for rootedness and identification to these and, above all, more 'cosmopolitan' groups through what Ortiz terms 'o imaginário colectivo mundial' or world collective imaginary.[9] This collective imaginary is, in effect, a symbolic repertoire made up of familiar international consumer products, imagery and names - the United Colours of Benetton, the face of Marlb'ro man or Marilyn, the Shell symbol, or the inevitable golden arches - a repertoire that enables 'modern' travellers to feel the persistence of their consumer past in the unstable present. To feel at home, that is, rooted despite their mobility, in the anonymous airport lounges or hotel rooms that Marc Augé elsewhere characterises as 'non-lieux'.[10] But both Augé and Ortiz are arguably only half-right. The fact that they are the final destination of very few people does not make international airports and hotels unanthropologised 'non-lieux' (especially for the people who work in them), but neither does the fact that travellers recognise international advertising symbols make these places universally homely. Such places are reassuring to the extent that their commercial legitimation of foreignness permits travellers who can afford it to feel at once foreign and at home, to assume their uncanniness as normal in a community of strangers. But while certain travellers will respond positively to their interpellation as members of a global consumer community others - for ideological, linguistic, economic or other reasons - will feel alienated, unable or disinclined to do so. Such (active or passive) resistance to 'global' marketing as it attempts to integrate individuals into consumer communities is one of a number of factors militating against widespread cultural homogenisation. In Ortiz's account,

9. Ortiz, *Mundializaçao e Cultura*, 1994, *op. cit.*, p145.

10. Marc Augé, *Non-lieux, Introduction à une anthropologie de la surmodernité*, Editions du Seuil, 1992.

11. As Banck notes in relation to *favela* dwellers, young consumers identify with certain products not simply to distinguish themselves from their parents but also from peer groups. This does not undermine Ortiz's point but it does highlight the fact that young and older consumers exercise an element of choice by choosing from the range of internationally marketed goods theoretically available to them. On the nature of this choice, see below.

12. On this see my 'From politics to culture ... and back?', *Latin American Perspectives*, forthcoming 2000.

13. See John Beverley and José Oviedo (eds), *The Postmodernism Debate in Latin America*, Duke UP, Durham 1993, and Anny Brooksbank Jones and Ronaldo Munck (eds), *Culture, Politics and Postmodernism in Latin America*, special issue of *Latin American Perspectives*, forthcoming 2000.

14. Like many other social and cultural theorists in the region, their analysis is informed by a somewhat uncritical respect for the notion of democratic renewal - a respect which can be traced to the years of authoritarian rule and the activities of 'new' social movements in the 1970s and 1980s.

the effects of supra-national market segmentation ensure that homogenisation, when it happens, affects not whole national cultures but different cultural levels across the planet. Across the world, he claims, the affluent and not-so-affluent young increasingly seek to differentiate themselves from older generations by adopting globalised referents - the Nike and Rayban symbols, Banck suggests, are as familiar and as sought-after in the São Paulo *favelas* as they are in my English home town. At the same time, the commercial success of Avon's sales team not only in the *favelas* but in isolated Amazonian settlements suggests that this desire to differentiate oneself within a community is not restricted to generational or Hollywood frames of reference.[11] Consumers are culturally levelled, Ortiz suggests, targeted by multi- and transnational cultural and other producers on the basis of lifestyles and aspirations, and regardless of locality or nationality. To this extent, he claims, globalisation works not by homogenisation but by differentiation. I would argue that it works by both. When MTV decided to launch its music channel in Europe, for example, it targeted young Europeans as a single homogeneous market. However, as David Morley noted recently, confronted with irreducible cultural differences among its target audience MTV has now been obliged to re-launch the channel with a more differentiated content. These differences remain limited, however, and are inflected according to region rather than nationality: programmes are designed for Scandinavia, for example, rather than Denmark, Norway or Sweden. No doubt this says more about the commercial strategies of multinational corporations than it does about the decline of national cultural difference; it nevertheless offers something like a 'market testing' of Ortiz's view that a certain cultural convergence takes place even as differences persist between levels of life.

Ortiz's study has been characterised by certain critics on the traditional left as a defence of global capitalism and cultural imperialism, as somehow prescribing rather than describing the mundialisation of culture. I would argue, rather, that his analyses can be read as a contribution to ongoing attempts by key Latin American intellectuals to construct a new critical left position attentive to the broader political claims of culture.[12] Their wider context is a decline of the region's more traditional left groupings accelerated, for eample, by: the fall of Soviet communism and the associated repositioning of Cuba; the consequences of externally-imposed neo-liberal socio-economic reform across the region; Latin American appropriations of postmodernist theory.[13] It is against this background that both Ortiz and Canclini highlight the relation of cultural consumption to democracy.[14] In particular, both agree that increased consumer choice and difference do not automatically make culture locally or regionally democratic. Despite a decline in the centralising effects of the nation state and national identity, the international concentration of ownership - in television, the cinema, publishing or more generally - in Latin America and elsewhere tends to preclude any significant increase in local cultural autonomy. By insisting on globalisation's solid base in flexible capitalism Ortiz also seeks to avoid 'una cierta ilusión posmoderna, como si el mundo estuviese compuesto por un conjunto de átomos sociales desconexos' (a certain postmodern illusion, as if the world were composed of a collection of disconnected social atoms).[15] He nevertheless insists on globalising features which are not reducible to the economic: 'la espacialidad de las cosas, los objetos, el medio ambiente y -¿ por qué no? - el imaginario colectivo' (the spatiality of things, objects, the environment and -why not? - the collective imaginary).[16] That embedded rhetorical question, like Banck's, marks a certain reticence which will be explored shortly.

The mundialisation, the de- (and partial re-) territorialisations and, above all, the hybridising processes described in broad terms by Ortiz are illustrated in the context of more specific cultural practices in the work of Canclini. In his groundbreaking *Hybrid Cultures* Canclini observes that traditional artefacts and vanguardist catalogues can routinely be found juxtaposed on élite coffee tables, while popular and élite cultural features commonly coexist in influential texts by García Márquez, Isabel Allende and others.[17] But this more or less incidental hybridisation coexists, he notes, with other forms. Traditional craftsmen and women are increasingly 'reconverting'[18] their knowledge and techniques, adapting them to urban culture and consumers: they are adopting new practices without simply abandoning older ones. Josefina Aguilar's makeshift display table, for example, juxtaposes images from Frida Kahlo with the type of traditional Mexican figures made by her grandparents before her and with models of sophisticated young 1990s women in sequinned microskirts. Traditional forms may be retained, as here, because they maintain a family tradition and/or because (like Aguilar's contemporary figures) they appeal to tourists. In other cases the persistence of traditional forms may reflect the producer's unequal access to cultural goods - such as the inspiration afforded by films or exhibitions - or the conditioning effects of hegemonic institutions and sectors. Canclini attributes these hybrid phenomena, willed or otherwise, to the fact that Latin American cultures are

> currently the result of the sedimentation, juxtaposition, and interweaving of indigenous traditions (above all in the Mesoamerican and Andean areas), of Catholic colonial hispanism, and of modern political, educational, and communicational actions. Despite attempts to give élite culture a modern profile, isolating the indigenous and the colonial in the popular sectors, an interclass mixing has generated hybrid formations in all social strata.[19]

Compounding this process is the fact that popular and élite cultures alike are being relocated within the logic of the market and can no longer claim to be the expression of creative, self-contained individuals. Art, for example, has become the point of intersection of journalists, critics, historians,

15. Ortiz, *Otros territorios*, 1996, op. cit., p54.

16. *Ibid.*, p55.

17. Néstor García Canclini, *Hybrid Cultures: Strategies for Entering and Leaving Modernity*, Christopher L. Chiappari and Silvina L. López (trans), University of Minnesota Press, Minneapolis 1995. (Mexican original 1989.)

18. The term 'reconversion', along with other key features of his analytic frame in this study, derives from Bourdieu. Canclini's reconversion of Bourdieu's terms tends to be flexible, however, and adapted to local circumstances.

19. García Canclini, *Hybrid Cultures*, 1995, *op. cit.*, p46.

museums, dealers, speculators and collectors.

The notion of hybridity tends to imply a prior non-hybrid state and (despite his explicitly historicised general definition) throughout his study Canclini tends to underplay the extent to which forms of hybridity have been a feature of Latin American culture since the Conquest.[20] The term's own hybrid history arguably reinforces his account of its contemporary form which (like Ortiz) he links primarily to deterritorialisation, understood here as the loss of the seemingly natural relation of culture to geographical and social territories. Canclini's example of partial and relative reterritorialisations of old and new symbolic products include the international market for Brazilian soap operas and migration across the Mexico/US border, where restricted but dynamic cultural production coexists with wide scale poverty and misery. Similarly, while popular culture takes the form of diverse tactics through which *favela* residents, and subaltern groups more generally, negotiate their identities and positions these may in turn be staged strategically by folklorists and anthropologists for museums and the academy, by sociologists and politicians for political parties, or by media workers for TV and radio.

'Decollection' is the second major hybridising process explored by Canclini, and marks a shift away from the traditional use of collections to order and hierarchise cultural artefacts and other symbolic goods. Today, these may be organised according to a range of mixed criteria , thereby reflecting the loss of a sense of overarching cultural order - a loss often (though decreasingly) associated in Latin America with postmodernity. The classifications that underpinned the separation of élite from popular culture and both from mass culture are disappearing - a tendency which is compounded by increasingly sophisticated reproduction techniques. More attuned here to Derrida than Benjamin, Canclini sees the associated reordering of cultural practices or performances and the crossings of identities as leading us to rethink in different and potentially positive ways how material and symbolic relations are organised among groups. He is nevertheless concerned that a tolerance of extreme cultural discontinuity is helping to consolidate the power of transnationals and states as they seek to understand and manage the production and circulation of symbolic goods. A certain commodification that follows from this ensures that cultural practices become more fragmented or specialised. Following Pierre Bourdieu, he notes that this process is eased by the fact that cultural goods possess no single, fixed meanings but are constructed within a field - including artists, markets, museums and critics - in which powerful inequalities allow particular interpretations to become dominant. To the extent that this is more often the result of willed or accidental complicities of society and state rather than simple imposition, however, Canclini (like Ortiz) sees cultural consumers as at least relatively autonomous. Although somewhat ambiguous in *Hybrid Cultures* (which has more to say on the power of globalising neo-liberal cultural and other networks), his assessment of

20. What distinguishes Latin American 'mestizo' versions of hybridity from the postmodern-inflected forms explored by Canclini and others is that the first retained some reference to legitimacy (with most giving priority to the European element). The second, by contrast, (and as reflected in Canclini's notion of 'decollection' below) (forgoes both author and script).

this relative autonomy becomes more positive in the later *Consumidores y ciudadanos* (Consumers and citizens).[21] Here he follows Ortiz in appropriating De Certeau's distinction between tactics and strategies to evoke the asymmetrical possibilities of subaltern and hegemonic groups where questions of culture and identity are concerned. De Certeau characterises a strategy as:

> the calculation (or manipulation) of power relationships that becomes possible as soon as a subject with will and power (a business, an army, a city, a scientific institution) can be isolated. It postulates a *place* that can be delimited as its own and serve as the base from which relations with an *exteriority* composed of targets or threats (customers or competitors, enemies, the country surrounding the city, objectives and objects of research, etc.) can be managed. As in management, every 'strategic' rationalisation seeks first of all to distinguish its 'own' place, that is, the place of its own power and will, from an environment.[22]

By contrast, a tactic is 'a calculated action determined by the absence of a proper locus. No delimitation of an exteriority, then, provides it with the condition necessary for autonomy. The space of the tactic is the space of the other'.[23] As noted in my conclusion, strategists are themselves tacticians in larger concentric circles. In De Certeau's terms, however, a cultural impresario advising local artisans to incorporate internationally-known images in their work acts on the basis of a strategic calculation and in pursuit of a particular objective: by contrast a cultural consumer reacts, offering a local, tactical response to the facts as she or he perceives them. A key tactical resource, Canclini suggests, is ritual, which functions as an 'oblique symbolic circuit' in the search for indirect ways of mediating and managing conflict. It is a salient feature of Latin American politics: where individuals cannot change their regional governor, for example, he (sic) may be satirised in Carnival dances or other metaphorical challenges. Rebellious popular sectors thus satisfy their needs tactically, participating in a system of consumption they do not choose, in a language they do not choose, demonstrating in squares made by and for others. Any resulting re-signification, any shift of power or meaning, is thus at best a temporary one. It is unable permanently to erase the old habits of either the demonstrators or their opponents. To this extent, Canclini suggests, popular sectors may indirectly support those who oppress them. It cannot be unproblematically assumed that they are untainted by the macrosocial, or that those lacking a voice could, if aided by an élite ventriloquist, be 'brought to discourse' and induced speak the pure and authentically radical truth of their condition. Poor women in the *favelas*, for example, are no more purely or inherently radical than any other social group. When radical means of action are available to them, they are more likely to opt for intermediate solutions. When ill, for example, they might consult both the doctor and the healer: trusting neither

21. Néstor García Canclini, *Consumidores y ciudadanos: conflictos multiculturales de la globalización*, Grijalbo, México DF 1995.

22. Michel de Certeau, *The Practice of Everyday Life*, trans Steven Rendall, University of California Press, Berkeley, California 1988, pp36-7.

23. *Ibid.*

completely, they put their faith partly in hegemonic and partly in popular knowledge.

For Canclini, all cultural practices involve acting rather than actions: they simulate social actions but rarely *operate* as actions. Yet sometimes, he acknowledges, new transformative practices do arise from metaphorical challenges. The Argentinian women who held up photos of their 'disappeared' children to the national and international gaze in the capital's Plaza de Mayo did eventually see some of those responsible punished. The wooden guns of the Zapatista insurgents, who confronted the Mexican government through the international media in January 1994, suggest another dramatic example of performance politics. And not only because the rebels were repeatedly assimilated by foreign commentators to characters in old Hollywood musicals or to sepia-tint (and thus supposedly authentic and unambiguous) revolutionaries. Although media exposure and repeatedly blocked negotiations have since colluded in a certain ritualisation or theatricalisation of their activities, these men and women were acting in deadly earnest. And if the repercussions of their actions - the crisis meetings of NAFTA signatories, the plummeting of the *peso*, international investors' panic - were swift and unambiguous it was partly because international politicians and investors took the television images at face value. The Mexican government responded by attempting first to suppress these images with an information blackout and second to suppress the rebellion itself with massive military force. The military repression permanently silenced many of the would-be political actors, but the news blackout was rendered ineffective by the rebel leaders' use of the Internet. Because this use was strategic as much as tactical, to the extent that all Internet users are in some sense on 'home territory', it has been widely (and *pace* Castells perhaps too readily) seen as a defining moment in contemporary popular resistance.[24]

As noted, for Canclini consumption itself has a ritual dimension as a compensatory practice which serves to neutralise the instability of the social. This compensatory dimension returns us to the secretive *favela* consumer. For although Ortiz and Canclini throw light on the globalising and hybrid local contexts in which such consumption takes place, none of the studies referred to can match Avon's penetration of their consumers' intimate spaces. Canclini's reticence on this point is partly political. Why, he asks, when global markets are increasingly powerful, do Latin America's postmodernists see fit to celebrate individual desires and to represent the social as an erratic coexistence of impulses and desires.[25] This does not amount precisely to a denial of the work of desire or the unconscious in the social. Like Bourdieu he acknowledges that '[t]he most fundamental principles of class identity and unity [are] those which lie in the unconscious' while implying that it is individuals' 'relative positions in the social structure (or in a specialised field)' rather than their desires or any other fluid, unstructured impulses that govern their position in any given interaction.[26] In his study of consumption in the Latin American megacities, Canclini insists on the need

24. Manuel Castells, *The Information Age: Economy, Society and Culture, Vol. II, The Power of Identity*, Blackwell, Oxford 1997, pp72-83.

25. García Canclini, *Hybrid Cultures*, 1995, *op. cit.*, p46.

26. Pierre Bourdieu, *Distinction: a Social Critique of the Judgement of Taste*, Routledge, London 1984, p579.

(among less self-conscious consumers as well as intellectuals) to impose a structure and an order on indeterminacy and desires, and he accords consumption a privileged role in this process. For if he dismisses certain postmodernist celebrations of consumption he also rejects the claims of some voices on the region's left that consumption is necessarily passive and irrational. Even low income families who spend all their meagre income on a birthday celebration are behaving rationally, he claims, to the extent that they are fixing collective meanings and the flow of events, regulating their desires and opening them up to public judgements.

> Comprar objetos, colgárselos en el cuerpo o distribuirlos por la casa, asignarles un lugar en un orden, atribuirles funciones en la comunicación con los otros, son los recursos para pensar el propio cuerpo, el inestable orden social y las interacciones inciertas con los demás. Consumir es hacer más inteligible un mundo donde lo sólido se evapora.[27]

For Canclini, it is in this play of desires and structures, in which desires become demands and socially regulated acts, that consumption's political dimension is most evident. Like Arjun Appadurai, he sees consumption not as privatised, individual possession, but as part of a collective appropriation in relations of solidarity and difference of goods which satisfy symbolic and biological needs, as well as controlling desires' flux.[28]

But it is by no means clear to what larger intelligibility or public judgement the Avon consumer is appealing. She has, after all, spent money which we assume she can hardly afford on something that in the ordinary sense of the terms she neither needs nor uses, and which she hides away. The larger socio-political role of consumption is not in question here. At issue is whether this role exhausts consumption in the way Canclini tends to suggest. The structuring role of desires in the social is not their only role, any more than marketing's historical exploitation of desires renders them reducible to marketing. This does not mean, of course, that marketing has not played a part in the 'unbracketing' of desires within the social. However, their bracketing was arguably always less complete than Canclini (or Bourdieu) tend to assume. Coincidentally, perhaps, De Certeau and Gilles Deleuze both insist on this with reference to Fernand Deligny's 'lignes d'erre'.[29] For De Certeau, consumers are 'trailblazers in the jungles of functionalist rationality' whose poetic practices 'produce something resembling ... apparently meaningless [lines whose] indeterminate trajectories do not cohere' with the space through which they move.[30] These lines exploit the vocabulary of established languages and syntaxes yet remain 'heterogeneous to the systems they infiltrate and in which they sketch out the guileful ruses of *different* interests and desires'.[31] For Deleuze, Deligny's lines represent micropolitical 'folies secrètes'. Like the face powder of the Avon consumer, these follies are not dissociated from public powers simply because they are secret. Rather, they relate to these powers in heterogeneous

27. Buying objects, wearing them on our bodies or distributing them around the house, assigning them a place in an order, attributing functions to them in our communications with others, these are ways of thinking about our own bodies, about the unstable social order or uncertain interactions with other people. Consumption confers intelligibility on a world where all that is solid melts into air. García Canclini, *Hybrid Cultures*, 1995, op. cit., p48.

28. For Bourdieu this dimension is bracketed with/in the *habitus* - most evidently and invisibly in the formula ((habitus)(capital)) + field=practice. More than in Canclini's study, the reader seems to glimpse the intellectual's will and/or desire to regulate desires and meanings by subordinating them to his own sphere of action.

29. Gilles Deleuze and Claire Parnet, *Dialogues*, Flammarion, Paris 1977, p155 and de Certeau, *The Practice of Everyday* Life, op. cit., p34.

30. De Certeau, *ibid*.

31. *Ibid*, original emphasis.

ways that Canclini and Ortiz register only in passing, and that Banck sees but does not quite recognise. Unlike Bourdieu, however, Banck can see that what is at issue here does not fall exclusively within the realm of necessity.

Attention to these heterogeneous relations offers a way of reading consumption as a practice that is simultaneously private and social, linked both to individual life politics and to a broader emancipatory politics, neither a wholly determinate social ritual not wholly reducible to questions of personal necessity or desire. Avon's success in producing new consumers is arguably linked to its recognition and exploitation of this multivalence. As Ortiz observes, for example, although strategists (unlike tacticians) tend to operate on their home ground, many social or cultural actors are supported by an institution whose strategies push them onto the ground of others. Although Avon's sales staff conform superficially to this model, they sell not only by virtue of the institutional weight behind them, but also by blurring the distinction between alien and home ground, selling and socialising. Its methods enhance saleswomen's economic autonomy - and since Avon pioneered direct selling in 1886 its sale force has always , as a matter of policy, been composed of women - reinforcing contacts within communities while maximising peer pressure to consume and to meet payments. According to its corporate brochure, Avon's mission is to sustain growth by being 'the company that best understands and satisfies the product, service and self-fulfilment needs of women - globally'. This is not because it assumes that all women's needs are identical - and Avon itself insists on needs rather than desires - but rather that those of a particular 'level' of women world wide are similar enough to respond to this type of targeting. As Ortiz observes, this consumer mundialisation does not imply homogenisation, partly because its strategies vary and interact differently with different contexts. This tendency is obliquely underlined by Avon's product range. The make-up it markets gestures towards the possibility of a deeply personal or quasi-ritualistic self-invention or re-invention, even for those facing routine poverty and institutionalised exclusion. In particular, Canclini would suggest, it registers a growing awareness of the self as a consumer and a social actor. But from De Certeau's perspective make-up might also invoke a ruse or trickery irreducible to narcissistic masquerade, the possibility of consumer waywardness. In his account, the knowledge of the strategist is inextricable from a Foucauldian 'panoptic practice', a gaze which the tactician can elude only by hiding.[32] In the case of the enigmatic Avon consumer this hiding is transitive, I suggest, because it is transitional, marking her status as a becoming-consumer. For De Certeau (who would no doubt underline the non-conformity rather than the partial conformity of her actions) such micro-practices can, over time, wear down institutional frameworks by playing both with and against the order that contains them. Deleuze, too, acknowledges the force of micro-political pleasures, the lines that mark 'les fluxes moléculaires' - hairline cracks that, in certain circumstances, can do more damage than larger, molar, fractures.[33] While

32. *Ibid.*, p36

33. Deleuze and Parnet, *Dialogues*, *op. cit.*, p155.

Canclini broadly accepts the possibility of such conjunctions, he is more concerned with the interrelated networks of production, distribution and marketing that enable symbolic exchange and, in certain circumstances, cause it to compound social and economic inequities. With these in mind he counsels repeatedly against placing too much faith in the subversive potential of popular or neovanguardist cultural micro-practices. In this he is supported by the multivalence of the Avon consumer's own micropractice, which is pleasurable partly because of its privatised and cosmetic component. This pleasure is not a quasi-automatised response to the aura of the fetishised, self-present commodity, nor yet a simple reflection of what Avon tells consumers they will feel. It is a pleasure produced in this particular consumer's relation to her acquisition, and in the imaginative and other work she does on it, in the course of which the commodity becomes something else.

These hybrid pleasures, intensified by guilt, nevertheless facilitate the induction of low-income women into consumption. Avon interpellates them as consumers, appealing to an identity that is not yet (wholly) theirs and in the process helping them to assume it. TV and other symbolic networks refer these women to a legitimating frame in which they figure as merely virtual consumers. If they keep rather than consume the product in question, if the make-up (for example) remains pleasurably unspent, their consumer identity remains largely virtual: in Canclini's terms, acting remains unconverted to action. But this emergent identity itself registers a certain objectification of self, an awareness of a relation to social- and market- led norms of beauty, and a sense that something can (and ought to) be done to conform to them. It marks, that is, the beginning both of a certain self-identification and of alienation.

Supported by friends, neighbours and relations Avon is easing low income women across Latin America and elsewhere into global consumer practices. As noted, this process may compound already gross socio-economic inequities. But in the right conditions, Canclini suggests, with equitable access to and reliable and multidirectional information on a genuinely wide range of goods, and with all sectors participating in its organisation, consumption may contribute to the development of a genuinely reflexive citizenship.[34] In the meantime (and *pace* Bourdieu), it can ensure that women and men who enjoy equitable access to very few consumer goods are less likely to experience their lives as played out wholly within the realm of necessity even as they try to escape from it.

There are, in conclusion, compelling reasons for more systematically extending the notion of hybridity, which Canclini and Ortiz have done so much to popularise in Latin America, to analyses of consumption itself. First, and unlike consumerism, consumption is not avoidable. Nor is it necessarily passive or uncritical - though it can be both - or simply compensatory. It is not wholly reducible to a socio-economic practice nor to a manifestation of interactive socio-political or economic rationality. It may

34. García Canclini, *Hybrid Culture*, 1995, op. *cit.*, p52-3.

be a source of individual or group pleasure as well as a source of conflict and anxiety. And while it has a potentially key role in identification processes, this role tends to be constructed (initially at least) in the terms proposed by those who produce and market the commodity in question. This role in turn may have major social, political and economic implications and, depending on the individuals and groups, fields and forces concerned, these implications may be more or less subversive, conservative or hybrid. The success of transnational companies like Avon rests largely on the fact that they have been able to exploit aspects of this hybridity neglected elsewhere, conditioning and responding to the individual needs and desires of local consumers in a global frame. For this reason, any attempt to challenge less desirable aspects of transnationals' activities in Latin America and elsewhere, and to facilitate the conditions in which all the region's consumers have equitable access to citizenship in the terms described by Canclini, will also need to attend as seriously as has Avon to the microdynamics of consumption.

'You can sample anything': *Zebrahead*, 'Black' Music, and Multiracial Audiences

Gregory Stephens

An explosion of racialised commentary in 1999 about the 'white boy' rapper Eminem illustrated just how enduring is the notion of black music as a sort of 'racial property'. Eminem was often portrayed as having single-handedly invented a new archetype for 'culturally black' white performers. In fact, this archetype has been a recurring motif in popular culture for two centuries, and the specifics of Eminem's case (raised among blacks in Detroit) have already been prefigured in an under-appreciated independent film, *Zebrahead*. A bit of historical and cross-cultural perspective on this domain would seem to be in order. In this paper I use *Zebrahead* as a case study of the cinematic use of 'black' music as a contested 'third space' between racial collectives. *Zebrahead* dramatises how music often thought of as 'black' can serve simultaneously as a marker of both 'racial' difference and interracial commonality. In broader terms, I want to ask: if film genres evolve in response to the changing demands of their audience, then how do multiracial audiences help shape generic transformations? Fully engaging that question would require a study of audience reception that is beyond my scope here. But I do want to suggest that 'black' music can play a key role in re-visioning a 'hidden history' of interraciality in film.[1]

My study of multiracial audiences grows out of a realisation that multi-raciality has been rendered invisible by a sort of binary racial mythology in cultural studies in general, and film criticism, in particular. For instance, Hazel Carby analyses black characters in *Grand Canyon* only by way of the themes of white fear and resentment, ignoring the dynamics of a multiracial audience. Edward Guerrero and Yvonne Tasker both treat biracial Buddy Movies as if they were situated solely within a 'white' generic community, and 'co-opt' black characters which rightly belong in a 'black' generic community. Benjamin DeMott has dismissed films with interracial themes as 'white fairy tales of interracial harmony' that constitute a 'smiling but monstrous lie'. This tendency to pigeon-hole films and their audiences in 'racial' boxes needs to be examined critically.[2]

The pervasiveness of multiracial phenomena, encountered both personally and professionally, has led me to ask: How can we develop non-reductive ways to analyse (and engage) multi-raciality, so that we are attentive to persistent 'racial formations', yet are not blinded by the racial mythologies embedded in the language of race itself? Indeed, can we own up not only to racial formations, but to this historical reality of multiracial formations? My efforts to meet this challenge have centred on a study of communicative

1. Among the plethora of articles about Eminem obsessively focusing on 'the white boy thing', one of the most perceptive is Scott Poulson-Bryant, 'Fear of a White Rapper', *The Source*, June 1999, 174 fn. Most of this commentary admits that Eminem has 'authentic' style and real-life street credentials, yet still betrays an urge to portray him as an outsider - in order to maintain the comfortable binaries of racial mythology. This is quite similar to reactions to the character Zack in *Zebrahead*. For a perceptive study of blackface as an example of what Ralph Ellison used to call 'the true inter-relatedness of blackness and whiteness', see W.T. Lhamon, Jr, *Raising Cain: Blackface Performance from Jim Crow to Hip*, Harvard UP, 1998. An often reductive application of the blackface tradition to film is Michael Rogin, *Blackface, White Noise: Jewish Immigrants in the Hollywood Melting Pot*, University of California Press, Berkeley 1996; on interraciality's hidden history, see Werner Sollors, *Neither Black nor White yet Both: Thematic Explorations of Interracial Literature*, OUP, 1997. On 'third space,' see Homi Bhabha, *The Location of Culture*, Routledge, 1994.

2. Hazel Carby, 'Encoding White Resentment: Grand

Canyon - A Narrative for our Times,' *Race Identity & Representation in Education*, Cameron McCarthy and Warren Crichlow (eds), Routledge, New York 1993; Edward Guerrero, *Framing Blackness: the African American Image in Film*, Temple University Press, Philadelphia 1993; Yvonne Tasker, 'Black Buddies and White Heroes: Racial Discourse in the Action Cinema,' *Spectacular Bodies: Gender, Genre and the Action Cinema*, Comedia/Routledge, London 1993; Benjamin DeMott, 'Put on a Happy Face: Masking the differences between blacks and whites', *Harpers* 291, September 1995, pp31-38.

3. Michael Omi and Howard Winant, *Racial Formations in the United States*, Routledge, New York (1985) 1994. On 'double-voiced', see Mikhail Bakhtin, *The Dialogic Imagination*, Texas University Press, Austin 1981; Henry Louis Gates, Jr, *The Signifying Monkey: A Theory of Afro-American Literary Criticism*, Oxford UP, 1988; Homi Bhabha (ed), *Nation and Narration*, Routledge, 1990.

4. Gregory Stephens, "'Frederick Douglass' Multiracial Abolitionism: "Antagonistic Cooperation" and "Redeemable Ideals" in the 5 July Speech', *Communication Studies*, vol. 48 no. 3,

acts - artistic, political, and religious - which are addressed to a multiracial audience. In analysing 'double-voiced' texts in relation to the multiracial settings from which they emerged, and the mixed audiences to which they were addressed, I have tried to understand the implications of this process (speaking to a multiracial audience) for identity formation, and for constructing new definitions of community allegiance and national citizenship.[3]

Texts produced in multiracial contexts may be read as instances of a 'mutually created language'. These co-creations emerge through a process of 'antagonistic co-operation' between the different constituents of multiracial audiences, and the speakers, writers and performers who devise multiple discursive strategies in order to address them. My work has applied this perspective to abolitionist politics (Frederick Douglass), literature (Ralph Ellison's *Invisible Man*), music (Bob Marley, and multi-ethnic rap music), and film (the interracial romance genre).[4] Here I want to combine two domains of popular culture, looking at representations of multi-raciality in the interface between music and film.

The use of 'black' music for films with a multiracial audience is a common feature of late twentieth century cinema. This phenomenon manifests itself in several ways: as a central narrative feature, as an equivalent of a Greek chorus, as an atmospheric 'additive' and as a marketing tool, to name four examples. My central concern is with the ways in which 'black' music is used as a contested form of interracial symbolic interaction. I put quotes around 'black' for two reasons. First, to draw attention to the use in film of styles of music commonly thought of as 'black', but which are in fact hybrid, or 'biracial'; secondly, to foreground the socially constructed nature of 'racial' identity and cultural allegiance.[5] This has been a central theme of films, such as *Young Soul Rebels* and *Zebrahead*, which use music as a meeting ground for interracial friendships or romances.

In the films to be examined here, different characters use 'black' music for opposing purposes: both to mark divisions between 'racial' communities, and to claim an interracial common ground. After briefly sketching some of the broader cinematic uses of 'black' music, I will initially concentrate on films which use 'black' music as a pivotal narrative device, citing examples from films that will be familiar to many readers: *White Men Can't Jump*, and *Do the Right Thing*. I will then explore in depth a pivotal scene from a lesser-known independent film, *Zebrahead*, as an example of cinematic use of popular music to demarcate a racial frontier in which both conflict and co-creation take place.

An example of an 'atmospheric' use of 'black' music can be found in *Grand Canyon*: a white motorist leaving a Lakers basketball game has his car stall in a foreboding urban neighbourhood. The sound of rap music booming from a passing car is used to signify menace.[6] The soul music soundtrack of *The Big Chill* provides a different sort of ambience: of 'good times' or self-affirmation. The main characters are white, but they 'claim' Motown music as the soundtrack of 'my generation,' i.e., Baby Boomers. The lyrics of these songs also act as a sort of Greek chorus, commenting upon the characters' lives in a range of ways. Finally, the use of 'black'-oriented soundtracks as a marketing tool is commonplace in the 1990s, as, for example, in the best-selling soundtrack of the Michael Jordan vehicle, *Space Jam*.

Before exploring *Zebrahead*, a movie that uses 'black' music as an interracial narrative device, I want to introduce this topic by examining a scene from Ron Shelton's *White Men Can't Jump*, in which Jimi Hendrix' music functions in similar fashion. *White Men Can't Jump* is premised upon the tension between the ideal that you can't judge a book by its cover, and the reality that people judge each other's capacities by skin colour all the time. This plays out primarily within the realm of pickup basketball,[7] but is also dramatised in a scene where Billy Hoyle, the white character played by Woody Harrelson, pops in a Jimi Hendrix cassette in his convertible. When Sidney Dean (Wesley Snipes) hears 'Purple Haze' he insists that Billy cannot *hear* this music because he is white. Whereupon Billy and his Puerto Rican girlfriend Gloria (Rosie Perez) point out that the whole band aside from Hendrix is white. To dramatise the double-edged fallacy of equating skin colour with cultural capability, Billy puts in a country ballad. When Sidney raises a stink, this allows Billy to reverse roles, claiming that his black partner cannot 'hear' this music coded as white. This scene signals that domains like basketball and blues, which we tend to think of as 'black,' are actually multiracial: in their structural origins, and in the audiences which sustain them - both as participants and performers, and as consumers.[8]

Our popular culture is in fact pervaded by symbols of inter-raciality, or what one might call indicators of 'racial ambiguity'.[9] I want to enumerate several factors within this scene which problematise attempts to interpret it with 'racialised' language.

First: Is Jimi Hendrix' music, as a product or artistic style, 'black'? Hendrix had a career touring the United States with rhythm'n'blues bands, playing for predominantly black audiences, before relocating to England. However, the re-construction of his music and image in Great Britain went far beyond simply adding a white drummer and bass player - Mitch Mitchell and Noel Redding, respectively. Any comparison of Hendrix' style of dress, pre-and post-England, will dramatically illustrate his immersion in the 'swinging' London of the mid- to late 1960s. Some of this can be attributed to marketing efforts by Hendrix' label, Warner/Reprise. But the music itself is an analogue to his sartorial flair: the blues foundation remains, but is re-filtered through 'rock' and 'psychedelic' sensibilities. Certainly many of Hendrix' Afro-American peers wrote him off as 'white.' I believe that his music remained 'black-based,' if we want to use racial markers, but became thoroughly hybrid or 'biracial,' which could be expected after years of playing rock festivals. At any rate, the criticisms of having gone 'white' stung Hendrix and drove his late employment of a black rhythm section, bassist Billy Cox and drummer Buddy Miles. This context informs the debate over the 'racial'

Fall 1997; Gregory Stephens, *On Racial Frontiers: The 'New Culture' of Frederick Douglass, Ralph Ellison, and Bob Marley*, Cambridge UP, Cambridge 1999; Gregory Stephens, 'Interracial Dialogue in Rap Music: Call-and-Response in a Multicultural Style', *New Formations*, vol 16, Lawrence and Wishart, Spring 1992, and 'Romancing the Racial Frontier: Mediating Symbols in Cinematic Interracial Representation', *Spectator: The University of Southern California Journal of Film and Television Criticism*, vol. 16 no. 1, Fall/Winter 1995/ 96.

5. Loring Brace, 'Race has no biological justification', University of Michigan, Association for the Advancement of Science conference, 20.2.1995. Quoted in *Los Angeles Times* editorial, 22.2.1995. There is more genetic diversity among 'racial' groups than between 'races'. A good overview of this issue can be found in Kwame Anthony Appiah, 'Illusions of Race', Chapter Two of *In My Father's House: Africa in the Philosophy of Culture*, OUP, 1992.

6. Hazel Carby, 'Encoding White Resentment,' 1993, *op. cit.*

7. 'Pickup basketball' refers to the system of play in which the

player who has oral rights to the next game on a court 'picks up' or chooses his or her team-mates from among the available players. A classic study of pickup basketball is Rick Telander, *Heaven is a Playground*, Simon & Schuster, New York 1976. An excellent portrait of interracial dynamics on an Austin, Texas court is Michael Moran, *Nothing But Net! An Essay on the Culture of Pickup Basketball*, Full Court Press, 1991 (P.O. Box 12641, San Antonio, TX 78212).

8. For an opposing view on the hybridity of black music, see the story of jazz drummer Max Roach calling white writer Frank Owen a 'racist white cocksucker' after Owen declared that rap was not purely 'black' since it sampled white rock groups; Greg Tate, *Flyboy in the Buttermilk*, Simon & Schuster, New York 1992, p131.

9. Gregory Stephens, 'Interraciality in Historical Context: Return of the Repressed,' in *On Racial Frontiers*, 1999, *op. cit.* On interraciality, see also Sollors 1997 and George Hutchinson *The Harlem Renaissance in Black and White*, Belknap/Harvard, Boston 1995, and Shelly Fisher Fishkin, *Was Huck Black? Mark Twain and African American Voices*, OUP, 1993.

categorisation of Hendrix' music which we witness in *White Men Can't Jump*. Similar questions arise regarding other 'black'-identified musicians, such as the changes necessary to market Bob Marley to a multinational, multi-'racial' audience.[10]

Second: basketball in the United States is 'black-dominated,' but generally perceived as a common ground in which members of different 'races' get a rare opportunity to come together and play by the same set of rules. Yet my ethnographic research indicates that, while this 'interracial common ground' remains an ideal for many players and fans, the sport remains pervaded by racial tensions and stereotypes. On an amateur level, players often use racial stereotypes to bend the rules. The perception of whites being outsiders who don't 'know' the game is a persistent feature of *White Men Can't Jump* (*WMCJ*).[11]

Third: this scene (and the movie) constantly plays on racialised expectations. Is it a genetic limitation that 'white men can't jump'? The belief that this is true allows Billy and Sidney to pursue their hustle. Music functions here as a critical sub-text: expectations that whites can't 'hear' black music, and conversely that blacks can't 'hear' white music, serve to lampoon binary racial mythologies. (Country-western, it should be noted, also has significant 'black' roots).

Fourth: *WMCJ* is part of a sub-genre, the 'Interracial Buddy Movie' (amongst others the *Lethal Weapon* series, *48 Hours*, *Boys on the Side* and *Deep Cover*). Critics of this genre too often apply racial binaries, treating 'black' and 'white' audiences as if they were mutually exclusive. Black characters in these films are often described as if they had been hijacked from a 'black' domain, and forced into a 'white' narrative structure. Critics tend to treat representations of inter-raciality as if they were divorced from real-life multiracial audiences - and indeed, from the many interracial friendships and marriages in this audience. Such binaries selectively tune out the multiracial demographics of the 'generic community' to which such films are addressed. Transformations in cinematic genres follow and in some ways anticipate changes in social psychology. If we pay attention to 'how a filmic text is adapted to the "imaginative landscape" of our time',[12] then we must be attentive to how the expectations of audiences help to structure films, and to restructure the genres within which they are located. The 'imaginative landscape' of multiracial audiences will be given a characteristic voice and form in films, and other artforms.

Fifth: Shelton's film can also be located, to a lesser degree, within an emerging genre I have previously described as the 'Interracial Romance Genre.' This genre and its multiracial audience also problematises the notion of a discrete 'racial' community.[13]

Sixth: The character Billy Hoyle's love interest here, Gloria (Rosie Perez), is Puerto Rican. Would the relationship be considered more 'interracial' *vis à vis* Billy, the white guy, or Sidney, the black guy? Although the Latina presence is only implicit here, Latin American notions of *mestizaje* (cultural hybridity) undermine North American notions of a racial binary. Our census categories reflect this problematic: Hispanics can be 'of any race'.[14]

The widespread use of racially ambiguous symbols, as displayed in *WMCJ*, or as experienced through participation in multiracial contexts, results in a communicative culture that is fundamentally interracial. Spike Lee makes a similar point, in a different way, by emphasising the centrality of black culture in 'mainstream' America. In *Do the Right Thing*, Mookie, an Afro-American, gets Vito, a racist Italian American, to name his favourite 'culture heroes': Eddie Murphy, Magic Johnson, Prince. He then tells him with biting irony: 'All of your favourite people are so-called niggers'. Vito is immersed in a black/multiracial culture without understanding it, without it altering his ethnocentric views.

Lee uses rap music as a racial sign: specifically, the Public Enemy song 'Fight the Power'. Yet while Lee presents opposition to this song within Sal's Pizzeria as a marker of racial difference, in 'real life' it would more likely be generational difference. About 80 per cent of those who buy rap are non-black - mostly suburban white teenage males, but also many Latino and Asian youths. The tension between the 'black consciousness' message of some rap groups and their predominantly white audiences has led to ever more strident claims of 'real' blackness, and accusations of being a sell-out or 'white boy's hero'. This ambiguity, or communicative biraciality, is actively repressed, of course, so that Lee can present Public Enemy as an unadulterated signifier of black radicalism. Yet as Professor Grif, a former member of Public Enemy, observed somewhat hyperbolically: 'We didn't attract black people; we had all-white audiences. Black people didn't want to hear what we had to say'.[15]

The presence of black and biracial icons in recent cinema point to the need to understand their role in our 'psychological structure'.[16] Some participants in this domain, such as 'Billy Hoyle', maintain an uneasy foothold in there a sort of perpetually re-negotiated 'antagonistic co-operation.' Others, such as 'Vito,' are still in denial of 'the true inter-relatedness of blackness and whiteness,' as Ralph Ellison once wrote, and their own close relationship with black or biracial cultural icons.[17] Vito is Spike Lee's representation of the 'mainstream' culture's secret fascination with (and promiscuous sampling or 'co-optation' of) black culture, yet continued denial of the political and cultural implications of that sampling. While Lee presents most whites as invaders in his proto-nationalist black community, director Shelton crafts a sort of sojourner role for the character Billy, who is grudgingly tolerated as a short-term guest in this 'black' domain.

But Anthony Drazan, director of *Zebrahead*, and actor Michael Rapaport construct a new cinematic type with Zack, the hero of this movie. The title indicates a 'psychological structure' that is half-white and half-black. Rather than being portrayed as either an invader or a temporary guest, Zack is represented as a permanent resident of an interracial domain. Zack is

10. 'Bob Marley's Zion: A Transracial "Blackman Redemption"', in Gregory Stephens, *On Racial Frontiers*, 1999, op. cit.

11. 'Interracial Dynamics in Pickup Basketball: An Auto-Ethnography'. Unpublished manuscript written for Mike Cole seminar, UCSD, 1995. Another 1990s ethnography of pickup basketball with interracial dynamics, also in the San Francisco Bay Area, is Jason Jimerson, 'Good Times and Good Games,' *Journal of Contemporary Ethnography*, vol. 25 no. 3, October 1996. A more cynical view of 'racial theatre' in sports is John Hoberman, *Darwin's Athletes: How Sport has Damaged Black America and Preserved the Myth of Race*, Houghton Mifflin, New York 1996. I have witnessed occasions in sports bars in which fans' allegiances become racialised. A classic example is Larry Bird and the Boston Celtics being perceived as a 'white' team, while the Detroit Pistons or Los Angeles Lakers were coded as 'black.' As with most racial mythologies, this one has a selective historical memory. For instance, the Celtics were the first NBA team to win a title with an all-black starting line-up, and it was a white Celtics guard, Bob Cousy, who pioneered the showtime, fast-break style now often thought of as black.

12. On 'imaginitive landscape', see: Gary Edgerton, 'Introduction: Genre Studies Issue,' *Journal of Popular Film and Television*, vol. 12 no. 2, Summer 1985, p53. *Re* black characters in 'white' narratives: Tasker (1993) and Guerrero (1993) and DeMott (1995) are examples of this tendency, *op. cit.* DeMott is a particularly egregious example of what David Hollinger has characterised as a 'game of competitive disillusionment', *Postethnic America*, Basic Books, New York 1995. Hollinger refers to white liberals or leftists competing to see who can be most cynical about the motives of whites who promote interracial common ground.

13. 'Romancing the Racial Frontier: Mediating Symbols in Cinematic Interracial Representation,' 1995/1996, *op cit.*

14. Claudio Esteva Fabregat, *Mestizaje in Ibero-America*, University of Arizona Press, Tucson 1994. Idealist interpretations of *mestizaje* ('mixed-race' culture and identity) have a long history in Ibero-America. On the origins of this tendency in Spain's hybrid roots (about a third of Spanish words are of North African origin), see Carlos Fuentes, *The Buried Mirror: Reflections on Spain and the New World*,

certainly not a new figure in American or West European cultures (Norman Mailer's 'The White Negro,' the 'two-tone' movement; the 'wigger' phenemonon).[18] But he is sufficiently original in cinematic terms for it to be necessary first to theorise his 'type' before we can understand the nature of his agency within this film.

A THEORY OF 'INHABITABLE' INTERRACIAL CINEMATIC TYPES

Zebrahead presents a rather original approach to inter-'racial' friendship and romance, in that it accents generational ties to black culture that prepare the 'crossing over.' Zack (Michael Rapaport) is from a Jewish family with long ties to the black community. Zack's grandfather founded a record store in downtown Detroit specialising in jazz and blues; his career as a concert promoter has provided him with interracial alliances. Both Zack and his father grew up working in this store, surrounded by black music and images of black musicians on the walls. So Zack and his black friends (and girlfriend) employ 'shared cultural codes'.[19]

Zack on his first date with Nikki, in his family's black music store in Detroit. "This is my home. This is me".

In a scene I will discuss momentarily, Zack's black girlfriend comments that 'you're more on the homeboy side than the whiteboy side'. His response is that he's not trying to be anything he's not: his cultural referents are in part a product of living in a 'predominantly black' city. Such a hybrid identity would only seem strange to those who have not witnessed the huge influence of 'black' culture on a broad range of today's urban youth. It is commonplace, for instance, to encounter Asian youth in urban centres such as San Francisco or London who walk, talk, dance, and make music in ways that are usually thought of as 'black'.[20] Zack, rather than being a 'wigger' or a wanna-be, is a representation of this cultural phenomenon who just happens to be white/Jewish. Perhaps predictably, his identity is centred on music: not only selling 'black' music in the family store, or the consumption of music, but also the creation of rap music with his black partner.

Music, like sports and dance, often functions as a 'third space' that cannot be defined by 'racial' boundaries. This third space is a 'racial frontier',[21] a shared but contested trans-racial domain with its own exploding demographic reality. The visibility of this phenomena is to some degree dependent upon location as well as ideology: it would be much easier in a city such as Chicago to still imagine the racial divide as almost impenetrable. But inter-'racial' or international couples in multinational crossroads such as London, Paris, Rio de Janeiro and San Francisco are ubiquitous. Aside from forming a trans-racial demographic, occupants of racial frontiers also form an interpretative community with an appetite for interracial or multi-ethnic representations. These mixed publics project their desire into a public sphere in which the 'mainstream' can no longer be accurately thought of as 'white.'

One can also think of this third space as a 'contact zone' where members of different cultures rub up against each other, or a border culture. However, *racial frontiers* are situated less on a line or divide between groups than on an expanding margin, which in many cases is becoming a new centre. The cultures created for, fought over and shared by multiracial audiences exist not only in physical space, but are also a cultural mythology and a 'psychic territory,' as Paul Gilroy's concept of a *Black Atlantic* suggests. The 'psychic territory' of racial frontiers is peopled by representations of various inter-cultural relations that together make up a trans-racial collective. In the language of depth psychology, these representations are objects in the 'psychological structures' of residents of racial frontiers.[22]

The psycho-social context of artforms with a multiracial audience points to the limitations of reductive models of cultural analysis, in which one dimension, such as gender, 'race', or power, is reified. Indeed, an understanding of the 'iconography' of multiracial contexts requires a cultural psychology that allows for the inherent poly-vocality or 'double-voicedness' of symbols produced in these settings. Jung's distinction between symbols and signs can be useful in analysing how 'black' music functions in this double-voiced mode. In *Psychological Types*, Jung suggests that *symbols* refer to something that can be known only in part. They are bipolar or double-voiced, while semiotic *signs* point towards something with a fixed meaning.[23] I want to tie this distinction between semiotic signs and poly-vocal symbols to Stanley Cavell's discussion of *iconographies*. At a core level movies work not with individuals but *types*: vamps, villains, rebels without causes, etc. When films do not develop their characters beyond these types, then we are left with stereotypes. However, a film's creators can succeed, to varying

Houghton Mifflin, New York 1992. The classic pro-mestizo Spanish-language text is Jose Vasconcelos, *The Cosmic Race/La raza cosmica*, John Hopkins, Baltimore (1925) 1997, a source of inspiration for Chicanos. Some of the most fascinating work on *mestizaje* is being done by Mexican feminists who are probing the life and legend of Malintzin, or Malinche, Cortes' interpreter and lover, who was the literal and figurative 'mother of the Mexican nation.' See for instance Fernanda Nunez Becerra, *La Malinche: de la Historia al Mito*, Instituto Nacional de Antropologia e Historia, Mexico 1996.

15. *Daily Texan*, 23.6.1990. On 'hero', see: Chuck D on KRS-One, in Mark Derby, 'Public Enemy: Confrontation', *Keyboard*, September 1990.

16. Moshe Halevi Spero, *Religious Objects as Psychological Structures*, University of Chicago Press, 1992. Jung also referred to psychological structures, as in the Terry Lectures at Yale University in 1938, when he remarked that religious texts are 'not only a sociological and historical phenomenon' but are also a function of the 'psychological structure of human personality.' *Psychology and*

Religion (CW11), Princeton UP, (1958)1969, p1.

17. For 'true inter-relatedness', see Ralph Ellison, 'Change the Joke and Slip the Yoke,' *Partisan Review* 25, Spring 1958, pp212-22;, p109. On 'antagonistic co-operation', see Ellison, 'The World and the Jug,' *Collected Essays*, Modern Library, 1995, p188.

18. 'Wigger' means 'white nigger' - an unfortunate choice of words, in my view, but certainly nothing new under the sun. Jack Kerouac and the Beats often romanticised black people and culture, without exhibiting much awareness of the repressive 'racial formations' Afro-Americans had to endure. The 'two-toned' movement was at its height around 1978-1980 in Great Britain, centred around an interracial 'ska' musical movement (not to be confused with the original 'ska' in Jamaica). The typical multiracial composition of the two-tone movement is evident in the documentary *Dance Craze*. This alliance between punks and British West Indians was pioneered by Bob Marley, who left a testimony to this fusion in his song 'Punky Reggae Party' (co-written with Lee 'Scratch' Perry).

19. Stuart Hall, 'Cultural Identity and Cinematic Representation,' *op. cit.*, p69.

degrees, in breathing life into these types. Then an *individuality* emerges on a middle ground between pure type and a living individual. Cavell speaks of these individualities as projecting 'ways of inhabiting a social role'. [24]

Cinematically, a type which has not been 'inhabited' is reduced to a stereotype, a frozen persona which functions as a semiotic sign with more or less pre-determined meaning. By contrast, a type which has been 'inhabited' becomes an 'individuality,' projected as a symbol which audiences read in multiple ways. We would tend to think of 'uninhabitable types' in connection with stereotyped representations of women, blacks, Asians, and Latinos. But it also applies to mixed race roles - witness the long life of the 'Tragic Mulatto' mythology.[25] And it can also be applied to certain sorts of white characters: John Singleton's use of Rapaport as a college freshman-turned-white-supremacist-terrorist (in *Higher Learning*) certainly fits the bill. The issue of representation - creating 'inhabitable types' - is crucial not just for people located clearly within one 'racial' group or another. More accurate representations are also needed for those who live on racial frontiers or cultural borderlands. Census figures show that nearly three million of US citizens are currently partners in an interracial marriage. The offspring of such mixed unions number in the tens of millions, confirming Albert Murray's claim that 'the mainstream is not white but mulatto'.[26] Within this context, it is inevitable that more films are attempting to devise a cinematic language capable of giving more accurate representation to life lived on racial frontiers.

In contrast to the impenetrable divide portrayed by Spike Lee and other racial romantics, some filmmakers have provided clues that the racial divide is in fact quite fluid. Their 'narrative and visual coding' suggests that there is a common culture, or 'shared cultural codes,' to repeat Stuart Hall's wording - a mutually accessible tradition upon which interracial relations can be based. Directors such as Mina Nair, whose work I have examined elsewhere,[27] or Anthony Drazan, in *Zebrahead*, present us with glimpses of an interracial common ground in domains such as music, sports, language and various icons of popular culture. Musical expression as an interracial and international *lingua franca* has been an especially dominant theme in many movies with interracial plots.

ZEBRAHEAD: 'BLACK' MUSIC AS AN AFROPEAN DOMAIN

Zebrahead is primarily about an interracial relationship in a Detroit high school, and is based upon director Anthony Drazan's memory of an interracial friendship. Yet according to Drazan, the film's final form leans on the improvisations of a largely non-professional, multi-racial cast.[28] Thus the film itself is in a real sense an inter-racial co-creation. As indicated earlier, Zack inherits his love of black music from his father and grandfather, who maintain a blues and soul record shop in downtown Detroit. Zack makes rap music with his best friend, Dee (DeShonn Castle), and sells tapes to his black classmates. He also works as a DJ. It is understandable in this context that Zack is in many ways culturally 'black'.

Zack selling rap cassettes made with his best friend Dee. He charges more to his white classmates.

Zack DJ-ing at a high school fashion show rehearsal for multiple audiences. "You can sample anything", he tells Nikki.

In the first of two scenes I want to analyse, Zack is mixing records in an auditorium for a fashion show rehearsal. As Zack stands behind his turntables,

20. Hence one criticism of the Oakland 'Ebonics' controversy (in which the school board defined 'black English' as a genetically inherited language) was the point that many non-black students spoke 'Ebonics,' while some black youth spoke 'standard' English. Oakland city council member Ignacio de la Fuente observed: 'Standard English derives its richness from the many cultures that are part of this nation. To deny African-American children ownership of standard English is to rob them of their cultural heritage one more time', *Oakland Tribune*, 17.1.1997. On Oakland/California's hysterical racial politics, see Todd Gitlin, *Twilight of Common Dreams*, Henry Holt, New York 1995.

21. Robert Park, *Race and Culture*, The Free Press, 1950, p91; Everett and Helen Hughes, 1952: *Where Peoples Meet: Racial and Ethnic Frontiers*, The Free Press, 1952, p19.

22. The concept of 'psychic territory' was articulated by Donald Winnicott in 'Morals and Education,' from *The Maturational Processes and the Facilitating Environment: Studies in the Theory of Emotional Development*, International Universities Press, Madison, CT 1965, p94. It has been

adapted by Moshe Halevi Spero, 1992, *op. cit*; Paul Gilroy, *The Black Atlantic: Modernity and Double Consciousness*, Harvard UP, 1993. On the 'contact zone', see: Mary Louise Pratt, 'Linguistic Utopias,' in *The Linguistics of Writing*, Nigel Fabb and Derek Attridge (eds), Methuen, New York 1987; 'Criticism in the Contact Zone: Decentering Community and Nation,' in *Critical Theory, Cultural Politics, and Latin American Narrative*, Steven Bell, Albert Le May, and Leonard Orr (eds), Notre Dame University Press, 1993. Among many scholars writing about border cultures, one of the most influential in American cultural studies has been Gloria Anzaldua, *Borderlands/La Frontera: The New Mestiza*, Spinsters/ Aunt Lute, San Francisco 1987.

23. C.G. Jung, *Psychological Types*. Princeton UP, 1971, pp473 fn.

24. Stanley Cavell, *The World Viewed*, Harvard UP, 1979, p33.

25. On 'tragic mulattos', see: Werner Sollors, *Neither Black Nor White but Both*, 1997, *op. cit*; Donald Bogle, *Toms, Coons, Mulattoes, Mammies and Bucks: an interpretive history of Blacks in American Films*, Continuum, New York (1973)1989.

he is approached by Nikki (N'Bushe Wright), the new (black) girl in town. Asked what he is playing he says: 'Could be Frank Zappa, could be Captain Beefheart'. 'Captain Beefheart?' she asks sceptically. He 'scratches' the record and cuts in a new theme, whereupon Nikki smiles. 'I know that, my mother listens to that'. 'You like that?' Zack asks. 'Yeah.' She throws up her arms and starts dancing. In the background we see models prancing on a runway - Asian, Italian and black. More students approach Zack's table. 'Check this out,' says Zack, dropping in a hoe-down fiddle on top of the same drums. Zack's partner Dee is euphoric at this mix, but Nikki, sceptical, gives Zack a look and turns away. 'You're making faces - now hold on, hold on,' Zack pleads.

At this moment a black student with Malcolm-style glasses and 'funky dreads' launches into a tirade. This nationalist (Al) lives in a rich white neighbourhood. The sight and sound of this white boy mixing a fiddle with rap beats sets him off: 'Perpetrator, that's all you are, a perpetrator! You don't know anything about the drums, the drums are *African*. You went into Africa, took our music, took our people, now here in America, you're gonna take rap? Bull!' Zack drops some heavenly voices into the mix, and looks at Nikki meaningfully. 'Puccini,' he says. 'Puccini?' she repeats, before catching a groove again. The models' movements become more stylised. Another black student named Nut takes offence and begins to 'dis' Zack: 'Weak mother-fuckin'-ass beats ... He needs to go to the Simpson show with that shit. Punk ass nigger caint DJ.'

"The drums are African!" Zack's antagonistic audience, the rich black nationalist Al (Abdul Hassan Sharif).

As the models continue to improvise a semi-classical dance, Nikki is beaming. *'You can sample anything,'* Zack tells her. The camera cuts to Nikki's face, her eyes down. She looks up at him in a new way as he repeats: 'Anything!'

On the surface, there's not much going on here, just a bunch of kids goofing off, listening to music and talking trash. But this scene is dense in symbolic interaction. The music itself structures this slice of the racial frontier, functioning simultaneously as a poly-vocal symbol of commonality and as a semiotic sign of unbridgeable difference.

There are two main activities going on in this scene: playing records and a fashion show rehearsal. The music is there in theory to support the rehearsal, but it is the contested terrain through which everything in the room flows. The fact that a white guy is mixing the music offends some people, while for most it is a non-issue. There are four audiences who react to Zack and the music he is playing in four distinctly different ways. First are the models, whose movements are structured by the music Zack plays. The second audience is a large group of onlookers, both black and white, who are enjoying the music and the performance of the DJ, and also seem unconcerned with 'racial' dynamics. The third audience is the black youths who object vociferously to 'their' music being 'stolen' or co-opted by a 'white boy.' Zack's fourth and preferred audience is Nikki. We sense that Nikki is intrigued by the fact that it is a white guy playing music which she associates with primarily 'black' referents. But she is certainly not offended.

Significantly, both black antagonists 'go off' when Zack introduces 'white' music into the mix. It is at the instant that Zack mixes in a hillbilly violin that Al rants about the African-ness of the drums. 'Black' music is assumed to be a racial property that can only be distorted or destroyed by whites. The explicit comparison of the 'borrowing' of the drums with the stealing of slaves will sound familiar to anyone who participated in black-oriented popular culture during the late twentieth century. During this period many cultural icons became racially coded, and there was intense conflict over attempts to construct or claim trans-racial symbols. This context amplifies the meaning of Nut's comment, at the moment when Zack mixes 'white' Puccini with 'black' drums, that Zack 'needs to go to the Simpson show with that shit.' The Simpsons were manifestly white (or 'yellow'), yet young blacks took note of Bart Simpson's anti-establishment attitude and attire and began wearing 'Bart is Black' T-shirts. The *latent* content, at least of Bart's behaviour, was claimed to have been drawn from or modelled on black sources. Director Drazan allows the anti-white characters like 'Al' and 'Nut' to introduce a degree of oppositional dialogism into a movie which clearly doubts the validity of 'racialised' readings of cultural symbols and personal relationships. The racial commentary of these black characters is presented as a marginal if inescapable component of the part of the racial frontier being dramatised. Most of the students we see do not agree with their racial essentialism, in which claims of cultural superiority and social victimisation are paired. But

26. Albert Murray, *The Omni-Americans: New Perspectives on Black Experience & American Culture*, Dutton, New York 1970, p112.

27. Gregory Stephens, 'Romancing the Racial Frontier', *Spectator*, 1995/1996, *op. cit.* On 'visual coding,' see: Tom Schatz, *Hollywood Genres, Formulas, Filmmaking, and the Studio System* Random House, New York, p22.

28. Taped telephone interview with Drazan, March 1995.

they cannot be dismissed or tuned out completely, if for no other reason than that their racialism poses a threat to the uneasy existing equilibrium in this multiracial student body.

Zack seems to tune out this racialised commentary. His performance has been directed to an audience of one: Nikki. By 'sampling' both African and European musical fragments, he has created what we might call an 'Afropean' collage. His musical collage is meant to demonstrate that 'black' and 'white' musical/ cultural forms can co-exist in the same space. Zack clearly intends for Nikki to understand that there is an interpersonal analogue to the hybrid aural space he is 'occupying.' His comment, 'You can sample anything,' when read along with the soundtrack he has re-created, suggests that, just as music is inevitably hybrid, with different traditions cross-fertilising each other, so are human relations capable of being mixed in an endless variety of ways. Yet there are limits to this hybridity, as is evident even in the way that Nikki reacts to his mixing. She is willing to accept Frank Zappa or Puccini, when combined with the 'black' drums. But the introduction of a hillbilly fiddle causes her to instinctively turn around as if to walk away.

In the last scene I will examine, Zack's musical/cultural 'promiscuity' convinces Nikki to see him romantically. They go out on a date, which begins in Zack's domain, riding in his jeep and playing his music. As they drive down a Detroit street and Zack clowns, Nikki laughs, saying: 'You're different than what I expected ... You're more on the homeboy than the whiteboy side.' Zack explains: 'This is Detroit, you know. This is where I live. I may not live downtown, but this is still a predominantly black city.' He shrugs, and adds: 'This is me, though. This is who I am.' As if his identity as a 'Zebrahead' (Afropean) can only be fully articulated through music, he pops a rap song into the jeep's cassette player. 'I made this with Dee,' he says.

This segment provides a good illustration of the multiple uses to which rap music, in particular, can be put. In *Grand Canyon*, rap is used to signal a *black* threat to a white interloper in an urban domain. By contrast, Drazan, and his lead actor Rapaport, use rap as a mediating tool, to facilitate interracial inter-subjectivity: both personal interaction and cultural co-creation. Furthermore, rap is not isolated from other forms of music. The sequence I am analysing here ends when Zack takes Nikki into his family store, 'Saul's Medley Land.' Here Zack puts on the Johnny Mathis record recommended by his father. Nikki soaks in all the pictures, murmuring 'so much music ... history'. They kiss under the gaze of a gallery of black musicians.

I want to comment on two 'mediating symbols' which structure the jeep scene. The first is the image of the 'Zebrahead' driving his black date through a 'black city' while listening to 'black' music made in fact by an 'interracial' team. The 'zebra' is 'driving' not only his jeep, and his date, but also the film's narrative. Yet the 'zebra' is also being driven by a context in which it is not clear where the boundaries of 'black' culture and community should

"You're more on the homeboy side than the white boy side", Nikki tells Zack on their first date.

29. Angela Davis, Speech to the 'Students of Color Conference' at University of California - San Diego, Spring 1993. On the symbolism of the 'zebrahead,' see Bernard Weinraub, 'Little Film That Could: A Hollywood Cinderella Goes to the Festival'. *New York Times*, 18.8.1992, C13. Jung speaks of 'mediatory symbols' as arising from 'The confrontation of the two positions' which 'creates a living, third thing' - i.e., a 'third space' of synthesis. He emphasises that this synthesis cannot occur so long as the opposites are 'kept apart ... for the purpose of avoiding conflict'. Therefore, symbolic interaction through mediatory symbols presupposes both conflict and co-creation; 'The Transcendent Function,' in *The Structure and Dynamics of the Psyche*, Collected Works 8, Princeton UP, 1969, p90.

be drawn. Zack wants to demonstrate his familiarity with 'black' cultural forms, and to insist that he is not trying to be something that he is not. He is participating in a multiracial call-and-response with the cultural tools available to him in the socio-cultural environment in which he has been raised. So the 'zebra' is not only a sign for interracial couples or mulattos, but a symbol for a biracial or *Afropean* domain: a portion of the racial frontier in which white people are neither centred nor excluded, as Angela Davis has said.[29]

The second 'mediatory symbol' is Zack's choice of the family record store as the space in which to romance Nikki, and the use of a Johnny Mathis song to set a romantic mood. Again, symbols of 'black culture' are used to carve out space in which interracial romance can occur: to legitimise this space as an interracial domain, and to set a mood in which both partners feel at home. Yet the 'black culture' Zack uses has been partially structured by non-whites: his grandfather packaged black music for the public, while Zack not only markets but co-creates this music.

My analysis of *Zebrahead* has been shaped by two different life experiences. During the 1980s I was a songwriter for a multiracial dance band, which inclined me to see Zack as a broadly realistic character. But when I taught this film, some students did not share my view of Zack's social realism. They were more inclined to 'buy into' the white supremacist character Rapaport played in John Singleton's *Higher Learning*. That many students found Singleton's hyperbolic film more 'realistic' than Drazan's debut told me that we are still largely unfamiliar with the *Zebrahead* type. Zack is in fact fairly common *in the culture*. But the images of the culture which we get through mass-mediated forums such as film are so saturated with a binary racial mythology that they effectively serve to screen out most representations of cultural hybridity.

Zack's claim to a biracial cultural space was interpreted as mere co-optation by a significant portion of this film's critical audience. The very fact that Zack is 'driving' this story is offensive to some white liberals, who read this not as evidence of the emergence of an interracial cultural domain, but as yet more proof that filmic representations of interracial relations continue to be centred on the agency of white males.[30]

One can sympathise with this argument, since many film-makers do not have faith that their audiences can identify with 'minority' themes unless they are mediated through 'white' eyes, unless a white character acts as a familiar referent on which to hang the narrative. Nevertheless this criticism is inadequate in relation to *Zebrahead*. As I have argued, Zack, the symbolic 'zebra', not only 'drives' this story, he is also being driven by its black and biracial constituents - especially the music. To characterise the agency of this character as merely 'white' is to remain blind to the inter-subjective and interracial (though 'predominantly black') nature of the culture in which he has been raised.

Zack's statement, 'You can sample anything,' is double-voiced, too. A reductive reading would view this as evidence of a white boy 'co-opting' black music. White 'borrowings' of black musical forms have a long history, from blackface to Elvis Presley, and in truth have often been a form of theft, since the 'sampling' usually did not result in either credit or payment for the black originators.[31] Yet to read Zack's words only as evidence of 'co-optation' would reflect a very narrow view of sampling. Popular music and cinema both incessantly sample, borrow, or quote from their antecedents. 'Black' styles of music have been particularly hybrid: from jazz' heavy use (and deconstruction of) 'tin pan alley' pop tunes, to rap's sampling from (and reconstruction of) rock and funk riffs. To suggest that white artists in this domain are only capable of theft, or co-optation, not only ignores the hybrid nature of the domain, but it also re-inscribes another form of racial mythology: that whites 'have no culture'. This would be to ascribe to all white artists a 'tourist mentality,' in which they move among cultures, borrowing or stealing as they go, without being rooted in any. This critique has often been directed at white artists who draw heavily from African and Ibero-American music, such as Paul Simon and David Byrne. (Black musicians associated with Simon in the documentary *Born at the Right Time* reject this critique as a denial of their own agency.) However tempting it may be to project this 'culture vulture' role onto a 'white' racial collective, this (stereo)type is not *inhabitable* for any 'white' actor with long-term experience in multiracial cultural and social contexts.

There is a double standard at work here. We may praise a black artist who samples heavily from his or her predecessors, saying that 'imitation is

30. Janet Maslin, 'A Racial Chameleon in a Hidebound World,' *New York Times*, 8.10.1992, C17, p21. My comments about *Zebrahead*'s critical reception are also based on discussion with academic peers. I have heard similar criticisms of the romances between white men and Asian women in *Come See the Paradise* and *Joy Luck Club*.

31. Eric Lott, *Love and Theft: Blackface Minstrelsy and the American Working Class*, OUP, New York 1993. W.T. Lhamon Jr. takes a more positive view of the interracial legacy of blackface in *Raising Cain: Blackface Performance from Jim Crow to Hip Hop*, Harvard University Press, 1998.

the sincerest form of flattery'. Yet we often reflexively dismiss a white artist doing the same thing as a 'cultural imperialist.' Recognising, once again, the partial truth of this perspective, I want to suggest other uses of 'sampling'. While some of those sampling cultural fares may view it as a 'taste test,' others may digest what they have sampled, may incorporate it into their cultural diet and their psychological structure. Sampling can be a temporary diversion, or a permanent integration. We should also ask: sampled into what? Certainly many white artists have 'sampled' black styles into a 'white' frame of reference, without either paying respect to their sources, or changing their Eurocentrism. Yet *Zebrahead* references a parallel history that requires an alternative reading: Zack samples a hybrid 'black' music into a biracial collage, does this in a multiracial context, and from a multi-generational perspective. The zebra's stripes are visible, so that respect is paid where respect is due. Yet the Afropean whole is something more than the sum of its parts.

A non-reductive analysis of interracial 'sampling' requires an understanding of popular culture and interracial communication as inter-subjective arenas. Ragnar Rommetveit has described inter-subjectively created forms of communication as a 'temporarily shared social reality'. Such a style of symbolic interaction 'aims at transcendence of the "private" worlds of the participants' by setting up 'states of inter-subjectivity'. Rommetveit argues that language employed in such contexts cannot be seen as using 'a fixed repertory of shared "literal" meanings', but rather employs something closer to 'negotiated drafts of contracts'. [32]

What I find appealing about Rommetveit's definition is the distinction between public and private life-worlds, and the transitory nature of shared social realities. To speak of the impossibility of privileging a mono- 'racial' interpretation of 'two-toned' symbols or texts, as I have done, is not to elide the continuing reality of 'racial formations',[33] nor to attempt merely to substitute an interracial semiotics for a racial mythology. My sketch of the pervasive use of 'black' music in American film is meant, rather, to insist on a both/and approach to sampling. Historically speaking, we have no 'pure' cultural sources. The sources we sample, as Zack's example shows, can play many roles at once: they can be socially constructed as 'racial,' given credit as 'black,' and yet employed for inter-racial or non-racial ends.

Just because audiences use the symbols of music and film in order to temporarily transcend their 'private worlds,' does not mean necessarily that the psychological reality of this private sphere is de-racialised. Yet when such 'temporarily shared social realities' are re-created repeatedly, over time, the language of race will prove inadequate to describe the consequences. These trans-racial realities may be temporary, but their continued re-construction also means that social, psychological, and material structures will emerge to 'house' these temporary trans-racial realities. Institutional structures will be built which produce and distribute interracial discourses. These multiracial formations are our co-creations, whether we want to take

32. Ragnar Rommetveit & Rolf Blakar, *Studies of Language, Thought and Verbal Communication*, Academic Press, London 1979, pp94, 97.

33. Omi and Winant, *Racial Formations*, 1994, *op. cit*; Gates 1988, *op. cit.*

34. Paul Gilroy, *Small Acts: Thoughts on the Politics of Black Cultures*, Serpent's Tail, London 1993, p9.

credit or assign blame. Multiracial audiences have a 'claim to ownership' on interracial culture that presents a historic opportunity.[34] In making such a claim, members of multiracial audiences have an opportunity to develop multi-centred forms of identity. For the multi-centred self, 'race' may be only one of several forms of community to which one claims allegiance and with which one communicates.

The work of international directors such as Mina Nair, or British directors such as Isaac Julien (in *Young Soul Rebels*) has given us a clearer picture than most North American cinema as to the role that music can play in constructing inter- 'racial' and multinational alliances. Drazan and his cast in *Zebrahead* have given us a sample of how the struggle for a post-racial language and culture is already underway, but often beneath our 'radar,' in North America.

FORMING MINORITARIAN COMMUNITIES: NOMADIC ETHICS FOR THE POSTCOLONIAL WORLD

Syed Manzurul Islam

Do we have any alternative to the current bipolar oscillation between naked individualism and authoritarian collectivity? Should the formation of a community always entail a reduction of difference and a static mode of organisation? Can we envisage a democratic community where subjects belonging to a multiplicity of difference can form a collectivity of mobile alliances? The idea of a minoritarian community is an affirmative response to these questions. Perhaps, this is a utopian idea, but if so then all visions of a future, daring to think otherwise, of desiring a community to come, are utopian. If not, are we not bound to condemn ourselves to remain where we are, caught in the static monotony of the status quo, leaving in place so many unjust relationships and apparatuses of power? However, the desire for a community to come need not be whimsical, or wilfully arbitrary. On the contrary, since the community to come cannot be legitimised on the authority of the habitual, a taken-for-granted conception of truth and rules of conduct, it requires a most patient and rigorous mode of thought, so that its infinitive tense can be activated, on the one hand, by locating its condition of possibility on a set of clearly thought out ontological presuppositions and, on the other hand, by grounding its practice on a set of scrupulously just and upright ethical criteria. These considerations take us to nomadic ethics. In fact, we cannot even begin to answer the question: 'how to form minoritarian communities?' without the presupposition of nomadic ethics. For minoritarian communities are nothing other than nomadic ethics in practice. This is a well-known position held by the schizoanalytical duo Gilles Deleuze and Félix Guattari. Yet, what is not clear is the relationship that nomadic ethics bears with the historically locatable nomads and minoritarian communities with the concrete minorities of our time. If nomadic ethics are to serve as the imperative for the formation of minoritarian communities in the postcolonial world, then these relationships need to be spelt out clearly. This essay is prompted by this task.

Any close engagement with Deleuze and Guattari's work reveals that their conception of nomadic ethics not only has a diverse provenance but spreads out onto an equally diverse mode of articulation. Given the task of this piece, my particular take on their work is focused on that line of articulation that concerns an ethics of encounter between difference, which, I think, is best exemplified in their conception of *aparallel evolution*. Again, the orientation of this piece drives me to pursue an aspect of Deleuze-Guattarian ethics that owes its origin to Spinoza's works and remains consistent with it. Furthermore, and beyond Deleuze and Guattari, in order to underscore the conception of the minoritarian community as a democratic collectivity based both on the mutuality of affection and the reflexive judgement of reason I need to visit Spinoza's work. So my usage of the idea of nomadic ethics would be just as much that of Spinoza as it is of Deleuze and Guattari. Yet this is not all, for the consideration of the location of historical nomads will add Ibn Khaldûn's thought to it. In fact, Khaldûn's work on nomads will pre-figure the nature of nomadic ethics. On a different level, my doubts about the efficacy of nomadic ethics in performing the task I want to assign to it, i.e. the formation of a minoritarian community in the postcolonial world, would require of me to subject it to a strategic/practical critique. Consequently, I will propose a modification to it by drawing on certain insights from Levinas's work. Perhaps, owing to the varied orientations of these ideas in their original habitats, their co-mingling may seem strangely paradoxical. Yet, the kind of nomadic ethics that I am interested in does work precisely through the negotiations of paradoxes. Not an unknowing paradox but a paradox that is reflexively aware of itself in its task of tracing a strategic route of arriving at the most practical state of the ideal.

For me, most importantly, the task of setting out the condition of a minoritarian community through the practice of nomadic ethics acquires value only against the persistence of exclusionary and absolutist models of inter-subjective relationship or community such as the national state formation and its relatively micro expressions found in the paranoiac sense of communities fixated upon their imaginary essences and the refusal of encounter. In other words, the project of a minoritarian community is proposed as a counter-thrust to sedentary fixities of state, nationalism, racial and cultural manicheanism, and the rigidity and the unity of the self. Yet if the project of minoritarian community were limited to a simple opposition to sedentary formations alone, then a binary logic would be left in place. Of course, without the differential structure which invariably partakes in the binary staging of arguments - as do our distinction between sedentary and nomadic formations - thought itself would be impossible. Yet the binary staging of an argument does not necessarily entail a subscription to binary logic. Hence, the imperatives of a minoritarian community - that is to say, nomadic ethics - cannot simply be a critical, deconstructive or counter-discursive move to sedentary formations. By breaking through the sedentary boundaries, it must not engage in a mimetic move to re-install binary logic, but proceed 'as if' this logic is redundant and move towards an affirmation of values where it ceases to be important to the way we form communities. Historically, at this juncture, despite the widespread presumption of an epochal shift - either with excited celebration or cries of despair - of a solid world melting in the air, of a world of simulacrum, of a capital that has gone triumphantly global, of proliferating techno-cyborgs and hyper-space, of roaming trans-national cosmopolitans, the old distinction between centre and margin, included and excluded, majority and minority, powerful and powerless remain as intractable as ever. However, this is not to say that these presumptions are false, rather that - irrespective of the extent of their occurrence - structures of domination have not disappeared. We still live in a world where many of the minorities of the age of modernity - racially, culturally, economically and politically subjugated others of a Euro-centric world - continue to find themselves in a minority location. Hence, a deliberate task of forming an ethical community is required where the question of justice for minorities is addressed but without re-producing the old majoritarian power structure.

Finally then, in order to sustain a mutual complication between historical location and the ideal of ethical imperatives, which is required if we want to make this exercise relevant to the Postcolonial world, I would engage in a four-pronged move involving nomads and nomadic ethics, and minorities and minoritarian communities. Only by proceeding in this way, I believe, we can conceive of an ethical thought measured by the practical question of justice, and a politics of right safeguarded by ethical considerations.

* * *

Let me begin with the nomads. But immediately we hit upon the dilemma: how can we know anything about the nomadic mode of life, let alone define it, since nomads do not speak in 'our' arena of conversation? Recently - owing to the impact of work done by postcolonial critics and critical anthropologists - we have become familiar with these questions. But sometime back, Arnold Toynbee - while playing the grand narrator of human destiny - became aware of the dilemma of any act of representation where the other subjects - the object of discourse - remained silent. Writing on the location of nomads in the unfolding of history, he observed: 'History of the nomads has been written almost entirely by observers belonging to one or other of the sedentary societies with which the nomads have happened to collide'.[1] No one writing about nomads, whatever innocence or noble intentions might inform their projects, can avoid this irony. Bruce Chatwin, feeling 'homelessness' in England and dreaming of 'homecoming' in the wonderland of other places, goes out in search of nomadic habitats. This takes him to Australia, to the outback of Aboriginal 'songliners', about which he writes: 'My reason for coming to Australia was to try to learn for myself, and not from other men's books'.[2] He would discover how the Aboriginals, as they went out on their dream-time walkabouts, and in the course of their labyrinthine wandering, mapped the continent with their musical refrains. Yet, without being aware of the irony of his gesture, Chatwin tells his readers that his insights into the 'songliners' came from Arkady Volchok, an Australian of Russian origin, 'who was mapping the sacred sites of the

1. Arnold J. Toynbee, *A Study of History*, Vol. 3, Oxford University Press, London 1934, p396.

2. Bruce Chatwin, *The Songlines*, Picador, London 1988, p14.

Aboriginals'.[3] Surely, what a perverse layering of representations we have here: Chatwin mapping novelistically Arkady's anthropological mapping of the Aboriginals' supposedly originary musical mapping. This raises the ethical dilemma of writing about nomads - where the position of the interlocutor, if not absent, is only provided by an ethnographic informer - which leads one to deal solely with the representations of representations. Yet, saying nothing about nomads is not a way out of this ethical dilemma, as it requires a much more complex response - which, I hope, will be apparent as we proceed through the essay. However, with this paradox in mind, I want to begin by attending to certain ways of mapping the composition of the nomadic mode of life, which might serve us as a model for nomadic ethics.

3. *Ibid.*, p94.

* * *

1375: suddenly cutting himself loose from the dynastic power politics of the Kashbah (fortified city) - of which he was a true Machiavellian prince - Ibn Khaldûn retreated deep into the solitude of the Sahara. Given sanctuary by a nomadic warlord at the citadel of Qalat Ibn Salamah, the would-be composer of universal history - perhaps looking far into the silvery shimmer of the sand dunes into which the Bedouin hordes would suddenly appear as a galloping organism - set out to shape his *Al Muqaddimah*, the finest piece of philosophy of history produced during the Middle Ages. But I do not want to talk about the life of the great Maghrebi historian - whose ancestors were the nomads of the Arabian desert, now exiled by the Christian *Reconquista* of 'Moorish' Spain- but about his analytic distinction between *Umran Haradi* and *Umran Badawi*. In other words, the distinction between sedentary and nomadic modes of life.

For Khaldûn, *Umran Hadari* never simply designates a sedentary settlement tied to the land or enclosed by the city walls, rather it results from the juridical and the pedagogical apparatuses functioning within the ambit of state formation. Frozen into stasis and 'oppressed by the law of restriction' the sedentary populace is moulded by the imperial state into, as Khaldûn says, domesticated gazelles, buffaloes and donkeys.[4] How these figures of animals remind one of Zarathustra's reactive menagerie of camels, apes and asses! Strangely, for so many, the lure of sedentary life becomes irresistible, perhaps because it offers seductive compensations in the form of increased luxury and the refinement of art and knowledge. However, sedentary people not only lose their fortitude but also are increasingly forced into 'remoteness from goodness'.[5] In order to understand why such a cruel destiny - despite all the apparent success of city life, civility and a powerful state - befalls sedentary people, it is essential to pay attention to the concept of *Asabîyah*. The loss of fortitude and the distance from 'goodness' that sedentary people suffer, argues Khaldûn, are the consequences of their loss of *Asabîyah*. Although *Asabîyah* is generally translated as 'group feeling' or

4. Ibn Khaldûn, *The Muqaddimah*, Franz Rosenthal (trans), Routledge and Kegan Paul, London 1967, p95.

5. *Ibid.*, p94.

6. Yves Lacoste, *Ibn Khaldun: The Birth and the Past of the Third World*, David Macey (trans), Verso, London 1984, p100.

7. Khaldûn, *The Muqaddimah*, 1967, *op. cit.*, p118.

8. *Ibid.*, p119.

9. *Ibid.*, p114.

'solidarity', it is also understood to be 'the vitality of the state' and 'the life force of the people' or '*Lebenskraft*'.[6] But before we can fully appreciate the concept of *Asabîyah*, it is necessary to explain the nature of *Umran Badawi* (the Bedouin or nomadic mode of life).

The nomadic mode of life, for Khaldûn, is linked dialectically to sedentary life both as its opposite and its precursor. If sedentary life is grounded in the stasis of the city, of the empire, of the body of the despot, then nomadic life seeks out the empty spaces of deserts and uninterrupted movement. Khaldûn writes: 'All customary activities of the Bedouins lead to wandering and movement. This is the antithesis of and negation of stationariness'.[7] Movement allows the nomads to live without the 'laws of government, institution', which leads, argues Khaldûn, to 'a state of anarchy'.[8] However, nomadic anarchy does not remain confined within the anonymous dunes of the desert, but spills over into the static tranquillity of sedentary regions. Having 'no homelands … and no fixed place', the nomads, writes Khaldûn, treat:

> All regions and places [as] the same … Therefore, they do not restrict themselves to possession of their own and neighbouring regions. They do not stop at the borders of their horizon. They swarm across distant zones.[9]

Despite their restless movement, anarchy, and destruction of the fruits of civilisation that sedentary people have built, Khaldûn treats *Umran Badawi* as possessing 'goodness.' Surely, this is an extraordinary position to be taken by a man of high learning and civil refinement, who spent much of his life in the sedentary politics of the Andalucian and Maghrebi courts. Khaldûn does not harbour any romantic fascination for the nomads, and having depicted their primitiveness and savagery, he continues to attribute 'goodness' to their way of life. Behind such a positive evaluation lies the singular belief - which Khaldûn never tired of repeating - that of all people it is the nomads who are in full possession of *Asabîyah*. Imbued with *Asabîyah* as if drunk on the elixir of life, the nomads not only display extraordinary fortitude - or, when least expected, storm out of the desert like 'beasts of prey' - but are capable of undertaking the most arduous of collective actions. For *Asabîyah* is a dynamic force that enables lonely nomads to release their power of affection, thus drawing the multitude into a collective assemblage. Sedentary civilisation, as it develops by according primacy to the individual, loses its vitality, because, argues Khaldûn, it is 'denied the affection caused by group feeling'.[10]

10. *Ibid.*, p99.

Whatever else *Asabîyah* may be, its most telling expression lies in its role as a political dynamic of collective power. Hence, argues Khaldûn, the nomadic formation is capable of founding great sedentary empires, states or dynasties. Historically, many nomadic tribes have indeed founded great imperial states on the strength of their *Asabîyah*. However, these forms and institutions of sedentary power politics do not agree with the nomadic *Asabîyah*. If a nomadic tribe acquires such powers, it not only becomes remote from 'goodness' but eventually also loses its capacity to sustain that kind of power. Despotic and royal authorities, with their demands for obedience to the law, and the consequent homogenisation and flattening out of difference, produce a form of power that never fails to be anathema to the nomadic *Asabîyah*. Left to themselves, the nomads form collective assemblages of democratic organisations, whose parts are never subsumed into one monolithic authority, yet are harnessed into a powerful composition that maintains a mobile and differential alliance between parts and whole. Khaldûn explains it in the process of expounding the mode of authority corresponding to nomadic and sedentary formations:

> Leadership means being a chieftain [nomadic formation], and the leader is obeyed, but he has no power to force others to accept his rulings. Royal authority [sedentary formation] means superiority and the power to rule by force.[11]

11. *Ibid.*, p108.

What is fascinating about Khaldûn's work is that despite being more than six hundred years old, his picture of the nomadic mode of life appears contemporary. Yet Khaldûn's nomads were always tied to the barren landscape of the desert, and it is as if their particular mode of life could only have emerged in response to its harsh challenge. It seems that without a Sahara, a Kalahari or a Gobi there would be no nomads - as if dry sand were the prerequisite or determining factor of a wandering life. Given the fact that Khaldûn only knew the camel-nomads of the Sahara, it was perhaps inevitable that he couldn't conceive of nomads without the spatial inscription of the desert.

Yet, despite providing a link between modernity and classical humanism, and despite inaugurating the modern materialist interpretation of history, Ibn Khaldûn is not a name that Western historiographers are familiar with - except a handful, amongst whom, surely, Arnold Toynbee has been the most prominent. Toynbee endorses much of what Khaldûn says about the nomads, without, however, judging their mode of life as closest to 'goodness' or seeing nomadic life as a dynamic formation because of its full possession of *Asabîyah*. For Toynbee, nomadic life simply reflects 'the tour de force' of geographical adaptation, where human ingenuity has devised a mode of survival in extreme circumstances. In spite of his admiration for the nomads' triumph in adversity, Toynbee, steeped in an 'Orientalism', which refuses to acknowledge dynamism in non-western societies, arranges them among his taxonomy of 'arrested civilisations'. Hence the nomadic 'tour de force', despite its virtuosity and sheer endurance, can only be, as Toynbee says, 'a feat in the realm of statics and not in the realm of dynamics'.[12] Yet, Toynbee has extended the nomadic range beyond the desert. He writes of the Polynesians who took up the challenge of the ocean, the Esquimaux who

12. Arnold J. Toynbee, *A Study of History*,1934, *op. cit.*

took up the challenge of the ice and the tribal bands of the grassy steppes: all nomads in their different ways. For Toynbee, the uncharted surface of the sea, the empty horizon of the snow-covered Arctic, and the endless waves of grass on the steppe are equivalent to the sand dunes of the desert. Since they are all nomadic habitats, their physical challenge gives rise to - irrespective of the specific nature of their demands - a very similar wandering mode of life. Yet nomadic wanderings, contends Toynbee, are neither random nor wayward. Rather, in their motions, they are pulled along the same repetitious orbit as if stuck in the same groove of the vinyl, keeping them 'moving perpetually within these limits'.[13]

13. *Ibid.*, p395.

If Toynbee's paradox of the dynamics of the static formation - where nothing seems to happen amidst a cornucopia of happenings - appears familiar to us, it is due to a long Orientalist tradition, whose general tenor can be glimpsed from the following extravagant but authoritative metaphor coined by Hegel: 'the repetition of the same majestic ruin'.[14] Yet, Deleuze and Guattari's 'affective' or 'minor' readings of Toynbee transform the paradox of the static-dynamic movement of the nomads into an intensive diagram of becoming. In *A Thousand Plateaus*, they write: 'Toynbee is profoundly right to suggest that the nomad is on the contrary he *who does not move* ... Of course, the nomad moves ... but in intensity'.[15] I will return to their writings later.

14. G.W.Hegel, *The Philosophy of History,* J.Sibree (trans), Dover Publication, New York 1956, p106.

15. Gilles Deleuze and Félix Guattari, *A Thousand Plateaus,* Brian Massumi (trans), The Athlone Press, London 1988, p381.

We must remember that Ibn Khaldûn's approbation of nomadic virtues is not based on an imaginary mode of life but abstracted from lives of the nomads of his own historical time. Now, we live in a time when the nomads, at least in Khaldûn's sense, have almost disappeared. Even though one still finds the Tuaregs tracking the sand dunes of the Sahara, they are no longer the force that once menaced the sedentary citadels of the Maghreb. The sedentary mode of life has brought most nomads - the camel-riders of the desert, the canoeists of the open sea, the horsemen of the steppe, or the barefoot-wanderers of the bush - within the orbit of its static organisation. The *polis* has finally triumphed over the *nomos* but in the shape of state formation - either the imperial states of former times or the nation states of the present. If the nomads have disappeared, then why bother about them? Is it simply because of the exotic fascination of the long lost savages? After all, Europe has had a long history of entertaining the strange virtues of noble savages who always lived in other times and other places. In a really cynical mood one could easily say: now that the nomads are dead, long live the nomads.

Yet, I believe that the nomads can serve as a model for an ethical practice for our own time. I believe this not because I think that the globalisation of capital with its trans-national movement, has made nomads of all of us, nor because of the techno-cultural phenomenon of what has been termed as 'postmodern'. We would do well to remember that the nomads were at the margin, beyond the walls of the citadel, located as the minority others. Yet, whilst the nomads of uncompromising landscapes and harsh places might have disappeared, quasi-nomadic living conditions are still thriving at the margins of modern nation-states, whose ex-centric subjects often dwell in the heart of the metropolis. Perhaps aspects of these minority lives resemble something of the nomadic lives of the past, but this does not preclude the nomadic becoming of all; indeed, the nomadic becoming of all is needed for the formation of a minoritarian community. For that a deliberate ethical practice is required. However, if we are simply content with a model of nomadic virtue as a matter of aesthetic sensibility - like Bruce Chatwin's hero Arkady, who is fascinated by the nomadic *Songlines* because of 'the beauty of this concept'[16] - then we are bound to reproduce once more the exoticism of the noble savages. Neither is it a question of setting off for the desert à la Rimbaud or Lawrence. Perhaps some of these predilections of contemporary culture have made James Clifford fling this rhetorical question at the cosmopolitan nomadologists: 'nomadology: a form of postmodern primitivism?'[17]

How can we, then, carry through the project of a nomadic ethics that does not fall back onto primitive exoticism and aestheticism? To begin with, there are the memories of the nomads, which Khaldûn helps us to remember, but without any romanticism. Nomads were not a people of phantasm but of history who almost vanished under the onslaught of the long march of the rational/paranoiac organisation of power - walled cities, states and empires - culminating in the national states and the colonial governance in the age of modernity. The memories of the nomads remind us of another way of organising a community; they offer a model of being otherwise. Yet, in order to avoid the nostalgia for, or the exoticism of, a lost world of 'primitive' virtues, and to make nomadism relevant to the task of forming a minoritarian community, at least two basic moves need to be made. First, we must distinguish the nomads of the past from nomadic ethics. Nomads of the past lived in a singular community - they were bound by the force of similitude - whereas the task of the present is premised upon the rupture of the singular community and the encounter of difference - to which nomadic ethics is a response. For the nomads of the past - being as they were a self-enclosed organism - self-difference or becoming-other was not a pressing issue. But nomadic ethics is driven precisely by this concern: how to become-other in an encounter so that a non-essentialist location for both the sense of the self and the place of dwelling can be realised? Second, the memories of the nomads of the past - which are the memories of the margin and the outside - impinge upon us to actively remember those who live in the margins of the modern national state formation. Without this active memory, which is to say, without bringing minorities of the present into the equation, without bringing their point of view to bear on the ethical project, nomadism cannot shed neither its exoticism nor its aestheticism and become a liberatory practice.

Before we discuss nomadic ethics, let us remind ourselves of Khaldûn's pre-figuration of it in his description of nomadic life. What are the nomadic

16. Bruce Chatwin, *The Songlines*, 1988, *op. cit.*, p3.

17. James Clifford, 'Travelling Cultures' in *Routes : Travel and Translation in the Late Twentieth Century*, Harvard University Press, Cambridge & London 1997, p39.

virtues that impel Khaldûn to evaluate the nomadic mode of life as a model of 'goodness'? Since Khaldûn - eschewing the romanticism of the noble savages - talks of the savagery, cruelty and primitive barbarity of the nomads in a disapproving tone, it cannot be on the grounds of moral judgement. On the contrary, it is the economy of the dynamic force of nomadic *Asabîyah* as a form of collective power that triggers off Khaldûn's affirmative evaluation. Surely what we have here is the materialist ethics of ethology and not the morals of transcendental judgement. Moreover the effective force of nomadic collectivity is derived, as we have seen, from the condition that demands perpetual movement. Consequently the nomadic location is formed as the effect of the force of movement itself, which enables the nomads to construct a political community of shifting alliances. The distinguishing feature of this political community, as Khaldûn pointed out, is its non-authoritarian, democratic organisation of power. Needless to say, these are some of the basic principles that would guide the formation of a minoritarian community.

* * *

Deleuze and Guattari's notion of *aparallel evolution* - as I have already indicated - best exemplifies the kind of nomadic ethics that I am pursuing in this essay. So it is necessary that I describe the notion as precisely as possible: its workings, its origin, its usefulness and limitations. Like Khaldûn's notion of *Asabîyah*, Deleuze and Guattari's *aparallel evolution* subscribes to an ethological ethics. Yet Deleuze and Guattari remain unaware of Khaldûn's work. Perhaps this is indicative of the Euro-centric limitations of even the most radical of Western thinkers.

Deleuze and Guattari's immediate source for their notion of *aparallel evolution* is Rémy Chauvin's work on reproductive biology, but its ethical provenance lies in Spinoza's idea of 'common notions' grounded in the physics of the body. At the end of this section we will see how closely Spinoza's ethics resemble Khaldûn's description of the nomadic mode of life. Before we examine closely the notion of *aparallel evolution*, let us begin with a clear statement of it, which Deleuze provides in a conversation with Clare Parnet:

> becomings: it is not one term which becomes the other, but encounters the other, a single becoming which is not common to the two, since they have nothing to do with one another, but which is between the two, which has its own direction, a block of becoming, an a-parallel evolution.[18]

18. Gilles Deleuze and Claire Parnet, *Dialogue*, Hugh Tomlinson and Barbara Habberjam (trans), The Athlone Press, London 1987, p7.

Deleuze's qualification of mutual-becoming as being aparallel is to insist on a non-imitative process. Here, it is never a question of two or more stable subjects - with their essential and fixed identities, which Deleuze calls 'molar' - mimicking one another. The mimicry between stable subjects keeps their fixity in place and leaves ample room for the *same* to appropriate the 'other' by turning it into a relative difference through the dialectical analogy of its own concepts. In other words, it brings into play the master/slave dialectic with its self-relational mastery of the 'other' through an analogical differentiation or othering, and its attendant *Ressentiment*. At a different level, within the ambit of parallel evolution - which subscribes to a process of self-mutation in a singular force-field - the question of an encounter between historically constituted differences does not arise. However, the notion of *aparallel evolution* does not stand in opposition to or as a rejection of parallel evolution; rather it is a complication of it. On the one hand it retains the function of parallel evolution as the ontology of virtual universal force - which is non-subjective, pre-social or ahistorical, and hence molecular - as a field of internal productivity; on the other hand, it brings in - in its composite formation - the question of socially constituted or rigid or molar subjectivity. Needless to say that the latter is the site of historical difference. But for the encounter between historically constituted subjectivities - either individual or collective - to take place and for mutual-becoming to be a possibility the ontological condition of parallel force is required. So the notion of *aparallel evolution* is meant to serve these diverse functions: on the one hand, to insist on the non-imitative process of becoming; on the other hand, to complicate the abstract ontology of creative force from a historical viewpoint. It is precisely for these reasons that *aparallel evolution* becomes a potentially valuable ethical idea for the postcolonial world.

In order to appreciate properly the value of the notion of *aparallel evolution,* it is necessary to proceed slowly to see the function of its different strands and their mutual complication. Let me begin with parallelism. Deleuze's expressionist reading of Spinoza deploys the Leibnizian term of 'parallelism' to explain the Spinozist idea of efficient difference of singular and univocal being.[19] For the Spinozist notion of *natura naturans* involves a process where the singularity of substance is seen not only to implicate or fold into itself attributes and modes, but also to explicate or unfold them into existence. Hence we find '*the same expression*' or the univocity at different levels of *natura naturata* or the universe.[20] Parallelism, therefore, expresses a univocal plane of creative force; it subscribes to an ontology of difference governed by its own internal, self-causing dynamics. Deleuze requires this ontological force as a pre-supposition to his conception of becoming, which he would translate in his own work into such terms as: 'molecular plane', 'plane of consistency', 'abstract machine', 'incorporeal', 'body without organs', 'continuums of intensities'. Although all evolution or becoming takes place on the parallel plane of forces or at the molecular level, it is necessary, as we have seen, to bring into the equation the socially constituted or rigid identity of the molar subjectivity in order to create a pathway for any practical becoming. To explain the process slightly differently, let us say that since individuations in the existing world are effected by being moulded into rigid or molar subjectivities as a result of being captured by regimes of signs and powers in their various configurations, mutual becoming

19. See in particular the introduction: 'The Role and Importance of Expression'; chapter IV: 'Expression in Parallelism'; and the conclusion: 'The Theory of Expression in Leibniz and Spinoza: Expressionism in Philosophy' in Gilles Deleuze, *Expressionism in Philosophy: Spinoza*, Martin Joughin (trans), Zone Books, New York 1992.

20. Gilles Deleuze writes, 'Substance already expresses itself in the attributes that constitute *natura naturans*, but attributes in their turn express themselves in modes, which constitute *natura naturata*.' *Expressionism in Philosophy: Spinoza*, p100

21. Deleuze and Guattari, *A Thousand Plateaus*, 1988, *op. cit.*, p11.

22. In order to avoid the connotation of descent and filiation, Deleuze and Guattari drop the term 'evolution'. Instead, to emphasise the process of complication they prefer the term 'involution', *A Thousand Plateaus*, 1988, *op. cit.*, p38.

23. Gilles Deleuze reworks the figure of the simulacrum in the sense in which I am using it here in his appendix to *The Logic of Sense* , 'The Simulacrum and Ancient Philosophy', trans. Mark Lester and Charles Stivale, Columbia University Press, New York 1990. Deleuze's analysis of Plato's procedures for arriving at the adequate grounds of representation or legitimate knowledge, shows how this project is fractured by its own phantasm. Plato's procedure is organised by the binary circuit of the model and the copy. Since the adequacy of representation or truthful knowledge depends on the nature of the copy, Plato's search for types of copies leads him to the most degraded or phantasmatic of all copies - simulacrum. However, Deleuze finds in the *Sophist* 'the most extraordinary adventure of Platonism', when 'Plato discovers, in a flash of an instance,

can take place only in conditions of destratification or deterritorialisation. Here the relationships between molar subjectivities should be seen as being non-parallel, on which deterritorialising movements act to cause breakdown, thereby allowing access to the parallel forces of the molecular, where real becoming takes place. It is the demand of the composite and the paradoxical process involving both the molar and the molecular that calls for the notion of *aparallel evolution* .

In the postcolonial study, the notion of mimicry - owing much to the work of Homi Bhabha - has been a familiar explanatory metaphor for the circuit of repetition in colonial encounter. Although mimicry is a complex notion - grounded as it is in the psychoanalytical speculation about the constitutive moment of subjective consciousness that attributes to it an ontological loss and fracture of perception - it draws its critical power from the-all-too visible effects of irony or parody. Which is to say that it claims its critical power by showing the ironical or parodic effects in the event of the mutual mistranslation or partial translation that invariably occurs in the site of colonial relationship. Furthermore, the ironic or parodic effects are then read both as a loss of authority in the coloniser's discourse and a gain in the colonised's agency in the form of counter-discourse. Whatever the merit of this mode of repetition, the fact remains that it operates entirely within the binary logic of oppositional dialectics: discourse/counter-discourse, gaze/counter-gaze, etc. Between loss and opposition, mimicry subscribes to the pathos of negativity, which fails both to overcome binary logic and to trace a pathway for affirmative becoming. It is, therefore, not surprising that Deleuze and Guattari would view 'mimicry [as being a] bad concept, since it relies on binary logic to describe phenomena of an entirely different nature'.[21] Of course - as I have already indicated - without a binary staging of arguments thought itself would be impossible. However, this does not mean that one needs to remain caught in the web of binary logic. For that an affirmative sense of ethics - which subscribes to a non-oppositional and non-specular mode of repetition - is required. I believe that the nomadic ethical notion of *aparallel evolution* provides that.

Aparallel evolution suggests a mode of encounter where none of the parties come before the other donning their mirror faces either to serve as a model or as a copy.[22] Hence the question of recognition/misrecognition, translation/mistranslation does not arise. For they maintain their absolute difference from each other, yet they form 'a single becoming' - a moving collective of alliance. Instead of mimetic repetition, *aparallel evolution* subscribes to a differential mode of repetition or 'doubling' as the process for the forming of 'a single becoming'. This mode of repetition not only suspends the reproduction of the model but also - like its rhetorical counterpart, the simulacrum - overturns the mimetic circuit of the model and the copy.[23] However, the repetition proper to *aparallel evolution* does not stop at the deterritorialisation of the mimetic circuit. Once the mimetic circuit of molar subjectivity is broken, the speed of repetition releases the molecular force -

belonging to parallel process - of becoming otherwise. Perhaps it is clear to see that the model of repetition that *aparallel evolution* subscribes to is not unlike the temporality of the aleatoric force that Nietzsche calls 'eternal repetition'.

Since *aparallel evolution* provides us with a non-mimetic mode of repetition, this, I would argue, offers a better model of encounter than the notion of mimicry, especially if we desire a Postcolonial world based on an ethical community in the mode of what we have been calling minoritarian community. Now, in order to see clearly the practical process of encounter implied in the notion *aparallel evolution* and to underscore its collective nature - without which one cannot conceive of a minoritarian community - we need to foreground its Spinozist genealogy.

We have already seen how Deleuze turned Spinoza's metaphysical speculations concerning parallel or univocal dynamics of creation into the presupposition for an ethics of becoming-other without the pathos of *Ressentiment* characteristic of the dialectical process where the subject produces the other through its own analogy of concepts. However, it is in Spinoza's demonstration of how 'common notions' are formed through affective encounters that we find the internal mechanism of *aparallel evolution*. At this stage it is worth pointing out that there is a remarkable similarity between Spinoza's criteria for ethical judgement and that of Khaldûn. Indeed, Khaldûn's *Asabîyah* seems almost interchangeable with Spinoza's conception of *Conatus* or striving. Spinoza neither defines the essence of being in terms of substance nor by its morphology but in terms of *Conatus* - the self-preservative dynamism that draws on the power of the body and the mind. Like Khaldûn, he rejects the transcendental or moral criteria of ethics. Indeed, his ethics is as ethological as Khaldûn's. Hence the evaluation of 'goodness' is conducted by Spinoza not on the grounds of moral worth but by the very productive force of *Conatus* itself - the extent to which a being has enhanced its power of action.[24] Let us take note that ethological judgement is one of the basic conditions of nomadic ethics.

If the essence of being is defined as a self-preserving *Conatus*, then how is it possible to form 'common notions' through mutual encounters? In order to answer this question we need to understand the complex circuit of the body: its mechanics and its power of affection. As with his conception of the essence of being, Spinoza never defines the body in terms of its identity of form, but by its power of action - its ability to do things. Since all bodies participate in the same force-field, 'all bodies agree in some respects'.[25] Spinoza identifies motion, rest, speed and slowness as being common to all bodies, which not only define a finite body, but also distinguish one body from another.[26] Deleuze's commentary on this dimension - which he prefers to call 'longitude' - of the body is to insist that these common dynamic elements subsist at the level of univocal forces. In other words, longitudinal aspects of the body can only be conceived at the level of *'unformed elements'*.[27] If the body were to exist only in its longitudinal dimension, it would have

that the simulacrum is not simply a false copy, but that it places in question the very notion of copy and model.' (p256) Moreover, by deterritorializing the mimetic circuit of model/copy, simulacrum releases the affirmative force of becoming. Hence, Deleuze sees in the simulacrum a form of repetition that Nietzsche conceived through the concept of 'eternal return'.

24. For instance, Spinoza writes: 'we neither strive for, wish, seek, nor desire anything because we think it is to be good, but, on the contrary, we adjudge a thing to be good because we strive for, wish, seek, or desire it.' Baruch de Spinoza, *Ethics*, James Gutmann (ed), W. H. White, A. H. Stirling and R. H. M. Elwes (trans), Hafner Press, New York 1949, pt.III, demons. to prop.IX, pp136 - 137.

25. *Ibid*., pt.II, lemma.II to prop.XIII, p91.

26. Spinoza writes: 'Bodies are distinguished from one another in respect of motion and rest, quickness and slowness, and not in respect of substance.' ibid. lemma. I to prop.XIII, p91.

27. Gilles Deleuze, *Spinoza: Practical Philosophy*, Robert Hurley (trans), City Lights Books, San Francisco 1988, p.127.

remained a self-enclosed entity, even though it would have mutated internally: it would never have encountered others. However, 'longitude' is only one dimension of the body, whose other dimension is 'latitude'. In fact, it is through the body's imbrication in the 'latitudinal' dimension, which is to do with the forces of affection, that one body encounters another. In other words, it is the body's immanent propensity towards affection - both affecting others and being affected by others - that activates the longitudinal mechanics of the body to encounter its outside. Furthermore, the nature of affection determines a body's power of action. Deleuze insists that, like 'longitude', the field of affection or 'latitude' is also constituted by 'the intensive states of an *anonymous force*'.[28] He combines Spinoza's 'longitude' and 'latitude' to form his own univocal field of forces - the plane of immanence or consistency - where all becomings take place.

28. *Ibid.*, p127.

Although Spinoza's 'common notions' as the basis of adequate knowledge, where the mind reflexively understands the causes of affection, is open to a rationalist-epistemological interpretation - indeed Spinoza's *Ethics* itself encourages it - Deleuze's minor reading would emphasise the mutual aggregation of bodily forces. The body understood in terms of 'longitude' and 'latitude' is a body that goes through its molar form - its genre or species - to the level of the molecular *unformed elements* , and consequently loses its rigid distinction from other bodies. Since the *unformed elements* are the site of univocal forces and dynamics, the 'common notions' can only be formed out of them. However, given the habitual regularity of the world, things do not run that smoothly: 'common notions' require chance, good fortune, and a series of complicated manoeuvres to be realised.

In order for the common characteristics of bodies to join each other in a mutual aggregation, a propelling force is required - a kind of quasi-causal agency - which is provided, as we have seen, by the power of affection. However, all powers of affection are not the same; they are distinguished into two broad categories: the *power of acting* and the *power of being acted upon*. Spinoza simply defines the former as *actions* and the latter as *passion*. Deleuze's commentary explains Spinoza's conceptual moves with extreme clarity:

> One needs first to distinguish between two sorts of affections: *actions*, which are explained by the nature of the affected individual, and which spring from the individual's essence; and *passions*, which are explained by something else, and which originate outside the individual. Hence the capacity for being affected manifested as a *power of acting* insofar as it is assumed to be filled by active affections, but as a *power of being acted upon* insofar as it is filled by passions.[29]

29. *Ibid.*, p27.

Affection in the active mode (*action*) is caused by a body's own essence - in other words, by its own immanent power of *Conatus*, which activates the mind to produce 'adequate ideas': the force of becoming. On the other hand, affection in the passive mode (*passion*) is determined externally, which separates the body from its power of acting, and consequently only gives rise to inadequate ideas. Deleuze finds a corresponding relationship of forces in Foucault's work: 'the power to affect other forces (spontaneity) and to be affected by others (receptivity)'.[30] Despite the immanent propensity of the active mode, the actual conduct of the being, insofar as bodies exist in mutual relationship, is overwhelmingly given to the passive mode: it is passional and receptive. Since the encounter between bodies, in the main, takes place at the receptive level, it seems that most encounters lead to the reduction of a body's power of action, and keep its force of becoming in check. Faced with the problem of showing how passional encounters can be transformed into the active mode, without which the project of a practical ethics would come to nothing, Spinoza distinguishes between types of *passion*, which can be classified under the general categories of sadness and joy. Again, Deleuze explains succinctly and clearly how these two *passions* function in the moment of encounter and produce their differential effects:

30. Gilles Deleuze, *Foucault*, Seán Hand (trans), University of Minnesota Press, Minneapolis 1988, p101.

> When we encounter an external body that does not agree with our own (i.e., whose relation does not enter composition with ours), it is as if the power of that body opposed our power, bringing about a subtraction or a fixation; when this occurs, it may be said that our power of acting is diminished or blocked, and that the corresponding passions are those of *sadness*. In the contrary case, when we encounter a body that agrees with our nature, one whose relation compounds with ours, we may say that its power is added to ours; the passions that affect us are those of *joy,* and our power of acting increased or enhanced.[31]

31. Deleuze, *Spinoza: Practical Philosophy*, 1988, *op. cit.*, pp27-8

In Spinoza's arena of passional encounters, it is neither through the sublation nor the mastery of the other, and definitely not by imitating others or reacting with *Ressentiment* that 'common notions' are formed. Only a joyous encounter can provide the passage towards forming 'common notions', where two bodies can join forces to compose a more powerful body. Hence, despite external determination, passional encounters of joy can turn a body's passive receptivity into an 'adequate idea', because this 'expresses the effect on us of a body that agrees with ours, it makes possible the formation of a common notion that comprehends the agreement adequately from within'.[32] Hence the affective encounter in its joyous form produces a self-understanding that leads to a necessary recognition of commonality between bodies, thereby prompting the multiple becoming of bodies. This is the basis of Spinoza's political notion of the formation of 'mass' (*Multitudo*) - the democratic collectivity. Now we can begin to see a clear convergence between Khaldûn's meditation on the historical nomads of the desert and Spinoza's articulation of a post-Cartesian ethics. Both Khaldûn and Spinoza, having conceived eminently ethological concepts - *Asabîyah* and *Conatus* respectively - give us the idea of internal movement, which through affective encounter leads to

32. *Ibid.*, p58

the formation of collective alliances.

Having traced the genealogy of *aparallel evolution* through Spinoza's 'common notions' we can see how a non-mimetic encounter can provide the basis for the formation of a collectivity through the reflexive understanding of a mutual conjugation of forces. In its turn, this reflexive understanding serves as the force of ethical obligation for striving for the minoritarian community to come.

* * *

Although Deleuze and Guattari's becoming-in-between in *aparallel evolution* involves the destratification of molar subjectivity, the question is: does this concept alone offer a sufficient safeguard against what Levinas calls 'the imperialism of the same'?[33] Levinas's critique of Western ontology demonstrates how its model of a rational life - given to the self-realisation of subjectivity in the valorisation of its own consciousness - not only reduces the otherness of the other but leads to the violent oppression of those who are different.[34] Against this egological ontology of self-mastery, Levinas proposes a radical form of passivity as the constitutive moment of subjectivity.[35] For Levinas, ethics - unlike Deleuze or Spinoza - is not ethological: it is not a question of affirmative becoming through bodily affection, although his idea of 'face-to-face' can be read affectively. Instead, his ethics works, like much ethical theory from Aristotle to Kant, through proposing a set of moral imperatives. However, unlike the dominant tradition of ethical theory, Levinas is not concerned with the rational inquiry into self-conduct that always leads to self-realisation and never fails to compromise the other. Instead, he proposes a set of moral imperatives that begins with a non-cognitive and non-ontological relationship with the other, where the other is neither thematised nor represented. In other words, the irreducible difference of the other is never compromised or translated into the self-same analogy of concepts. The other in its anonymity commands the 'subject' who must respond not only with absolute passivity but must feel obligated to the point of being a 'substitute' for the other's death. In this moral arena, moreover, there is no reciprocity, but only the process whereby one simply presents her/himself before the other by saying *Me Voici* (Here I am) to bear witness to its commands and be traced by its anonymous presence.

It seems that there is a fundamental divergence between Deleuze and Guattari's affirmative ontology and Levinas's other-oriented moral imperatives: the former seems to be advocating the power of being; the latter, the abdication of this power. Yet, despite all the seeming differences, Deleuze's thought is not so very different from Levinas'. Although I cannot go into the details in this essay, suffice it to say, that Deleuze's critique of relative difference through the mediation of the identity and analogy of concepts coincides with Levinas's critique of totalising thought. Both these thinkers give us a sense of the outside or the other in its absolute difference

33. Emmanuel Levinas, *Totality and Infinity*, trans. Alphonso Lingis, Dusquesne University Press, Pittsburgh 1969, p.39.

34. Levinas thus draws the historical consequence of egological ontology: 'My being-in-the world or my 'place in the sun', my being at home, have these not also been the usurpation of spaces belonging to the other man whom I have already oppressed or starved, or driven out into the world; are they not acts of repulsion, excluding, exiling, stripping, killing?' in Emmanuel Levinas, 'Ethics as First Philosophy', in Seán Hand (ed) *Levinas Reader*, Basil Blackwell, Oxford 1989, p82.

35. Levinas writes: 'The identity of the subject comes from the impossibility of escaping responsibility, from taking charge of the other ... the most passive, unassumable passivity, the subjectivity or the very subjection of the subject, is due to my being obsessed with responsibility for the oppressed who is other than myself'. In Emmanuel Levinas, *Otherwise than Being and Beyond Essence*, Alphonso Lingis, Martinus Nijhoff (trans), The Hague 1981, p14 and p55 respectively.

and without a representational image. Moreover, both of them situate the need to think through the event of encounter with this irreducible other at the centre of their philosophical projects: Deleuze propels his idea of affirmative becoming out of it, and Levinas, his non-egological ethics. However, despite basing himself on Spinozist passive emotions or receptivity, Deleuze's affective becoming promotes, no doubt under the influence of Nietzsche and Bergson, too affirmative an ethics. This becomes a particular problem in the negotiation of rigid or molar identities that constitute social and historical reality. Although Deleuze and Guattari argue that all mutual becomings take place upon the destratification/deterritorialisation of molar identities, and that these processes do not involve the imitative circuit of model and copy, it is still difficult to see how affectivity alone can withstand the counter-thrust of egocentric passions and mimetic drives. In order to secure the deterritorialisation of an egocentric and essentialist self, and to safeguard against the mastery and appropriation of the other in an encounter, I believe a certain deliberate moral positioning is required.

It seems to me that Levinas's ethics of extreme passivity which positions the 'subject' into a relationship of obligation with the other without prior thematisation and representation, leaving the other to its absolute difference, is a necessary moral preparation for both effective deterritorialisation of molar subjectivity and a safeguard against the return of the territorialising drive. Hence, I would propose Deleuze and Guattari's *aparallel evolution*, which allows continuous becoming-other in affective encounters and the formation of shifting alliances of 'in-betweens', as the most appropriate nomadic ethics for our time - with the proviso, however, that their active and affirmative ethological ethics is sufficiently safeguarded by the passivity of Levinas's moral ethics. Of course, this produces a paradox. Yet, for an effective nomadic ethics, the question is not how to resolve it, but - like Levinas's paradox between 'saying' (*le dire*) and the 'said' (*le dit*) - to work productively through it.

Wilson Harris, in his novel *The Four Banks of the River of Space* (1990), shows that being passive or active are not mutually exclusive states but parts of the same paradoxical process of cross-cultural becoming. Anselm, the narrative voice of this text, asks himself in his dream-monologue: ' What balance divides heroism into sheer possession of the other, the sheer hunt, on the one hand, and necessary burial of the stranger one bears who brings news of chains that bind us [?]'. His answer murmurs as if Levinas were whispering through the leaves of the tropical canopy of the Guyanese rain forest, where the orchid still blossoms in its primordial harmony despite the taxonomic territorialization of colonial botanists: ' To break those chains we need to see ourselves as captives in the hand of the stranger.'[36] Contrary to commonsensical expectation, Anselm's passivity, his being the captive of the other, does not imprison him in the pathos of abjection but only frees him of his egocentricity - characteristic of molar subjectivity - and clears the passage for his affirmation of the 'cross-cultural capacity to bear the dual,

36. Wilson Harris, *The Four Banks of the River of Space*, in *The Carnival Trilogy*, Faber and Faber, London 1993, p423

triple (sometimes self-reversible) content'.[37]

37. *Ibid.*, p313.	

If nomadic ethics is not merely content to remain an aesthetic vision of a sublime life, or to choose not to entertain the whimsical fantasy of 'exotic primitivism', then, as I have already argued, it must allow itself to be questioned from the point of view of historical minorities. Deleuze and Guattari are not unaware of this problem; they point out that: 'there is no becoming-majoritarian; majority is never becoming. All becoming is minoritarian'.[38] Here it is worth pointing out that 'minority' is not meant to be a numerical figure; rather, for Deleuze and Guattari, it indicates the force of the outside - a contrapuntal note to the molar harmony of dominant stratification. Furthermore, the figure of 'minority' brings with it the multiplicity of contingent connections, and disrupts the axiomatic of majoritarian subjection - its transcendental principle of the 'one', its secure subject of enunciation, and its fixation upon repressive power. Historically, of course, the 'minority' articulates a relationship within a regime of power where the 'minority' is on the margin - othered by the majoritarian discourse and subjected to its power. Hence, in Deleuze and Guattari's becoming-minority - the trajectory of all becomings - there is no room for becoming-man, becoming-Whiteman, becoming-European; only for becoming-woman, becoming-Black, etc. Yet they also argue that 'even blacks ... must become black. Even women must become women'.[39] Within the context of nomadic ethics, this antinomy is understandable but is also, from the minority point of view, slightly troubling.

38. Deleuze and Guattari, *A Thousand Plateaus*, 1988, *op. cit.*, p106

39. *Ibid.*, p291.

First, let me establish the positive side of this argument: since numerical, historical or subaltern minorities are not reducible to nomadic or molecular minorities, they do not form automatic rhizomatic multiplicities. If minorities were to stay where they are - the fixity assigned to them by the majoritarian power - they would continue to play the slave to the master. Moreover, without a vision of the 'outside' and the affirmative movement of becoming, there is no guarantee that minorities would not be trapped within mimetic desire, reactive politics, and the sad passion of *Ressentiment*. How else could one prevent the birth of a new majority once the present majority is vanquished? The formation of a comprador bourgeoisie in neo-colonial nation-states - who not only serve the interests of the neo-imperialists but also replicate the same old power structures - is a good example of this. Having foreseen these dangers, Fanon advises the colonised minorities: 'do not imitate Europe ... so let us stop envying her'.[40] Furthermore, a minority subject-position constituted at one level does not automatically prevent the same subject from assuming majoritarian positions at many other levels: a colonised man may share the same minority position with his wife or sister in a colonial society, but that may not be a guarantee that he wouldn't assume a majoritarian position in relation to her at the level of gender. Similarly, a bourgeois black woman in a white supremacist society may share a number of minority positions with her black maid, but would assume a majoritarian relationship with her at the level of class. Furthermore, a heterosexual man

40. Frantz Fanon, *The Wretched of the Earth*, Constance Farrington (trans), Penguin, Harmondsworth 1967, pp252-3.

or woman placed at the margin of society because of her/his particular location in relation to class, race or gender may find her/himself in a majoritarian role in relation to her/his queer neighbour. Apart from the ones I have so far catalogued, it would not be difficult to add to them a number of other multiple and contradictory locations that a single unitary subject finds her/himself being placed in. Yet, in the urgency of having to fight against the minority location that one finds oneself in, one often forgets the minorities in respect of which one has majoritarian relationships.

Finally, if historical or subaltern minorities opt out of nomadic or minoritarian becoming, this can easily lead to the valorisation of experiential plenitude, and, consequently, to the fixity of essential difference. Essentialism thus embraced by a minority may not only give rise to the fantasy of purity of origin, but also to an odious form of nationalism. Are we then not likely to produce another Bosnia or Rwanda? Perhaps this perception has prompted Nicolás Guillén - the Afro-Cuban poet - to write:

Soy impuro ¿qué quieres que te diga?
Completamente impuro.
Sin embargo,
creo que muchas cosas puras en el mundo
que no son más que pura mierda.[41]

41. I am Impure, what can I say? Absolutely impure. But, I think there are many pure things in the world that are nothing but pure shit. Nicolás Guillén, Digo que yo no soy un hombre puro (I Declare Myself an Impure Man), in ¡Patria o Muerte! The Great Zoo and Other Poems, Robert Márquez (trans), Monthly Review Press, New York 1977, pp210-211.

Moreover, if historical minorities - either on account of their racial, sexual or colonial subjection - allow themselves to remain fixed in the imaginary purity of their essence, then how can they question the authority of colonial or racially supremacist discourses? For these supremacist discourses premise their legitimising authority on the assumptions of immobile essence and purity of origin. At best, if a historically subjected minority does not undertake a nomadic or minoritarian becoming, it can only claim injustice within this imitative logic - we do not have what they have - and can only claim liberation by way of the reverse side of the same majoritarian principle - we must have what they have (for instance, creating our own nation-state by excluding those who are not pure like ourselves).

Nuruddin Farah brilliantly dramatises this danger in his novel, *Maps* (1986), which tells the story of Askar and Misra amidst the swelling nationalist paranoia fostered by the Ogaden war. Askar, who loses his mother at birth, becomes so close to Misra - his foster mother - that their bodies become one. Misra's love for Askar reaches such an intensity that he even replaces Allah and becomes the 'space and time' of her universe. Yet the fervour of nationalism fed on the fables of ethnic purity turns Askar - the Somali - into a warrior for the fatherland, and Misra - the non-Somali (Oromo) into a scapegoat, a traitor, and eventually 'a corpse [that] no one claimed.'[42] Reflective by nature, Askar becomes aware that behind the bodily separation, which assigns him and Misra their respective selfhood in the social landscape,

42. Nuruddin Farah, *Maps*, Picador, London 1986, p241.

lies the inscription of national belonging - the marker of an essential difference between 'we' and 'they'. In an imaginary interlocution with Misra, he tells himself that 'the other, i.e. the maps which give me the distance in scales of kilometre - [are] the distance that is between you and me'.[43] Now, given all these dangers, how could we refute the claim that a minority must also become minoritarian in the sense of embracing a nomadic becoming?

Despite making a case for why a minority cannot do away with becoming-minority, we haven't yet fully taken account of the point of view of 'historically determined' minorities. Deleuze and Guattari's equation of a minority with the anonymous force of the 'outside' makes it an abstract figure that does not have a necessary bearing on historical or subaltern minorities. Moreover, since they see all molar politics of rights - of which minority demands for self-identity and self-determination form a part - as negative or reterritorialising from the point of view of molecular politics, they may be seen to be blind to the specific condition of historical minorities. It is true that in response to feminist demands, they concede: 'It is, of course, indispensable for women to conduct a molar politics, with a view to winning back their own organism, their own history, their own subjectivity: "we as women ... " makes its appearance as a subject of enunciation'.[44] But this is done almost in passing, and without giving proper consideration to how it might affect the idea of molecular politics.

It would seem that it is Deleuze's over-eager anti-Hegelism that pushes the argument to a purely aesthetic politics of the sublime. As a consequence of this, the politics of liberation engaged in by historically determined minority subjects - those who have been placed in a subaltern position and denied their own voice, their self-determination, their place of dwelling, their rights to form a community of their own - are seen as a reactive or Hegelian corruption of the pure model. This is because this kind of politics works within the limiting framework of determinant oppositions rather than beyond all oppositions. Hence, 'feminist' nomadologists have complained about Deleuze-Guattari's idea of becoming-women for women because - from women's point of view - the renunciation of their specific difference in the name of overcoming all differences does not enable them to redress the historical injustice done to them. Moreover, the ego-power-centric subjectivity of the molar type, whose deterritorialisation nomadology calls for as a precondition of affirmative becoming, has never been the lot of women or, for that matter, of any other historically determined minority groups. Thus Rosi Braidotti, following Luce Irigaray, points out that, 'one cannot deconstruct a subjectivity one has never been fully granted'.[45] This 'feminist' critique of Deleuze-Guattarian nomadism is legitimate, only if it is understood within patriarchal territoriality, and only insofar as it concerns gender relationships. Since women are located in a diverse set of relationships - where they may find themselves in a number of majoritarian positions, such as colonial women in relation to the colonised, white women in relation to black subjects in a racially structured society, and bourgeois

43. *Ibid.*, p18.

44. Deleuze and Guattari, *A Thousand Plateaus*, 1988, *op. cit.*, p276.

45. Rosi Braidotti, *Patterns of Dissonance*, Elizabeth Guild (trans), Polity Press, Cambridge 1991, p122.

women in relation to the working classes in a class-based society - minoritarian destratifications are still needed by women subjects. However, the voiceless must have a voice; the subaltern, no matter how inaudible their voices are, must be heard; and the homeless must have a home. Our critique of Hegelianism must not throw the baby out with the bath water.

Following on from the strategy of passive/active positioning in the event of mutual encounter that I have already argued for, it seems to me that a paradoxical engagement with both molar and molecular politics is required. There cannot be a purely sublime model of affirmative becoming. Perhaps Levinas's last major text, *Otherwise than Being and Beyond Essence*, brings home the unavoidable nature of this paradox. His critique of totalising ontology and egological thought, forcefully announced in *Totality and Infinity* and continued in much of *Otherwise than Being and Beyond Essence*, not only endeavours to reject the cognitive or propositional language of rational knowledge (*le dit*) but also attempts to find a way to give expression to a purely ethical language (*le dire*). However, in the latter text, Levinas comes to realise that the response to the other in a purely ethical language is not possible since it can only be given expression in cognitive language. Hence, *le dire* is always compromised and betrayed the moment it is expressed. Therefore, the ethical task is not to do away with cognitive language, but to bear witness to the other in it or to make room for *le dire* in *le dit*.[46] Similarly, the task of a nomadic ethics is not to reject molar politics but to find a way through it so that the affirmative becoming of the molecular type becomes possible.

Finally, how should the nomadic ethics of *aparallel evolution* that I have proposed - with the Levinasian modifications - be conducted in relation to a historically determined majority and minority? In other words, how can a majority and a minority encounter each other to produce a community of 'in-betweens'? Although Deleuze and Guattari allude to betrayal as being a nomadic trait, they do not consider its role in relation to historically determined majorities and minorities. Juan Goytisolo, the Catalan writer, on the other hand, devotes much of his work to this question. For Goytisolo, 'active betrayal' is a pre-condition for the encounter with the outside; without becoming-traitor, the majority can never conjugate with the minority. Exiled from his Spanish homeland to Tangier, where he gives himself up to nomadic wandering through the labyrinthine alleyways and teeming chaos of the *souks*, the narrator of *Count Julian* (1970) finds himself repeating the 'Moorish tableau' of the Manichaean order that his homeland has nurtured for centuries.[47] Yet looking out at the Spanish coast, the contemporary narrator entertains the fantasy of being the double of Count Julian - the Visigothic governor whose betrayal supposedly allowed Islam to enter Spain in the eighth century. It is as if only by becoming a traitor of the abominable magnitude of the count, that the narrator can begin to deterritorialise the Manichaean order of Spanish majoritarian culture and open the pathway for an encounter with its erstwhile demonic minority. Of this moment of

46. 'The *Otherwise than being*', writes Levinas, 'is stated in a saying that must also be unsaid in order to thus extract *Otherwise than being* from the said in which it already comes to signify but a *being Otherwise*.' *Otherwise Otherwise than Being and Beyond Essence*, p7.

47. In his essay, 'From Count Julian to Makbara', Goytisolo, in his reading of his own novel through Edward Said's *Orientalism*, points out how the orientalist doxa that has constructed the 'Moors' as other provides the mise-en-scène in which his work is set. His justification for re-enactment of orientalist stereotypes is that in order to 'battle ... against [this] tradition' they must be repeated, because, otherwise the 'grotesque ... deform[ation] ... of the 'white' imagination', (p227), can't be dramatised. Juan Goytisolo, *Saracen Chronicles*, Helen Lane (trans), Quartet books, London 1992.

betrayal, Goytisolo writes:

> the pleasure of betraying: of freeing oneself of that which
> identifies and defines us: of that which converts us,
> against our will, into spokesmen of something: of that
> which pins a label on us and fashions a mask for us:
> what homeland?: all of them: those of the past, the
> present, and the future: large and small, powerful or
> miserably poor and helpless: selling one's homeland into
> bondage, an endless chain of scales, an unending crime,
> permanent and active betrayal.[48]

48. Juan Goytisolo,
Count Julian, Helen
Lane (trans),
Serpent's Tail,
London 1989, p112.

Active betrayal is not a whimsical 'going native' or savouring of the exotic pleasure of cross-dressing, but a relentless questioning and rejection of the principles and the conditions that have constituted one into a majoritarian subject.

We see a similar dramatisation of 'active betrayal' in J.M.Coetzee's novel, *Waiting for the Barbarians* (1980), where the figure of the Magistrate, a long-serving functionary of the Empire - obviously echoing the internal colonialism of South Africa under apartheid - tries to find a way to conjugate with the barbarian other. First, as an amateur archaeologist, he collects the long-buried secrets of the desert, then he sets himself the task of deciphering the secrets of the barbarian girl - a prisoner in his encampment. These attempts, however, only further consolidate his imperial/majoritarian self. It is only when in an affective encounter with the barbarian girl - who then ceases to be an 'interior' to be penetrated and deciphered and presents herself in her irreducible difference as a pure 'surface', and he himself, in turn, appears in her gaze as 'a blur, a voice, a smell'[49] - that he begins to shed his molar/majoritarian self. Even so, this encounter is not enough for an effective deterritorialisation of the historic position allotted to him, let alone for the forming of a minoritarian community with the barbarians. The Magistrate needs to betray actively the law of the Empire, which he does by escorting the barbarian girl back to her people across the desert. Yet, even this is not enough, because without performatively undergoing the minority conditions through his own body, the betrayal remains only formal. So in a series of deliberate attempts he brings to bear on his body 'the traces of a history her body bears'.[50] Only when he suffers the humiliation, imprisonment, torture and starvation which the Empire habitually metes out to its barbarian other, does he feel that his betrayal is active enough to destratify his imperial self. Hence, it is as a result of his becoming-minority to the imperial regime that the Magistrate enters the threshold of *aparallel evolution*. However, in the end the novel does not manage to carry through this process and allow conjugation with the barbarians to form a minoritarian community. Perhaps because of Coetzee's

49. J.M.Coetzee,
*Waiting for the
Barbarians*, Penguin,
Harmondsworth
1982, p29.

50. *Ibid.*, p64.

ambivalence about the future of South Africa, and in order to keep his narrative safe from any directly political entanglement - to maintain its aestheticist aloofness intact - the novel ends in a nihilistic gesture of self-loss that goes 'nowhere'. Yet, in the affective encounter through which the Magistrate forms a micro-alliance with the barbarian girl, we can find an embryonic model of a collective evolution towards the formation of a nomadic or minoritarian community. However, the point here is that without betrayal there is no becoming-nomad for the majority.

Let us also remember Isabelle Eberhardt: if between her romantic exoticism inspired by Pierre Loti at the beginning of her North African adventures and her naive complicity with the *Mission Civilisatrice* towards the end of her destitute life, Eberhardt becomes a nomad, it is not by wandering through the desert but by the extent of her betrayal of her European origin.[51]

If a historically determined majority can only enter the process of *aparallel evolution* by turning itself into a traitor or betraying actively, how about the minority? We have already explored the dangers of a molar stasis for historical minorities: they also need to become nomads and molecular minorities. However, the course that the minority needs to follow is not the same as for the majority, since the biggest danger for the minority is the mimetic seductiveness of the majoritarian power structure. Yet, I have argued that historical minorities need to conduct their molar politics of self-determination or struggle to win back what is due to them, not as something peripheral, in the way Deleuze and Guattari seem to suggest, but as an integral part of a total liberatory movement. Obviously, any molar politics incurs the danger of majoritarian reterritorialisation - the recreation of repressive and exclusionary power structures. Hence, for a historically determined minority what is required is a paradoxical engagement with molar and molecular politics all at the same time. To give up molar politics would amount to historical suicide; but if they are conducted without the imperatives of nomadic ethics the result is most likely to be the formation of a new majoritarian power. Therefore, in order to remain just, and to avoid sedentary stasis, the politics of rights and self-determination conducted by a historically determined minority need the nomadic ethics of becoming-minority. On the other hand, a nomadic ethics that does not go through the molar politics of minority rights not only remains a form of pure aestheticism but also loses its power of action in the existing social formations. From the point of view of the minorities, what then is required is a continuous movement between molar reterritorialisation and molecular deterritorialisation

Finally, when a traitorous majority and a non-mimetic minority affectively meet each other - which cannot fail to be a joyful encounter - *aparallel evolution* between them becomes a real or historical possibility; and, consequently, leads to the formation of a powerful community of shifting 'in-betweens'.

51. See Isabel Eberhardt, *The Passionate Nomad: The Diary of Isabelle Eberhardt*, Rana Kabbani (ed), Nina de Voogd (trans), Virago, London 1987; and Isabel Eberhardt, *Departures: Selected Writings*, Karim Hamdy and Laura Rice (trans), City Lights, San Francisco 1994.

For an image of a minoritarian community, I leave the final words to the *Omeros* of the New World - Derek Walcott:

... History has simplified
him. Its elegies had blinded me with the temporal
lament for a smoky Troy, but where coral died
it feeds on its death, the bones branch into more coral,

and contradiction begins. It lies in the schism
of the starfish reversing heaven; the mirror of History
has melted and, beneath it, a patient, hybrid organism

grows in his cruciform shadow. For a city
it had coral pantheons. No needling steeple
magnetized magnetized pilgrims, but it grew a good people.[52]

52. Derek Walcott, *Omeros*, Faber and Faber, London 1990, chapt. LIX, sec.II, p297.

The Techniques Of Ecstasy: Writing The End Of The Century

Andrew Blake

Erik Davis, *TechGnosis: Myth, Magic and Mysticism in the Age of Information*, Serpent's Tail, London 1999, 368pp; £14.99 paperback. Kodwu Eshun, *More Brilliant than the Sun: Adventures in Sonic Fiction*, Quartet , London 1998, 222pp; £10 paperback. Jeremy Gilbert and Ewen Pearson, *Discographies: Dance/Music/Culture and the Politics of Sound*, Routledge, London 1999, 195pp; £12.99 paperback. Ben Malbon, *Clubbing. Dancing, Ecstacy and Vitality*, Routledge, London 1999, 256pp; £55 cloth, £17.99 paperback. Simon Reynolds, *Energy Flash: A Journey Through Rave Music and Dance Culture*, Picador, London 1998, 512pp; £12.99 paperback. David Toop, *Exotica: Fabricated Soundscapes in a Real World*, Serpent's Tail, London 1999, 304pp; £12.99 paperback.

Most accounts of dance culture offer some reflection on the quasi-paradoxical production of ecstasy through the high technologies of computerised music and massive PA systems. The rituals of the evening out are, to many participants, precisely that: a sacralised sequence of events and experiences. Erik Davis - in a text devoted to the general state of contemporary technospirituality - moves through many of the spatial, graphic, sonic and power relations of the new technologies focusing, predictably, on the PC and the internet, and producing a book which speaks for a generation almost lost in cyberspace but determined to hang on to structure and value, if not identity as we used to know it. Drawing on a vast range of material which connects science, technology and other forms of thought - from the Masonic insignia still adorning the dollar bill, through the early theorisation of electricity, to the paranoid fictions of Philip K. Dick - Davis reminds us that the spiritual and the technological have always been, and still are, intertwined, and insists that if we are to continue to glean meaning from information, they'd better remain so. We have to learn not just to surf, but precisely to thresh and glean, from the vast amounts of information available. To underline the point, Davis makes one of a number of striking musical analogies. 'We must learn to think like DJs, sampling texts and voices from a vast cornucopia of records while staying true to the organic demands of the dance' (p332).

Kodwu Eshun would doubtless agree. *More Brilliant than the Sun* is an incandescent evocation, its polished filigree work reflecting, and reflecting on, swathes of post-war Black music/history. And above all it is an attempt to renew knowledge by writing anew. Starting with an impassioned denunciation of lazy and ignorant (white British) music journalism, too ready to confine rhythm to the mysterious, the natural, and by implication, the jungle, Eshun insists on the science in his sonic fictions, the learned performance and learned technological manipulation in sounds from the free jazz of the 1960s through hip-hop to techno's mutations through to Hackney's jungle. Blackness here becomes performativity, not directly related to parenthood or skin colour; likewise, machines are made to perform Blackness. To express this adequately Eshun kicks hard against the poststructuralist fantasies that would inhibit language by denying its relationship with the real (including that lazy music journalism he detests). Neologising and reordering, he generates new grammars, inscribes new meanings: 'But Nirvana's never enough. The End of the Century Dancefloor is a series of paradoxical psychedelias that introduce immersive inversions and fleeting reversions. The phuture is a series of synthetic sensations, artificial emotions, tense presents' (p99).

David Toop tries to do something similar, sampling from his encyclopaedic knowledge of music and musicians to offer a new set of connections, and alongside, sampling from various genres to produce a text which is by turns analytical, descriptive, confessional, fictional, and a tripped-out mix of all the above. The book explores a central conceit, the paradoxical place of the 'Exotic' in a globalising world in which there is, increasingly, no 'there' there, but only touristic simulacra, the remains of a colonial relationship which had simultaneously defined the exotic and destroyed it. He focuses on the middle of the road exotica albums of the prolific Les Baxter (almost all made in LA recording studios by people who had not visited the places depicted), and surrounds his discussion with a wealth of explorations of jazz, avantgarde, blues and country musics. Like much of Toop's previous work, *Exotica* simultaneously impresses in breadth of knowledge, while short of breath in argument. Reprinted interviews, some of them scarcely relevant, give the text the well-padded feel of the Victorian novel, while the excursions into Conradian quasi-fiction (highlight: a dialogue with a very rational Lassie) prompt the usual injunction: don't give up the day job.

London. The Heart of Darkness. Clubland, thriving, makes the centre as alive at four on a Sunday morning as at four on a Saturday afternoon. Ben Malbon now works in advertising, but did an ethnography of 'clubbing' as a PhD project, and here it is (it's worth mentioning that there's a sad story about contemporary academia here). Like Sarah Thornton's account, this is a brisk bop through the clubber's experience, rather than the delirious hypertheorised trancedance offered by Kodwu Eshun, Simon Reynolds, or indeed the majority of academic and journalistic commentators on contemporary music/culture. Malbon worked with a number of clubbers who discuss how they feel, what they do and occasionally accompany him on nights out. Unlike Thornton, Malbon makes no bones about being a participant observer, but he presents a cool look at his and their experiences - including their views on 'cool', which reinforce Thornton's conclusions that clubbing is an élitist practice stratified by the fear of an imagined mainstream 'other' to the authentic experience. Malbon updates a few Cultural Studies assumptions - insisting that even the most elitist metropolitan clubbing experience can be read as 'resistant' to certain social norms, he enthusiastically, evangelistically represents the energy and vitality of the experience - and he says more about music and dancing than most other club culture books have done. But he does not say enough, partly because his discussion is resolutely rooted in the present, and is too insistent that pleasure should not be written off as mere hedonism, despite a text framed by images of queues, bouncers, pickers and other apparatuses of social control.

Jeremy Gilbert and Ewen Pearson provide the ideal companion to Malbon's ethnography in *Discographies*. Structured by deep knowledge of history, theory, and actual musical practice (like Toop, Pearson is a musician), their account delves more deeply into the political darkside of the dance music force than any previous sympathetic account. This is partly because Gilbert and Pearson are concerned to establish a critical popular-musicology which goes beyond the spotterish list or the fanzinesque flourish, and in order to do so they have to deal with profound legal and political structures. Their discussions of drugs and music technology are necessarily backed up with the legacy of Puritanism, and while they confirm Malbon's claim for clubbing as resistant, the metropolitan experience is set in a far broader spatial and historical context. They end by tying in the politics of Britpop to the rise of the New Lad, that implicitly white anti-clubber of the retropresent, and by contrasting the positive place of club cultures against that demonised identity.

Which is of course one aspect of a patriarchal continuum. When Acid House took off in the late 1980s the British music press remained resolutely 'rockist', supporting the white-boy guitar bands who were to emerge in the Britpop era. But one of its more intelligent writers changed the terms of rock criticism from self-righteous analysis to self-dissolving appreciation, grasping remembered moments of epiphany which reflect those celebrated by Malbon, Gilbert and Pearson; since then, he has come to echo them exactly. Simon Reynolds insisted in *Blissed Out: The Raptures of Rock* that rock bestows a lack of control, enabling the listener to escape from the socially constructed repressions of everyday subjectivity.[1] He responded coldly to acid house. There followed a reversal, worked out in two further books. First, with Joy Press, Reynolds wrote a sustained, theorised analysis of rock which cuts savagely across *Blissed Out*. *The Sex Revolts* offered a Freudian fix on rock's gender relations. Fascism, misogyny, cyborgism, and the escape from relational 'commitment' of life on the road, are critiqued in their catch-almost-all category of male 'rebel rock'.[2] Having dissed most rock, in *Energy Flash* Reynolds reverts to the adoration found in *Blissed Out*, but with dance

1. Simon Reynolds and Joy Press, *Blissed Out: The Raptures of Rock*, Serpent's Tail, London 1990.

2. Simon Reynolds, *The Sex Revolts: Gender, Rebellion and Rock'n'Roll*, Serpent's Tail, London 1995.

music as the new object of desire. The preface locates the moment of epiphany through which the author was converted:

> The last place I'd expected to find a Dionysian tumult was in the cool-crippled context of dance music. But that's what I saw in 1991 at Progeny, one of a series of DJ-and-live-band extravaganzas organized by The Shamen. They were pretty good, and Orbital's live-improvisation around their spine-tingling classic 'Chime' was thrilling. But what really blew my mind were the DJs whipping up a Sturm und Drang with the Carmina-Burana-gone-Cubist bombast of hardcore techno, the light-beams intersecting to conjure frescoes in the air, and, above all, the crowd ... This was the Dionysian paroxysm programmed and looped for eternity (pxvi).

Energy Flash appeared in association with Reynolds's internet website (http://members.aol.com/blissout), which straddles the commercial/informational potential of the internet, presenting information culled from the book with much of Reynolds's published journalism, alongside hyperlinks to online booksellers and interviews with a predictable litany of British rave-culture peripherals: novelist Irvine Welsh; cybertheorist Sadie Plant; her erstwhile partner Nick Land and his Cybernetic Culture Research Unit; and Kodwu Eshun - each of whom are visited with Reynolds's approval. (He also reviewed *TechGnosis*, positively, for the *Guardian*). This lineup of wannabe weirdside intellectuals might lead one to expect from *Energy Flash* an exploration of rave as the new Counter-Culture. Far from it. The argument running throughout is that the more basic and repetitive the music, and the more it confers on dance participants that state of release from routine mental operations Reynolds dignifies with the term 'bliss', the better. This is consistent with his *Blissed Out* apotheosis of noisy rock, but not with the criticisms of rock masculinities offered in *The Sex Revolts*, nor with Land's numerate cybermysticism. So for example the homosocialities of hardcore techno, gabber and so on are not dismissed as yet more protofascist escapism, but praised because of their bestowal of irrational mass response, while less populist forms such as 'intelligent techno' are dismissed as a 'reversion to older ideas of musicality'(pxvii).

In assembling these connections to form another matrix of physical-musical response, Reynolds is implicitly acknowledging the first wave of academic readings of club cultures. Steve Redhead, Hillegonda Rietveld and Antonio Melechi, among others, explored the ecstasies of dance through theoretical models which used British subcultural studies and French cultural theory alike, as do Gilbert and Pearson and Eshun.[3] All these accounts prefigure Reynolds's concern with the disappearance of the individual will during the dance event. The ecstasy of disappearance, in the utopian moments of these accounts, is related to the first disappearance of an Ecstasy tablet down the throat of the participant. There follows the epiphanic

3. See Steve Redhead (ed), *Rave Off: Politics and Deviance in Contemporary Youth Culture*, Avebury Press, Aldershot 1993; Steve Redhead (ed), *The Clubcultures Reader*, Blackwell, Oxford 1997; Hillegonda C. Rietveld, *This is Our House*, Ashgate Press, Aldershot 1998.

experience in which 'the Dionysian paroxysm' seems to the willing participant as if it has been both achieved and 'programmed and looped for eternity'.

Of course it wasn't, and isn't. The world continues to turn, even when those who are up for it are up. As Ben Malbon admits, dance events, even festivals, come to an end, the lights come on, and most of the participants - however much they have achieved a state of amorphousness on the dancefloor - remember who they are, resolve into individual human beings once more, return to school, University, or the office, and continue to play their parts in the current system of production, distribution, exchange and consumption - of which the production, distribution, exchange and consumption of dance music and Ecstasy are component parts. Matthew Collin, in the most careful of the late-1990s journalistic accounts of the dance decade, notes that economic forecasters The Henley Centre claimed in 1993 that the dance scene in Britain was worth £1.8 billion annually, about the same as book publishing; in 1996 the British Tourist Board's attempts to recruit younger visitors to Britain focused on the provision of clubs and rock music;[4] the new Leicester Square 'superclub' Home is one result. Even in the techno which Reynolds fetishises as the ultimate music of 'resistance', as in the wider frame - the clubbing experience recounted by and to Malbon, or indeed the tranche of technospiritualities recounted by Davis - there is no necessary or sufficient connection to the end of that, commodity-capitalist, world as we know it.

4. Matthew Collin with John Godfrey, *Altered State: The Story of Ecstasy Culture and Acid House*, Serpent's Tail, London 1997, pp267-271.

MAKING SENSE

Alan Durant

Jean-Jacques Lecercle, *Interpretation as Pragmatics*, Language, Discourse, Society series, Macmillan, London 1999, 251pp; £45 cloth, £16.99 paperback.

As Jean-Jacques Lecercle reminds readers on page one of this thought-provoking book, the word 'representation' (in this respect like 'interpretation', 'reading', and even 'analysis') has both a practice and also a result, or product, sense. Arguably in cultural and literary studies these days, less interest is typically shown in investigating the practice or mechanisms of representation and interpretation than in what you can say, within a cultural argument, by advancing a particular 'product' interpretation of a discourse. Many valuable insights are undoubtedly produced along with this relative emphasis on generating readings, rather than examining what the evidence for supporting them (and so their degree of legitimacy) might be. In a polemical aside in *Interpretation as Pragmatics*, however (an aside which echoes arguments acknowledged from Umberto Eco's *The Limits of Interpretation*, 1990), Lecercle goes so far as to suggest that much interpretation in literary and cultural theory today is not 'interpretation' at all according to his own definitions; rather it is a variety of other kinds of use of texts, informally triggered by whichever text is being discussed.

As regards explanation of how meanings are produced, two major traditions within recent cultural analysis might be distinguished, with significant differences - as well as fairly uneasy relations - between them, especially in terms of the notions of subjectivity and cognition they assume. The first may be associated with Anglo-American linguistics (especially pragmatics), and is underpinned by analytic and so-called 'ordinary language' traditions in the philosophy of language. In terms of the everyday practice of interpretation, such work is reflected most directly in linguistic stylistics and discourse analysis, as well as in psychological work on discourse comprehension. The other major tradition you might associate with continental, especially post-structuralist, theory. Eminent in this tradition are Michel Pêcheux's Althusserian accounts of discourse meaning and interpellation in the 1970s; other, cognate paradigms include Lacanian understandings of meaning production and aspects of the work of Bakhtin, as well as more general derivations from Saussure, often via Barthes. Lecercle suggests that, as a result of developments since the 1970s, these two broad traditions have become more accessible to each other, and that Judith Butler's highly innovative work, on the 'politics of the performative' (especially in *Excitable Speech*, 1997) brings together the best of each. However you view this specific assessment, there is little doubt that significant discrepancies between the two traditions remain.

One reason *Interpretation as Pragmatics* is as interesting as it is, accordingly, derives from its efforts to cut across the intellectual divide. The book energetically critiques what it characterises as the 'tin-opener' version of interpretation (open the tin, find the sardines of meaning laid out for you), as well as the conduit metaphor for communication on which that tin-opener model relies (ideas are objects; linguistic expressions are containers; communication is sending). Instead, Lecercle develops an alternative account of interpretation as a public practice of construction: ascribing meaning involves intervening; successive interpretations constitute a chain of such interventions or social moves, with each fresh interpretation reworking the interpreted discourse in a variant form. As well as emphasising interpretation as a social practice, the reader's act of translating discourse into ever new - always selective - versions, rather than notionally restating the same thing, shifts responsibility for meaning from the speaker (as origin of the text) onto work carried out by the reader. What nevertheless prevents this line of argument slipping into the interpretive relativism implicit in much contemporary audience ethnography is Lecercle's close attention to questions of precisely how interpretations are derived from specific discourse features and styles.

In order to explain how meanings are constructed, rather than merely recognised, Lecercle develops a model consisting of four (conceptually distinct, if temporally merged) interpretive procedures: glossing (of clichés and tropes, as well as of words and idioms); solution and disclosure (involving inferences of varying kinds); translation or re-description ('into a theoretical language of our own choice'); and intervention (taking part in ongoing social action, for some given purpose, in some specific set of circumstances). Together, these procedures contribute to a more general account, which Lecercle calls his ALTER model of communication (the ALTER acronym follows from respective slots in the communication structure: A = author; L = language; T = text; E = encyclopaedia; R = reader). ALTER is broadly based on the communication model presented by Roman Jakobson in his celebrated 'Closing Statement: Linguistics and Poetics' (delivered 1958, published 1960), but has been modified in the light of ideas from Greimas and the Swiss logician J.B.Grize.

Chapters Four to Seven of *Interpretation as Pragmatics* develop the overall account by discussing individual positions in the ALTER model (though not in ALTER sequence): reader (imposture), author (intention), language (interpellation), and encyclopaedia ('pragmatics of literature').

Lecercle's account of authorship and intention, to take perhaps the strongest chapter, draws on a critique earlier in the book of E.D.Hirsch's view of intention. But shifting the ground of debate - and loosely following Pêcheux's critique of Jakobson - Lecercle emphasises a need to distinguish between people, as actors within any act of representation and interpretation, and the subject positions these people come to occupy. Because utterances have given grammatical forms and vocabulary, Lecercle insists, they carry an already-specified potential for generating some meanings and not others. Even so, whatever meaning an utterance takes on in a given context depends on a process of realisation which involves, among other things, the interpellation of people into author and reader slots within the overall communication structure: 'The reader is interpellated by the representation she constructs in the place of the author; the author is interpellated by the representation of the readers she fantasises' (p75). Authorial intention in this framework is a necessary illusion: a place for ascriptions of meaning to ascribe meaning to, rather than the content of a unified and directing consciousness or identity.

According to Lecercle, insisting on slots or positions in this way is not necessarily inconsistent with how we intuitively think of communication occurring, if we posit a continuous process of adjustment of representations exchanged between the interpellated slots. Such adjustment is geared towards maximising intersection between the inevitably differing models which authors and readers bring to any given utterance of the language in question (which varies between regions, social groups, and periods) and of background cultural assumptions (what Lecercle, taking a term popularised by Eco, calls an 'encyclopaedia' of background knowledge and presupposition).

Perhaps surprisingly, given the interest of the 'author' chapter, the account offered of the reader position is rather less persuasive. Lecercle proposes a notion of necessary 'imposture', based on the idea established earlier in the book that interpretation involves risk-taking rather than mere recognition or reconstruction of meaning. From this fairly uncontroversial view, however, he then extrapolates the further notion that, in some sense based on subjection, all reading is misappropriation. Whatever the inherent strengths of this view, Lecercle's description of such 'imposture' is confused by a long and apologetic account of Louis Althusser's reported impostures (as related in his autobiography), prefaced by Lecercle's own admission of 'pious as well as theoretical aims' in the chapter (p95). The precise relationship between interpellation and imposture remains, to my mind, the least satisfactorily presented step in the book's overall argument.

Striking insights into the social circulation of interpretations do nevertheless follow from Lecercle's ALTER model. These include his sharpening of a central paradox of communication: 'We must invent a meaning for the text in the hope that this invention will be archaeological rather than merely imaginative' (p5). Lecercle's ALTER model also prompts four provocative, more general claims about meaning: all interpretations are possible; no interpretation is true; some interpretations are just; and some interpretations are false. These claims regarding the status of interpretations gain extra urgency when publicly contested interpretations are at stake, in that, as Lecercle puts it (alluding to Lyotard), 'True interpretation is at best an innocuous fantasy entertained by a glib and gullible interpreter, at worst a terroristic claim in an interpretive dispute, or differend' (p12).

Lecercle's interest in the social consequences of publicly contested interpretation is evident throughout. His description of the Derek Bentley case, for instance ('Let him have it, Chris') is mostly compelling; and his emphasis on the importance of relating construction from a text back to the text is enthusiastically linked to the legal concept of intentional rather than intended meaning - ascriptions of meaning that might reasonably be made, rather than whatever meaning was actually held in mind at the time of utterance. Lecercle's exploration of this distinction leads into further discussion of differences between textual meaning, use and effect, and an assessment of how confusion between these different forms of response to texts can undermine efforts to adjudicate between controversial readings. (Lecercle takes as his main case studies for this section the *Satanic Verses* fatwa and Charles Manson's claimed interpretations of Beatles songs as explanation for the murder of Sharon Tate).

As I have described it so far, *Interpretation as Pragmatics* is a challenging work. Erudite and allusive, its readings of individual texts (of a classroom Graham Greene story, glossolalia in John Barth, and Lewis Carroll's *Through the Looking Glass*, all in Chapter One; of oracles and traditions of midrashic reading; of Edward Lear, Willoughby's letter in *Pride and Prejudice*, or Joseph Wright of Derby's vacuum pump painting) are impressive and memorable. Nevertheless, I'm not fully convinced by the overall 'theory' advanced. While the ALTER model certainly offers persuasive description, there is at the same time a tendency, more characteristic of deconstructive philosophical arguments than of model-building ones, to short-circuit argument from marginal or perverse cases onto all cases (hence Lecercle's special interest in glossolalia, malapropisms, nonsense verse and slips of the tongue). Equally problematic, the book's use of diagrams is accompanied by suggestions of visual metaphor and heuristic which obscure exactly what kinds of force, procedure or cause the various arrows are supposed to represent. Despite use of the word 'pragmatics' in the title, too, *Interpretation as Pragmatics* hardly engages with contemporary debates in any of the major versions of that field. And, finally, it is puzzling how apparently uninterested the author is, despite explicitly expressed loyalty to Althusser, in pursuing questions of the relationship between the encyclopaedia of background knowledge which language users draw on in interpretation (how - in a more hermeneutic vocabulary - people 'live in' their language) and issues of ideology.

All in all, it is tempting to say that, despite these limitations, *Interpretation as Pragmatics* remains a serious work to engage with. It is. To some extent, though, the book's allusive one-liners, register-mixing, and local pastiche - all highly entertaining - make such a comment slightly inappropriate; occasionally these features tend to destabilise the book's more serious theoretical ambitions.

TYPISTS AND OTHERS

Tim Youngs

Casey Blanton, *Travel Writing: The Self and the World*, Twayne, New York 1997, 148pp; £22.95 cloth. Patrick Holland and Graham Huggan, *Tourists with Typewriters: Critical Reflections on Contemporary Travel Writing*, University of Michigan Press, Ann Arbor 1998, 261pp; £24.95 cloth.

Of these two additions to the fast-growing number of books on travel writing, Blanton's is the least satisfactory. This is due not so much to its several grammatical mistakes and typographical errors, annoying though these are, as to the format of the series in which it belongs: Twayne's 'Studies in Literary Themes and Genres'. It would be difficult enough to do justice to the history of travel writing, as a theme and genre in a single volume, but to succeed in fewer than 150 pages is impossible. Rather like modern travel writers, Blanton struggles against the limitations of her chosen form.

Restricted as her space is, Blanton attempts to trace the evolution of the genre and identifies exemplary individual works. Her first chapter provides an historical overview of self and other in travel writing from the ancient Greeks to the present. Although she is properly wary of generalisations and of tracing an uninterrupted pattern of evolution, she detects a gradual but fundamental change away from object-bound accounts of those who travelled with a purpose or for a cause to the 'more explicitly autobiographical travel books' of today (p4). A great problem with her formulation, however, is that it tends, wrongly, to consign political motivation to the past and to assume that the more subject-oriented narratives of recent years engage less with the external world.

Blanton follows her survey chapter with one on James Boswell and his 1760s Grand Tour journals. These, according to her, mark the beginning of the modern travel book, whose features include: 'a narrator/traveller who travels for the sake of travel; a narrative organization that owes much to fiction; a commitment to both a literary language and a personal voice; and thematic concerns of great moral and philosophic import' (p30).

A chapter on Mary Kingsley as an exemplar of Victorian women travellers follows. Interestingly, Blanton finds Kingsley's self-effacing humour, often claimed by critics to be a sign of her gendered oppression at home, 'rather tedious' (p54). She notices Kingsley's opposition to women's suffrage and asserts that Kingsley was free neither from Eurocentrism nor from racism. Blanton joins feminist critics of Kingsley in finding in her work a duality between authority and submissiveness but she departs from some in thinking it dangerous to insist on essential differences between women's and men's texts; rather, she urges, we should

1. Barbara Greene, *Too Late to Turn Back: Barbara and Graham Greene in Liberia*, Settle and Bendall, London 1981; Penguin, Harmondsworth 1990.

see them both as 'part of the conversation that is travel writing' (p58).

Chapter Four, on the modern psychological journey and Graham Greene's *Journey Without Maps*, is notable for two failings. The first is Blanton's reading of the text entirely in terms of Greene's own psychology. She ignores the many criticisms Greene makes of English society for its suppression of the instincts and of the fears he finds reawakened in Liberia. Second, while Greene hardly mentions the existence of his cousin Barbara, who accompanied him on the trip, Blanton refers to her even less. Coming straight after a chapter on the subordination of women, this reticence is baffling. Had she dealt with Barbara Greene's narrative, *Land Benighted*, 1938, in its reissued form, *Too Late to Turn Back*, she would also have been able to consider its introduction by Paul Theroux, who is a subject of her final chapter.[1]

In a refreshing, if perhaps critically generous chapter on Peter Matthiessen and the travel writing of nature, Blanton regards *The Snow Leopard* as being raised to another level by its author's spiritual and emotional quest: his efforts, as a Zen Buddhist, to accept suffering. The Zen perspective has the book reversing the 'traditional naturalist-explorer's monarch-of-all-I-survey position' (p77). Matthiessen gains 'an entire new way of seeing and of thinking' (p78).

Chapter Six looks at V.S. Naipaul, of whom Blanton is a good deal more tolerant than many critics, pointing out that his voice is consistently that of an outsider. She concedes that Naipaul may sometimes be unlikeable but argues that his travel books reveal him exploring the self in 'painful and explicitly autobiographical ways ... It is as though Naipaul can find a place for himself only if he resolves the problem of difference, only if he can understand where and how others differ from him' (p83). Naipaul is a critical figure in Blanton's sketch of travel writing, representing the 'elegant writing' and 'deep introspection' of its heyday and suggesting its future, 'toward paradox, inscrutability, and openness' (p94).

The chapter on Bruce Chatwin is more predictable. Blanton follows those admirers who deny that Chatwin romanticises the nomad and who claim that he has taken the genre perhaps as far as it can go. More dubious judgements on Chatwin haunt the final chapter, which is concerned mainly with place and displacement in Paul Theroux and Roland Barthes. Incredibly, Blanton insists that 'Chatwin maintains an ongoing dialogue with the world's citizens about the nature of human restlessness', that he has an ability to be decentred or displaced, and that he is able to leave his 'very British life' at home (p107). It might be truer to say that his dialogue is with himself, that he is a ventriloquist, and that his cultural and ideological baggage identify him wherever he is. Otherwise there would hardly be a sense of a very British life to be left at home. Yet there is a tension in this final chapter. Blanton reiterates her conviction that there has been in travel writing a growth of concern with the problems of representing the other. However, she now admits to major exceptions and points to Paul Theroux as a prominent example of a writer who remains centred in a conventional way. Her plea that we should constantly negotiate the entangled space between us, and her suggestion that it is our task to treat travel texts as culturally biased, do seem to qualify some of her earlier, more confident pronouncements on the status of travel writing now. Suddenly we have a sense of contemporary travel writing as in process and not as a summation; and that is how it should be.

Blanton is sparing in her use of endnotes but more than twenty pages at the end of her book are devoted to a useful bibliographical essay and to a selective but wide-ranging annotated list of travel titles to send interested readers on their way.

Patrick Holland and Graham Huggan modestly describe their book as 'an introductory critical survey' (px). It is much more than that. True, their study is about twice the length of Blanton's, they do not have to conform to the format of a series, and their focus is solely on contemporary travel writing, but their sharper critical edge is apparent from the start. Their thesis is that 'travel writing frequently provides an effective alibi for the perpetuation or reinstallment of ethnocentrically superior attitudes to "other" cultures, peoples, and places' (pviii). Aware of the defamiliarising strategies adopted by travel writing as it attempts to keep up with new ideas about the representation of the other, they are less sanguine than Blanton about the successes that have been achieved. They exempt neither general readers nor theorists from their scrutiny, seeing readers of travel writing as 'eager consumers of exotic - culturally "othered" - goods' (pviii) and regarding the 'ubiqitousness of "traveling theory"' as indicating 'a utopian impulse that is arguably the product, not of the world itself but of a "worldly" intellectual elite' (pix). More than Blanton, also, Holland and Huggan note the 'wider structure of representation' of which travel writing is a part (pviii). In particular, they point to the economic context of travel and travel writing, often undercutting the narratives' nostalgia and spiritualism by uncovering the material conditions that make travel possible and by reminding us of the economic arena into which the texts enter.

If '[t]ravel narratives strive to express the unfamiliar, but also to contain it' (p24), the tension inherent in this dual function seems especially intense in this '"postimperial"' age (p23) and is perhaps responsible for the air of cultivated eccentricity and disownable self-irony that *Tourists with Typewriters* notes so well. The affected individuality of contemporary travellers is in fact the mark of their conformism, Holland and Huggan suggest. The play on the myth of the English gentleman abroad, together with a pervasive nostalgia, helps create a 'regressive cultural nationalism [that] has sinister implications, yet these are side-stepped by recourse to parody and pre-emptive self-critique' (p23). Redmond O'Hanlon and Eric Newby are the targets here. Discussion of them leads to an original consideration of camp in travel writing, including a suggestive angle on Bruce Chatwin as dandy, whose 'hyperconscious posturing is a useful rhetorical strategy:

it grants him performative license and a dilettante's range of ideas and opinions; it also gives him a freedom to assimilate his personal experience to aesthetic whim' (p38). Perhaps, as Holland and Huggan claim, Chatwin's awareness of his voyeurism and consumption of the exotic leads to the self-parody of *The Songlines*, but they are probably right when they complain that 'Parody notwithstanding, Chatwin's work is unashamedly romantic; and with that romanticism comes a certain tendency to cultivated naïveté: a propensity to homogenize different peoples and cultures; to discover psychic or instinctual similarities rather than accounting for social or historic differences; and, at worst, to reduce an infinitely complex world into a random display of beautiful collector's items' (p39).

An admirable feature of Holland and Huggan's writing is its independence of thought. Its ambivalence towards postcolonial theory and practice generates a welcome unpredictability. Praising, as they should, the contribution of postcolonialism to uncovering the complicity of travel writing with imperialism and to encouraging narrative strategies of resistance to earlier models, they are nevertheless suspicious of 'the totalizing, ironically dehistoricized vocabulary it often deploys in order to talk about irreconcilably different cultures and cultural issues' (pp47-48), and of the 'increasing - mostly academic - commodification of the postcolonial' (p48). They are thinking of academics, not just of travel writers, when they observe that '[i]n a postcolonial era', "otherness" is a profitable business' (p65).

Contemporary travel writing can, like much in this age of postcoloniality, be both conservative and questioning. A carefully-argued section on Caryl Phillips, Jamaica Kincaid, Amitav Ghosh, Vikram Seth, and Pico Iyer reveals this. In Holland and Huggan's eyes, postcolonial travel writers are caught in a double-bind. They perpetuate the exotic, views about which they might wish to change; and the genre in which they work has a legacy at odds with what they want it to do. Cultural otherness is still produced for consumption.

On gender Holland and Huggan's approach is similar to Blanton's. Like her, they warn that certain anthologies risk essentialising women's travel writing and believe that not all women's writing is emancipatory in its politics. Two contemporary women travellers they especially admire are Robyn Davidson, for resisting the mythicisation of Australian Aborigines and of herself, and for exposing travel writing to internal critique; and Sara Suleri, whose *Meatless Days* 'interrogates the kind of national (travel) narrative that it associates with ethnocentric vision and a patriarchal view of place' (p129).

In the final chapter (though there is a postscript after it), *Tourists with Typewriters* asks how innovative travel writing can ever be. Some find an answer in eco-travel, New Age and nature writing but Holland and Huggan are critical of these 'commodified expressions of environmental angst' (p178) and of the 'postmodern commercialization of narratives of disappearance' (p179).

Tourists with Typewriters is one of the very best books on travel writing and the best I have read on contemporary travel literature. It is impressive in its range of references and perceptive in its readings. In showing how travel writing has flourished through late-capitalist hyper-commodification it avoids the pseudo-radicalism of criticism that looks only at the rhetoric and tropes of texts. And in admitting its own role in the market whose flow it seeks to disrupt, it should give pause to all of us who make a living this way.

BOOKNOTES

Fred Botting, *Sex, Machines and Navels: Fiction, Fantasy and History in the Future Present*, Manchester University Press, Manchester 1999, 240pp; £40 cloth, £13.99 paperback.

Fred Botting begins his book by self-consciously navel-gazing. He stares hard at that button on the belly, perhaps even his own, 'collecting fluff', and transforms it, like many have before him, into metaphor. And of course when it comes to metaphor, the navel is a literary theorist's dream. It is a scar, a hole, a knot, a node. It is a somatic memory of separation, of the lost maternal, of the confused boundaries between self and not-self. As Botting argues, the navel in the title is not merely a quirky addition to the suitably fashionable terms 'sex' and 'machines', it 'becomes strangely central to their articulation.' Or at least it does here.

   The Introduction comprises a survey of celebrity navels: from the theological puzzle of Adam and Eve to Madonna, *Star Trek*, and the 'appropriate hyperrealism' of the Teletubbies. The following chapters then consider various epistemological navels: the navel of psychoanalysis, the navel of history and the navel of cyberspace. The first of these chapters sets the tone, as later arguments and literary analysis draw heavily on Lacan. (It seems rather odd that whilst this book has a title packed with reference-friendly terms, the word 'psychoanalysis', which strikes me as central to its thesis and its readership, is missing.) The final chapters provide extended readings of classic, if somewhat dated, SF texts and films (*Bladerunner* and *Neuromancer*), alongside more recent works (Rucker's *Wetware* and Gibson's *Idoru*).

   Botting's readings of, and through, his metaphorical navel are provocative and often entertaining. After all, navel gazing can be fun. But only for so long. In the end, those multiplying metaphors can overwhelm us, masking the point like so much fluff. And then it's time to look up.

Amanda Boulter

Rex Butler, *Jean Baudrillard: The Defence of the Real*, Sage, London 1999, 172pp; £12.99 paperback.

Rex Butler is the first to think Baudrillard's work is a 'defence of the real.' To sustain the thesis he suggests first that Baudrillard does not really understand himself (for example: fourth order simulacra - there is no such thing); and second, one must draw conclusions from Baudrillard's analyses that are quite different from his own.

   If there are three phases of Baudrillard's work - the first explores limits of scientific reason, the second examines the consequence of these limits for his own work, the third examines language and thought as the fundamental limits by their 'power to affect and create the real' - there is here no attempt however to show any evolution in his thought. The discussion in the three main chapters (entitled Simulation, Seduction, and Doubling) moves back and forward across writings of the 1960s to 1990s as though there were perfect continuity. Thus simulation is 'not finally distinguishable from ... seduction.'

Butler's reading is caught in a delirium. Baudrillard 'repeats the same essential paradox throughout his work' so in Butler's own book 'there can finally be no sequence to it or logic to the separation of its chapters.' Baudrillard is concerned throughout with 'a real that is the limit to all systems, a real that no system could ever entirely capture or explain' and this 'real upon which the system cannot reflect ... is only the sign itself'. This clarifies things. Butler is 'reading against' Baudrillard's concept. He admits at the end of the book that his purpose has been to 'produce an unrecognizable Baudrillard', a metaphysics of semiosis strangely closer to that which Baudrillard once identified as the game of hide-and-seek with the real to be found in the thought of Lacan.

Mike Gane

Hazel Carby, *Race Men*, Harvard University Press, Cambridge, Mass, 1998, 228pp; £14.95 cloth.

Hazel Carby has been at the cutting edge of African American studies ever since her landmark 1980 essay on early black women writers and the blues helped many died-in-the-wool literary critics see the importance of the vernacular in black culture. *Race Men*, her intelligent and timely study of black public figures from W.E.B. Du Bois to Danny Glover, is often rightly acerbic especially when describing the machismo underpinning the work of Miles Davis, the disturbing racial implications of the *Lethal Weapon* series, or the stuffed-shirted public position of Cornel West (literally as he prescribes a dress code for black intellectuals).

There are problems in her analysis, however; not least her attack on Du Bois for using a debilitating gendered discourse which she feels undermines his critique of American materialism and its most famous African American proponent Booker T. Washington. Yet Du Bois's startlingly effective critique is now nearly a century old and to judge it mainly by the standards of our time does a grave disservice to his difficult position as a relatively new and isolated intellectual figure in America having to bludgeon himself into a debate where few prisoners were being taken.

In comparison, in Carby's treatment of her heroes, C.L.R. James and Paul Robeson, gendered language is not interrogated nearly so closely or given what amounts to an ahistorical frame. The work on both is really dynamic with the close critique of the depiction of Robeson's body and the performance of Robeson's singing of spirituals particularly astute. Moreover, her understanding of cricket in the section on James is particularly welcome, showing how the 'history of cricket as a political biography of colonial manhood' literally can define James's project. However, Robeson's naive relationship to Soviet Russia and the Communist Party in America and the effect this might have on his abilities to function as a 'Race Man' are not problematised at all. In fact Carby seems happy to offer his film *Proud Valley* as exemplar of a growth to an independent moment after the tribulations of Modernism even though its syrupy sentimentalism and one-dimensional propogandist tone surely undermines any claims it might have to being taken as seriously as Carby wants us to. It seems that Robeson's siding with an international proletariat forgives him errors of male hubris which could and should have been traced to make the book more even-handed.

Race Men reveals many insights in its groundbreaking investigation of the usually unspoken symbiosis of race and masculinity, but it is only the opening salvo in a discussion which will run and run.

Alan Rice

BACK ISSUES

1 Peter Wollen on fashion and orientalism / **Denise Riley** on 'women' and feminism / **Dick Hebdige**'s sociology of the sublime / **Laura Marcus** on autobiographies / **John Tagg** should art historians know their place? / **Franco Bianchini** on the GLC's cultural policies / **Homi K Bhabha**, **Stephen Feuchtwang** and **Barbara Harlow** on Fanon

2 Mary Kelly, Elizabeth Cowie and Norman Bryson on Kelly's Interim / **Greil Marcus** on subversive entertainment / **Georgina Born** on modern music culture / **Geoffrey Nowell-Smith** on popular culture / **Ien Ang** on 'progressive television' / **Alan Sinfield** on modernism and English Studies in the Cold War / **Tony Bennett** on Eagleton.

3 *TRAVELLING THEORY* – **Julia Kristeva** on the melancholic imaginary / **David Edgar** on carnival and drama / **Kobena Mercer** black hair – style politics / **Jacques Ranciere** on journeys into new worlds / **Peter Hulme**'s Caribbean diary / **Bill Schwarz** on travelling stars / **Ginette Vincendeau** on *chanteuses realistes* / **Steve Connor** on Springsteen / **Christopher Norris** on Gasché's Derrida.

4 *CULTURAL TECHNOLOGIES* **Out of print**

5 *IDENTITIES* **Out of print**

6 *THE BLUES* – **Jacqueline Rose** on Margaret Thatcher and Ruth Ellis / **James Donald** how English is it? / **Benita Parry** on Kipling's imperialism / **John Silver** on Carpentier / **Mitra Tabrizian** and **Andy Golding**'s blues / **Barbara Creed** on *Blue Velvet* / **Joseph Bristow** on masculinity / **Graham Murdock** on Moretti's *Bildungsroman* / **Edmond Wright** on post Humptydumptyism.

7 *MODERNISM/MASOCHISM* – **Victor Burgin**'s Tokyo / **Linda Williams** on feminine masochism and feminist criticism / **John Tagg** on criticism, photography and technological change / **Geoff Bennington** *l'arroseur arrose(e)* / **Emilia Steuerman** on Habermas vs Lyotard / **Paul Crowther** on the Kantian sublime, the avant-garde and the postmodern / **Mark Cousins** on Levi Strauss on Mauss / **Iain Chambers** being 'British' / **Adrian Forty** on lofts and gardens / **Lisa Tickner** on Griselda Pollock.

8 *TECHNO-ECOLOGIES* – **Peter Wollen** cinema: Americanism and the robot / **John Keane** on the liberty of the press / **S.P. Mohanty** on the philosophical basis of political criticism / **David Kazanjian** and **Anahid Kassabian** naming the Armenian genocide / **Paul Théberge** the 'sound' of music / **David Tomas** the technophilic body / **Felix Guattari** the three ecologies / **Margaret Whitford** on Sartre.

9 *ON ENJOYMENT* – **Slavoj Zizek** the undergrowth of enjoyment / **Peter Osborne** aesthetic autonomy and the crisis of theory / **Rachel Bowlby** the judgement of Paris (and the choice of Kristeva) / **Joseph Bristow** being gay: politics, identity, pleasure / **Gail Ching-Liang Low** white skins black masks / **Christine Holmlund** I Love Luce / **Line Grenier** from diversity to indifference / **Mark Cousins** is chastity a perversion? / **Simon Critchley** review of Christopher Norris.

10 *RADICAL DIFFERENCE* – **McKenzie Wark** on the Beijing demonstrations / **Paul Hirst** on relativism / **Cindy Patton** African AIDS / **Anna Marie Smith** Section 28 / **Tracey Moffatt** something more / **Susan Willis** Afro-American culture and commodity culture / **Hazel V. Carby** on C.L.R.James / **David Lloyd** on materialist aesthetics / **Peter Redman** Aids and cultural politics.

22 *POSTCOMMUNISM* – **Vitaly Komar and Alex Melamid** monumental propaganda / **Michael Holquist** cultural criticism for Russian studies / **Ted Levin** reimagining central Asia / **Mark Slobin** sight-reading St. Petersburg / **Svetlana Boym** 'Back in the USSR' to 'Bye-Bye Amerika' / **Mikhhail Yampolsky** Chekhov / Sokurov / **Katerina Clark** Russian Intellectuals post perestroika / **Nancy Condee and Vladimir Padunov** Pair-a-dice lost.

23 *LACAN AND LOVE* – **Joan Copjec** the invention of crying / **Renata Salecl** love: providence or despair / **Juliet Flower MacCannell** love outside the limits of the law / **Mladen Dolar** *la femme-machine* / **Alenka Zupancic** what's love got to do with *id*? / **Miran Bozovic** on Lacan and Spinoza/**Jane Malmo** on Milton's *Samson Agonistes* / **Slavoj Zizek** on Otto Weininger.

24 *ON NOT SPEAKING CHINESE* – **Ien Ang** on not speaking Chinese / **Ghassan Hage** locating multiculturalism's other / **Rob Wilson** Hawaii and cultural production in the American Pacific / **C.J.W.-L. Wee** Kipling and the 'colonial condition' at home / **Julia Emberley** simulated politics / **Iain Chambers** the judgement of the angels / **Neil Roughley** on the phenomenology of *Camera Lucida* / **Gillian Swanson** on national character in the Profumo Affair / **Johan Fornas** on authenticity in rock, rap and techno music.

25 *MICHEL FOUCAULT: J'ACCUSE* – **David Macey** *J'Accuse* / **John Rajchman** Foucault ten years affer / **Kate Soper** forget Foucault? / **Alan D. Schrift** reconfiguring the subject as a process of self / **Sue Golding** the politics of Foucault's poetics / **James Miller** from Socrates to Foucault / **Robert J.C. Young** on Foucault, race and colonialism / **John Marks** a new image of thought / **Wendy Wheeler** after grief / **Nick Couldry** on Rachel Whiteread's *House*.

26 *PSYCHOANALYSIS AND CULTURE* – **Malcolm Bowie** Memory and Desire in Civilisation and its Discontents / **Lesley Caldwell** Interview with Andre Green / **Dominique Scarfone** Conflictuality / **D.W. Winnicott** The Psychology of Madness /

Jim Hopkins Wittgenstein and Interpretation / **Clare Pajaczowska** Art as a Symptom of Not Dying / **Alex Tarnopolsky** Loss and Mourning in *Rigoletto* / **Christopher Wintle** *Rigoletto*'s Bottle / **Special Section – Revisiting Psychoanalysis and Feminism**: Ann Scott, Juliet Mitchell, Margot Waddell, Joanna Ryan, Joan Raphael-Leff.

27 *PERFORMANCE MATTERS* – **Simon Frith** Popular Performance / **Lydia Goehr** The Perfect Musical Performance / **Nicholas Cook** Rock, Theory and Peformance / **Martin Stokes** Arabesk in Turkey / **Sally Banes** and **John F. Szwed** Dance Instruction Songs / **John Stokes** Frank Norman / **Gill Frith** Gender and Performance in Women's Fiction / **Karen Lury** Television Performance / **Les Back** Apache Indian and the Cultural Intermezzo.

28 *CONSERVATIVE MODERNITY* – **Harriet Guest** feminism and sensibility / **Geoff Eley** German exceptionalism before 1914 / **Janet Wolff** Mark Gertler / **Paul Gilroy** revolutionary conservatism / **Lynne Segal** feminism in psychoanalysis / **Bill Schwarz** British Conservatism / **John Kraniauskas** Eva Peron / **Peter Osborne** times (modern), modernity (conservative).

29 *TECHNOSCIENCE* – **Rosi Braidotti** cyberfeminism / **Andrew Barry** the European network / **Nell Tenhanf** machines for evolving / **Terri Kapsalis** Norplant: contraceptive technology and science fiction / **Simon Penny** the Darwin machine / **Tiziana Terranova** Digital Darwin / **Sue Owen** chaos theory and marxism / **Cheryl Sourkes** genes and genesis / **Janine Marchessault** the secret of life.

30 *CULTURAL MEMORY* – **Michael Rowlands** sacrifice and the nation / **Tony Kushner** memory of Belsen / **Anna Vidali** political identity / **Susan Taylor** classifications / **Imruh Bakari** Caribbean cinema / **Sylvie Lindeperg** memory to allegory / **Mamadou Diouf** terrorism as social identity / **Erica Burman** false memories / **Tricia Cusack** carnival and patriarchy.

Schubert's sexuality / **Barbara Engh** after 'his master's voice' / **Herbert Scnadelbach** the cultural legacy of critical theory / **Sean Homer** the Frankfurt school, the father and the social fantasy / **Deborah Parsons** flaneur or flaneuse? / **Graeme Gilloch** the return of the flaneur / **Esther Leslie** space and west end girls / **Eamonn Carrabine and Brian Longhurst** mosaics of omnivorousness / **Kate Soper** despairing of happiness.

Back issues cost £14.99 each
Make cheques payable to *Lawrence & Wishart* and send to:
Lawrence & Wishart, 99a Wallis Road, London E9 5LN

Vhy not Subscribe?

New Formations is published three times a year. Make sure of your copy by subscribing.

SUBSCRIPTION RATES FOR 2000 (3 ISSUES)

Individual Subscriptions
UK   *£35.00*
Rest of World   *£38.00*

Institutional Subscriptions
UK   *£70.00*
Rest of World   *£75.00*

Please send one year's subscription
starting with Issue Number _____

I enclose payment of _____

Please send me _____ copies of back issue no. _____

I enclose total payment of _____

Name _____

Address _____

_____ Postcode _____

Please return this form with cheque or money order (sterling only) payable to *Lawrence & Wishart* and send to: Lawrence and Wishart, 99a Wallis Road, London E9 5LN